Political Theory and the

Displacement of Politics

CONTESTATIONS

A series edited by

WILLIAM E. CONNOLLY

Political Theory and the Displacement of Politics

Bonnie Honig

Cornell University Press

Ithaca and London

First published 1993 by Cornell University Press

International Standard Book Number 0-8014-2795-9 (cloth)
International Standard Book Number 0-8014-8072-8 (paper)
Library of Congress Catalog Card Number 92-56772
Printed in the United States of America
Librarians: Library of Congress cataloging information appears
on the last page of the book.

For Michael

Democratic ages are times of experiment, innovation, and adventure.
                                                    —Alexis de Tocqueville

The hero's gesture has not accidentally become *the* pose of philosophy since
Nietzsche: it requires heroism to live in the world as Kant left it.
                                                    —Hannah Arendt

Not long ago I became acquainted with the Kantian philosophy—and I now have
to tell you of a thought I derived from it, which I feel free to do because I have no
reason to fear it will shatter you so profoundly and painfully as it has me.—We are
unable to decide whether that which we call truth really is truth, or whether it
only appears to us to be. If the latter then the truth we assemble here is nothing
after our death, and all endeavor to acquire a possession which will follow us to
the grave is in vain.
                                                    —Heinrich von Kleist
                                                    (in a letter to his fiancée)

Contents

Acknowledgments

In the process of writing this book, I have often been astounded at my good fortune in having so many friends and colleagues who were willing, in the midst of their own busy schedules, to read and comment on drafts of chapters and, in some cases, on the whole manuscript (which, in its early stages, was *very* long). Their interest in the project and their encouragement were critical to its completion, and I am delighted finally to repay their kindness with the written acknowledgment it deserves.

Let me begin with the colleagues with whom I am most recently acquainted. I am indebted to the late Judith Shklar for reading several chapters in early draft form and for responding to them insightfully and critically while leaving me the space to figure out how best to address her concerns. Her recent, untimely death made me realize anew the extent of my debt to her scholarship and her example. Michael Sandel responded with generosity and magnanimity to my critique of his work, pressing me to come to terms with my own conceptions of the good while defending his position in ways that sought to encourage rather than deflect further debate and exchange.

Fred Neuhouser's careful reading nudged my thinking about Nietzsche along just when I was beginning to be too satisfied with it. My arguments on Rawls's *A Theory of Justice* were improved by the comments and queries of Patrick Neal, Geoff Smith, and Adam Swift, all of whom were willing to wrestle with some unfamiliar ideas rather than dismiss them out of hand. Michael Shapiro and Stanley Cavell also commented on the Rawls materials to my profit. Sally Gibbons responded to my reading of Kant, and she checked the translations of Kant that I use. I am most grateful to her, though, for her constant support in the final four months of revision. Her unerring instinct for an argument stipulated but not quite made was my most valuable resource during that period. Thanks also to Jim Grant, who helped me keep in touch with the book in its last stages.

Glyn Morgan commented on the whole manuscript with his usual care, intelligence, and attentiveness. Our recently begun conversation about political theory and politics was one of the perks of the revision process. Thomas Dumm's reading of the manuscript was also the occasion of a new friendship and a new conversation. I value both and am grateful to him for his extensive and thoughtful comments on the work. David Mapel took on the whole manuscript as well and responded to it with characteristic encouragement and insight, making me realize how I have come to rely on our professional and personal friendship over the years. Peter Digeser, another old friend and colleague, has read and quarreled tenaciously with arguments and readings from their earliest to their latest stages of development. I am grateful to him for his continual support and friendship. My thinking has also profited from conversations over the last couple of years with Marcie Frank, Steve Johnston, Jeff Isaac, Tom Keenan, Uday Mehta, Dana Villa, Stephen Macedo, and, especially, Kirstie McClure.

I presented early versions of Chapters 4 and 5 at the American Political Science Association conventions in 1989 and 1991, at Northwestern University's series in political theory in the spring of 1990, and at Tulane University's Murphy Institute seminar on liberty in April, 1991. I am grateful to all the discussants and participants in those meetings, including George Kateb, James Johnson, Jane Mansbridge, and Nancy Rosenblum. Parts of these two chapters draw on material that appeared as "Arendt, Identity and Difference," *Political Theory* 16 (1988), 77–98, copyright © 1988 by Sage Publications, Inc., and reprinted by their permission; "Declarations of Independence: Arendt and Derrida on the Problem of Founding a Republic," *American Political Science Review* 85 (1991), 97–113; "Toward an Agonistic Feminism: Hannah Arendt and the Politics of Identity," in *Feminists Theorize the Political*, ed. Judith Butler and Joan Scott (New York: Routledge, 1992); and "Rawls on Politics and Punishment," in *Political Research Quarterly* 46, no. 1 (1993). Thanks to all these journals and publishers for permission to use these materials here. Thanks, too, to the people at Cornell University Press, to Kay Scheuer, Teresa Jesionowski, Mary Lash, and Linda Wentworth, to Roger Haydon for being a supportive editor and for allowing me to decide the colors for the cover of this book, and to John Thomas for his rigorous copyediting.

I am indebted to the National Endowment for the Humanities and to Tulane University's Murphy Institute of Political Economy for a one-semester leave in 1991 that enabled me to complete a draft of the manuscript. Thanks, in particular, to Richard Teichgraeber III for being a welcoming and considerate host and to Ruth Carter for providing supportive staff assistance. I am also grateful to the Harvard government department for a one-semester paid leave in 1992 that allowed me to finish the final revisions of the book.

I first explored many of the issues treated here during my graduate studies at Johns Hopkins University. I am indebted to the late George Armstrong Kelly for encouraging my early work on Kantian respect and for sharing his own unfairly bad book reviews with me. For their guidance then, and for their collegiality since, I am deeply grateful to Richard Flathman and William Connolly. Bill Connolly joined the department at Hopkins just as I had run out of ways to account for what seemed to be inexplicable oddities in Arendt's thinking. He provoked me to read Nietzsche, and the mysteries of Arendt's account of action began to make a certain kind of sense. I am particularly indebted to Bill for his comments on this manuscript. His influence and the traces of the arguments we continue to have are evident on most of the pages that follow.

Also noticeable are the traces of a rather different set of arguments I continue to have with Richard Flathman, who also commented helpfully on the whole manuscript. It was he who first suggested that I pursue my interest in Arendt's political thought beyond the bounds of a seminar paper. I am grateful to him for that and more: for ten years now (a shocking realization), I have had the great good fortune to be guided by his consistent examples of candor, distance, wit, and insight in his scholarly work and in his relationships with students as well as colleagues. It is the best kind of debt to owe and I acknowledge it with pleasure and gratitude.

Finally, I would like to thank my husband, Michael Whinston, whom I met the week I began work on this project. I dedicate this book to him for believing in "life after the book" and for supporting me in this work as in all my endeavors with love, indescribable patience, and some excellent suggestions for revision.

Bonnie Honig

Lincoln, Massachusetts

Abbreviations

IMMANUEL KANT

KPW   *Kant's Political Writings.* Ed. Hans Reiss. Cambridge: Cambridge University Press, 1970.

FRIEDRICH NIETZSCHE

AC   *The Antichrist.* Trans. R. J. Hollingdale. New York: Penguin, 1969.
BGE   *Beyond Good and Evil.* Trans. Marianne Cowan. Chicago: H. Regnery, 1955.
GM   *On the Genealogy of Morals.* Trans. Walter Kaufmann and R. J. Hollingdale. New York: Vintage Books, 1969.
GS   *The Gay Science.* Trans. Walter Kaufmann. New York: Vintage Books, 1974.
HAH   *Human All-Too-Human.* Trans. R. J. Hollingdale. Cambridge: Cambridge University Press, 1986.
TI   *Twilight of the Idols.* Trans. R. J. Hollingdale. New York: Penguin, 1969.
TSZ   *Thus Spake Zarathustra.* Trans. Thomas Common. New York: Modern Library, 1960.
WP   *The Will to Power.* Trans. Walter Kaufmann and R. J. Hollingdale. New York: Random House, 1967.

HANNAH ARENDT

BPF   *Between Past and Future.* Enlarged ed. New York: Penguin, 1977.
HC   *The Human Condition.* Chicago: University of Chicago Press, 1958.
LM   *The Life of the Mind.* 2 vols. Ed. Mary McCarthy. New York: Harcourt Brace Jovanovich, 1978.
OR   *On Revolution.* New York: Penguin Books, 1963

JOHN RAWLS

TJ   *A Theory of Justice.* Cambridge, Mass.: Harvard University Press, 1971.

MICHAEL SANDEL

LLJ   *Liberalism and the Limits of Justice*. Cambridge: Cambridge University Press, 1982.

Political Theory and the

Displacement of Politics

CHAPTER ONE

Negotiating Positions: The Politics of Virtue and *Virtù*

[Virtù] rouses enmity toward order, toward the lies that are concealed in every order, institution, actuality—it is the worst of vices if one judges it by its harmful effect upon others.

—Friedrich Nietzsche

As a child, I used to read the last page of mystery novels first. Freed of the need to find out whodunnit, I could then read the book at a more leisurely pace, appreciating its detail, examining its clues, getting to know its characters. But reading the last page first had its costs: my reading was punctuated by fewer surprises. Less vulnerable to the text, I was also less drawn in by it.

To put the last page first is the conventional responsibility of introduction in academic texts. The reassurance of narrative is taken to an extreme in this convention, which requires that the first chapter tell the reader precisely whodunnit, why, and how. Here the author must outline the project, explaining what its goals are, where it is going, what it will find when it gets there, and by what roads it will travel en route. Academic audiences (and publishers) demand these reassurances even as they resist them. Straussian, analytic, and deconstructive readers, like the best inspectors in the detectivel literature, interrogate the author's directions and explanations, always on the lookout for false leads or secret codes. Introductions, these readers know, are an author's last-ditch attempt to control and limit the field of interpretative possibilities.

Political Theory and the Displacement of Politics is not a mystery novel, but it has its own share of suspects, of traps and false leads, and it yields, albeit somewhat reluctantly and fitfully, to the pleasures of narrative resolution in the end. Along the way, it conducts a series of engagements with some authors whom it suspects of having something to hide but also something to contribute to the resolution of the book. These engagements are occasioned by my observation of a mysterious phenomenon: the displacement of politics in political theory. Most political theorists are hostile to the disruptions of politics. Those writing from diverse positions—republican, liberal, and communitarian—converge in their assumption that success lies in the elimination from a regime of dissonance, resistance, conflict, or struggle. They confine politics (conceptually and territorially) to the juridical, administrative, or regulative tasks of stabilizing moral and political subjects, building consensus, maintaining agreements, or consolidating communities and identities. They assume that the task of political theory is to resolve institutional questions, to get politics right, over, and done with, to free modern subjects and their sets of arrangements of political conflict and instability.

Why and how did this become the project of political theory? What are its costs? Can it succeed? And should we—particularly those of us who support a democratic politics—want it to? I consider these questions conceptually and textually. Focusing on three political theories that displace politics, I ask in each case, what are the pressures within the theory that drive the theorist from a theorization of politics to its displacement? what fear, anxiety, or need is so great that the disruptions of politics cannot be risked? onto what sites and subjects is politics displaced and what are the consequences of that displacement?

Immanuel Kant, John Rawls, and Michael Sandel are the theorists whose displacements of politics I take as exemplary. I look to Friedrich Nietzsche and Hannah Arendt to provide the contrasting alternative, a perspective from which agonistic conflict is celebrated and the identification or conflation of politics with administration is charged with closing down the agon or with duplicitously participating in its contests while pretending to rise above them. By way of this alternative perspective, I ask whether the displacement of politics does not pose its own risks. Do the theories that promise safety from the disruptions and conflicts of politics harbor dangers and violences of their own? More important still, are they open to the suggestion of this critical possibility?

The theories that displace conflict, identify politics with administration and treat juridical settlement as the task of politics and political theory I call virtue theories of politics. The theories that see politics as a disruptive practice that resists the consolidations and closures of administrative and juridical settlement for the sake of the perpetuity of political contest I call *virtù* theories of politics. The terms "virtue" and "*virtù*" may call to mind Aristotle and Machiavelli but they are my own terms of art, drawn from Nietzsche and Arendt with Machiavelli in a minor, supporting role. I use them to stabilize the positions from which I define and negotiate the issue of displacement. They are my negotiating positions, positions that enable the negotiation of dominant assumptions about politics that have sedimented so firmly into place that they appear to be indubitably true.

Virtue theorists of politics assume that the world and the self are not resistant to, but only enabled and completed by, their favored conceptions of order and subjectivity. This assumption undergirds their belief that modern disenchantment, alienation, pain, and cruelty would be diminished if only we adopted their principles of right, established just institutions whose fairness is ascertainable from a particular (rational) perspective, or yielded to the truth of membership in a wider community of meaning and value. In short, each of the virtue theorists examined here believes, mistakenly, that his own theory soothes or resolves the dissonances other theories cause. Each yearns for closure and each looks to politics, rightly understood, to provide and maintain it.

Unfortunately, the assumptions, goals, and yearnings of the virtue theorists tend to erase the resistance from political orderings and the struggle from subjectivity, eliminating the excess that haunts the formation of the self into a subject and expelling the disruption from politics. These are the sites on which *virtù* theorists make their stand. Whereas virtue theorists assume that their favored institutions fit and express the identities or the formations of subjects, *virtù* theorists argue that no such fit is possible, that every politics has its remainders, that resistances are engendered by every settlement, even by those that are relatively enabling or empowering. It is for the sake of those perpetually generated remainders of politics that *virtù* theorists seek to secure the perpetuity of political contest.[1]

As Nietzsche uses it, *virtù* is an ethical perspective that calls attention to the remainders of system, to the insistences, cruelties, deceits, and inconsistencies, of virtue as a system of values. That is why Nietzschean *virtù* "rouses enmity toward order," because the efforts of political and moral orders to stabilize themselves as the systematic expressions of virtue, justice, or the telos of community drive them to conceal, deny, or subdue resistances to their regimes.[2] Moral and political orders must work to maintain the fittednesses they presuppose, daily. To that end, they rely on such practices as respect, responsibility, punishment, and friendship to discipline dissonances and resistances ranging from the criminal to the idiosyncratic. Nietzschean genealogy supports *virtù*'s disruptions by unmasking the extraordinary means by which these practices secure the would-be ordinarinesses of moral and political life. But the promise of Nietzschean *virtù* is not only negative; Nietzsche looks to *virtù*'s disruptions to create spaces of possibility for a new table of values in which *virtù*, in its more positive dimensions, takes the place of virtue as an excellence in an alternative ethic of self-overcoming.

Arendt, too, looks to *virtù* to disrupt the closures of moral and political system and create new spaces of possibility. But she departs from Nietzsche in celebrating *virtù* as an excellence of *political* founding, a practice of which Nietzsche despairs. She prizes *virtù* for its unique capacity to found new regimes, generate political power, and set up the institutional conditions for its maintenance and regeneration. Whereas Nietzsche unmasks the extraordinary underpinnings of ordinary life, Arendt leaves them in place in order to focus more forcefully on making the "extraordinary"—in this case, virtuosic political action—"an ordinary occurrence." Virtuosic action relieves the oppressive repetitions of nature, enabling Arendt's actors to "establish relations and create new realities" rather than merely repeat old ones. And it subverts the "rise of the social," the forces of normalization that discipline multiple selves into modes of subjectivity whose homogeneity disables the individuality Arendt celebrates.[3] Arendtian *virtù* is more political and more institutionally located than the Nietzschean variety, but it too has a role to play in a kind of transvaluation of values, one that might embolden citizens for the ruptures, the genuinely discomforting pleasures and uncertainties, of democratic political action.

The ruptures and uncertainties that mark democratic politics make it more consonant with *virtù* than with virtue theories of politics. The virtue theorists' assumption that it is possible and desirable to contain or expel the disruptions of politics has antidemocratic resonances, if by democracy one means a set of arrangements that perpetually generates popular (both local and global) political action as well as generating the practices that legitimate representative institutions. Because virtue theorists displace politics with bureaucratic administration, jurocratic rule, or communitarian consolidation, they tend to remove politics from the reach of democratic contest. Because they assume that their accounts of subjectivity fit the self without excess, they also exhibit an undemocratic insensitivity to the remainders of their politics, even as they depend on those remainders to stabilize their orders. For example, in the virtue theories of Kant, Rawls, and Sandel, the consolidation of the self into a law-abiding democratic citizen *depends* on the projection of the subject's dissonant impulses onto a stable, exteriorized other. The other is then dehumanized, criminalized, or ostracized by an (otherwise inclusive) political community. But virtue theorists neither acknowledge nor theorize this dependency in their treatments of respect, responsibility, punishment, and friendship. They depoliticize the remainders of their politics, disavowing their political genealogy, function, or significance. The democratic arrangements they envision do not cross the fundamental line that distinguishes "us" from "them"; they hold fast to it. It is the line that claims some for democratic citizenship while remaindering others.

Are *virtù* theorists right, however, in their assumption that the formation of subjectivity engenders resistances in the self? Are they right to assume that all sets of arrangements are invariably troubled by remainders? Are they right to think that a democratic politics, in particular, is energized by these assumptions? Or are virtue theorists right in thinking that resistances and remainders, when they do surface, are either unfortunate accidents that no system can control or the symptoms of an ill-conceived, dysfunctional politics? The conflict cannot be settled at this general level. Instead, I analyze the particular contributions of virtue theorists annd ask, do their own theorizations of politics and subjectivity fit and express selves or communities without remainder? or do their conceptions generate remainders that they then disavow, conceal, or subdue?

In Chapters 2 through 6, I adopt the perspective of a *virtù* theory of politics in order to pose these questions. I find that the expressivist assumptions of virtue theorists (the assumption that their political orders express and fit the selves and communities for whom they are designed) do quite a lot of unacknowledged theoretical work. I challenge the virtue theorists' view of their institutional arrangements as fulfilling, meaningful, just, or self-realizing by calling attention to the moments in their own accounts that belie these assumptions: the mechanisms that enforce the order on those for whom it is not meaningful, the rifts and fissures that mark the identities virtue theorists cherish for their seamlessness, and the disappointment, incomprehension, and alienation of those who find that, in their case, anyway, the promise of self-realization is false.

To render problematic the assumption of fittedness is not to say that these virtue theories of politics do not fit some of their subjects quite well; it is, instead, to focus on the depoliticizing effects of their *assumption* of fittedness. The assumption occludes the processes that daily produce selves into subjectivity. Once those processes are occluded, the remainders they engender can be accounted for only as independent, prepolitical or apolitical artifacts. Little wonder, then, that virtue theorists seem to be truly bewildered when the remainders of their politics surface in their own texts. Their bewilderment animates their insistence that their regimes are not really responsible for those who do not fit the mold (though they do take credit for those who do), that their institutions of punishment are simply defensive and justified mechanisms necessary to protect citizens from a few inexplicable, idiosyncratic disruptions, that their identitarian closures do not threaten but rather enable and indeed consolidate the democratic character of their arrangements. In short, by denying their regime's role in the *production* of the well-fitted subjects it presupposes, virtue theorists manage to distance themselves from the remainders of their politics and that distance enables them to adopt a not terribly democratic intolerance and derision for the other to whom their democratic institutions are supposed to be (indeed, claim to be) reaching out.

As I develop the virtue-*virtù* debate further in the following chapters on Kant, Nietzsche, Arendt, Rawls, and Sandel, I hold *virtù* as well as virtue theorists to the standards of *virtù*, tracing the moments at which both sets of theorists close political spaces, seeking out the unacknowledged remainders of their politics. Along the way, I renegotiate and adjust the terms of the debate in order better to capture the concerns generated by the work of each of these theorists. My readings are occasioned by the problematic of the displacement of politics as the virtue-*virtù* opposition frames it, but that problematic is too broad a point of departure for each chapter, and so I approach each thinker initially by way of a concept or concern suggested by his or her own work. I intend each chapter to serve not only as part of the virtue-*virtù* debate arranged here but also as an independent contribution to existing debates about such practices as respect, responsibility, authority, punishment, and subjectivity as well as to interpretative debates about Kant, Nietzsche, Arendt, Rawls, Sandel, and others.

I begin with Kant and with Nietzsche, in Chapters 2 and 3, because these thinkers respectively represent relatively uncontroversial examples of virtue and *virtù* politics. Both respond to the Enlightenment's destabilizations of traditional values and beliefs, Kant by seeking new groundings for them, Nietzsche by celebrating their passing. Whereas Kant looks to politics to support his rational grounding of morals for modernity, Nietzsche debunks the idols (which include reason and the modern state) to which Enlightenment thinkers like Kant turn in their effort to fend off what they perceive to be nihilism. Nietzsche counters that to confront and affirm the fact that the human world is not inherently valuable or meaningful—to announce the death of God—is to take a step away from nihilism, not toward it. Nihilism, in Nietzsche's view, is the persistent belief in not the rejection of values that are empty or self-contradictory. Rather than consolidate and conceal the fissures created by a reason that does more than it can bear, Nietzsche calls for us to exacerbate them further. On Kant's account, however, God is not dead; reason has distanced him from the human world. His distance creates a rupture that causes alienation, disaffection, and confusion for the species but it also affords human beings a valuable opportunity to develop autonomy, to move from their naive stage of faith to one supported and enforced by reason, rightly used. In short, Kant soothes and seals the ruptures Nietzsche celebrates and aggravates.

I approach Kant's theorization of politics and its role in sealing the rupture of modernity through his account of the practice of respect for persons. I point out that the practice, which bridges Kant's moral and political theory, is directed not at persons but at the moral law in persons or at the moral worth of persons. Consequently, Kantian respect serves not simply as a principle of distance or negative liberty but as part of a broad and complex set of moral and political practices that consolidate selves into moral and political subjects. The consolidations secured by Kantian respect denigrate and even dehumanize those selves and those parts of the self that resist the moral law's imperatives. With those resistances out of the way, Kant displaces politics with a practice of juridical settlement that expresses the will of the more cooperative parts of the self and establishes the conditions for the moral improvement of the species and for the development of virtue in individual persons.

Kant's reduction of politics to law and his treatment of politics as an instrument of his moral project led Arendt to reject his account and to look to his treatment of aesthetics and judgment to ground an alternative, more political, theory.[4] I am sympathetic to Arendt's critique of Kant on this score but, rather than ignore Kant's political theory, I prefer to trace the unacknowledged moments of politics in Kant's own political writings, the moments of disruption and closure that resist, disturb, and occasion the legal-political theory Kant does provide. Kant is driven to reduce politics to law by his fear that, unless reason is harnessed to its proper uses by positive law (and, indeed, by reason itself), it will disrupt the beliefs, assumptions, and practices that make human life bearable under modern conditions. Properly used, reason conceals or bridges the gaps that mark agency, morals, politics, and also reason itself. I conclude that Kant's practice of respect plays an important role in this part of the Kantian project since it too relies on practices of (self-)concealment to stabilize the moral subjectivity—the idea of man as an end in himself—that Kant assumes as one of his starting points.

In Chapter 3, I turn to Nietzsche, whose critique and recovery of responsibility are part of a larger effort to displace Kant's ideal, the man of perfect virtue, with a counterideal, Nietzsche's controversial overman (the man of perfect *virtù*). Although both are ideal figures, each serves a different purpose. Kant's ideal seals into place prevalent but unstable moral practices, whereas Nietzsche's disrupts them further. Animated by his belief that traditional moral standards foster self-loathing in subjects who can never measure up to them, Nietzsche enlists the aid of the overman to create spaces for alternative forms of life and subjectivity in a terrain already closely settled by morality.

Virtù is one of the levers of critique on which Nietzsche relies, and his opposition of *virtù* to virtue partly inspires my own schematic. But I focus the chapter on Nietzsche's account of responsibility because responsibility is more significant than *virtù* in Nietzsche's writings but also, and more important, because Nietzsche's recovery of responsibility is pivotal in a reconstructive project to which too many readers of Nietzsche still attend too little. Nietzsche recovers responsibility as part of his transvaluation of values for a postnihilist world. He gestures beyond his well-known disruptions of established settlements and conventions to an alternative ethic that seeks to be more generous and creative—more responsive to the impulses, yearnings, and resentments that mark the human condition in modernity. Premised on a view of the self as an original multiplicity that is enabled by, but also resistant to, its formation into responsible subjectivity, Nietzsche's alternative ethic values not the construction and maintenance of any single form of subjectivity but a commitment to a perpetual process of self-overcoming that offsets and (artistically) engages the tendency of sedimented identities and forms of life to engender remainders. In matters of identity, Nietzsche insists, it is not possible to get it right.

These Nietzschean views about the self lead me to radicalize Nietzsche's account and to treat the overman as a personification of those aspects of the multiple self remaindered by its formation into subjectivity. To treat the overman as a part of all selves is to democratize the figure and its effects. It is also to suggest that the herd, to which the overman is repeatedly opposed, is a personification too, representing those parts of the self that prefer the familiar, predictable routines of the subjectivity that constitutes them to the unknowns of a Nietzschean self-overcoming. My radicalization of Nietzsche's overman and herd and my focus on the struggle between them in a single self prepare the way for my treatment of Arendt, who sees the self's internal struggles as one of the *sine qua non* of the politics she theorizes.

In Chapter 4, I turn to Arendt seeking the *virtù* theory of *politics* that Nietzsche never quite provides. I read Arendt from Nietzschean premises, highlighting her treatment of the self as an original multiplicity and her theorization of action as a kind of self-overcoming. I point out that, like Nietzsche, Arendt sees the self as a creature that is always agonistically engaged and implicated with established identities and subjectivities that never quite succeed in expressing it without remainder. And I note that both theorists treat the self's perpetual ill-fittedness as a site from which alternative ethical and political possibilities are generated. (Is it for these reasons that both are acutely sensitive to the processes that produce the remainders of politics, or is it because both write from a position of homelessness that only Kant, among the virtue theorists, comes close to capturing?)

When Arendt (unlike Nietzsche) takes these arguments to politics, she theorizes a practice that is disruptive, agonistic, and, most important, never over. In Arendt's *virtù* politics, as in matters of identity, it is not possible to get it right. She banishes rational, foundational truths from the public realm for fear that their irresistible compulsion will shut down the agon whose security, maintenance, and perpetuity she seeks. She pictures the possibility of founding, maintaining, and stabilizing a regime without the resources of antecedently established, well-fitting identities and without the rational or foundational truths to which most founding documents do reach. Drawing on Jacques Derrida's analysis of founding documents and practices, I criticize Arendt's belief that foundings can and indeed ought simply to dispense with foundational anchors. If regimes invariably reach for them, that is because they need to stabilize themselves with the support that comes from a place outside politics, the prepolitical or apolitical space occupied by natural law or self-evident truths. But are these foundational supports really pre- or apolitical? Do they really have the power to close spaces of politics, to hold politics at bay? Contra virtue theorists such as Kant, and contra Arendt herself, I argue that even foundationally secured foundations are always imperfect, fissured, or incomplete and that these imperfections are the spaces of politics, the spaces from which to resist and engage the would-be perfect closures of god, self-evidence, law, identity, or community.

My criticisms and amendments ought not to obscure the fact that Arendt's political thought forms the spiritual and conceptual center of this book. Her work inspires my governing distinction between virtue and *virtù*, and it animates my concern for the preservation of political space in late modern times. Toward the end of Chapter 4, however, I radicalize her own account of action to overcome the public-private distinction she establishes as one of action's necessary conditions. I suggest that the radicalization (to which she would no doubt have been hostile) is a good instance of Arendt's practice of authority in which citizens express their reverence for the authorizing texts or founding acts of their regime, not by enshrining them but by amending and augmenting them in perpetuity. Arendt's account of authority transforms Nietzsche's ethic of self-overcoming into a democratic politics of augmentation that perpetually reauthors a regime's constituting structures for the sake of the remainders that sedimentations (of identities and constitutions) would otherwise engender. When Arendt calls for the protection of political space, she does so largely out of the conviction that plurality and difference (and magnanimity toward them) are the first casualties of the displacement of politics and the closure of political space. I call not simply for the protection of political space but for the proliferation of political spaces, noting that plurality and difference are also the casualties of Arendt's own depoliticization of the private realm.

In Chapters 5 and 6, I ask whether Arendt's conviction about the consequences of displacement is borne out in the political theories of Rawls and Sandel, and I find that it is. Both these theorists displace politics (in Arendt's *virtù* sense of the term), Rawls for the sake of a justice that is well administered, Sandel for the sake of an identity that is sustained by stable communities. Both consolidate their displacements by remaindering—punishing, ostracizing, concealing—the moments of dissonance and otherness that disrupt their orders. But neither thinks that his arrangements are responsible for the production of remainders. Each depoliticizes remainders and treats the other as an outside agitator who comes from somewhere else to disrupt an otherwise peaceful and stable set of arrangements. Contra Rawls and Sandel, I argue that these remainders are potential sites of politics, that each has the power to disrupt and politicize established assumptions about agency, rationality, or the good, and that that is why each of these theorists is so anxious to exteriorize the remainders of his position rather than engage them.

Some readers may resist my application of this line of criticism to Rawls's liberal politics, in particular, because his liberalism seems so loose, so open, especially by comparison with Sandel's communitarianism. One of my goals in developing the *virtù* perspective is to disrupt that impression and the symbiotic arrangements—by which I mean the liberal-communitarian debate—that secure it. In Chapter 5, I trace the processes that daily produce the remainders of Rawls's politics, calling attention to the rationalist assumptions that ground the regime, its entrenchment of practices of justification that resist rather than invite augmentation, and its construction of citizens as passive consumers of the state's goods and services rather than as its active and vigilant interrogators. I focus, in particular, on Rawls's justification of punishment, noting that its completeness leaves his law-abiding citizens untouched by its violence. The completeness of punishment's justification is so important to Rawls that he grounds retributive justice in the very antecedent moral (un)worth he rejects as the basis of distributive justice. The antecedence of criminality relieves the system of any responsibility for the production of criminal subjects and provides the practice of punishment with the closure it craves.

I resist Rawls's attempt to make an exception of the criminal and the more benign others that keep surfacing in his regime by suggesting that they personify those parts of the self that resist its formation into a subject of justice. From this perspective, punishment and criminality cease to appear epiphenomenal. They, and the violences juridical institutions visit on them, are part of ordinary life in Rawls's liberal regime. The ethical response to that circumstance is not, as Rawls would have it, to deny or dissolve it or to reconcile ourselves to it but to politicize it, to engage the fact that we are implicated in it, indeed, constituted by it, too. This is what Rawls's difference principle aspires to in its best moments. But its aspirations are undermined rather than secured by Rawls's closures of punishment and politics, both of which disempower Rawlsian citizens to deal ethically with the others who surface among and within them.

Devoted to stabilizing the state as the privileged site of administrative politics and to centering the courts into their role as the arbiters of distributive justice, Rawls resists the *virtù* theorist's call to politicize relations to the other and proliferate the sites of politics. It is not until I turn, in Chapter 6, to Sandel that I find a virtue theorist who does both, in part by theorizing the self in its inter- and intrasubjective dimensions. Sandel's proliferations, though, turn out to be bound to a politics of identification and consolidation that integrates or exteriorizes the dissonances it encounters. According to Sandel, the status of the self as subject, of homosexuality, and of pornography can all be resolved by a community (or a court) that discerns (or fails to discern) in the other some likeness to itself or some sign of distinctive worth.

For Sandel, the problem posed by the other is a problem of knowledge or recognition: can "we" discern traces of ourselves in the other? When the question is cast in these terms, however, an alternative construal of the other—as a marker of radical undecidability—is lost. Contra Sandel, I argue that the political issue is not whether the community can identify the other as same or different, enough like "us" to be acknowledged, or not; it is whether the community that tries to discern patterns of sameness in the other will glimpse traces of the other in itself. The undecidable other disturbs the categories of identity and difference that a communitarian politics celebrates and consolidates, alerting already constituted subjects to undecidabilities within them. This is the source of the community's ongoing *need* to fit unruly others into neat categories of sameness and difference, friendship and enmity ("Halt! Who goes there?"). I interrogate that need from a perspective that aspires to its overcoming, and I suggest that Sandel's failure to engage that need critically leaves his subjects as ill equipped as Rawls's to respond ethically and maganimously to the dissonance and otherness within and among them.

Virtù theories of politics value—they do not try to soothe or efface— the undecidable other's disruptions of language, law, morality, and subjectivity because the other keeps the contest of identity and difference going. For that reason, a *virtù* politics goes beyond magnanimity to gratitude to the other. At the end of Chapter 6, I return briefly to Rawls to ask whether his later amendments of *A Theory of Justice* make room for this magnanimity and gratitude. If justice is now "political, not metaphysical," does that mean that Rawls's closures of political space are less insistent or thorough? It does not. The generality of the revised Rawlsian project is not capacious enough to accommodate the *virtù* theorists' politicizations of the other, and Rawls's commitment to the displacement of politics for the sake of justice remains steadfast.

I end with Rawls and Sandel because it was their liberal-communitarian debate that initially provoked me to think about the displacement of politics as a problem in contemporary political theory. My interest in their work led me back to Kant and then to the conviction that all three theorists subscribe to the same basic and problematically expressive assumptions about politics and the self. In an effort to substantiate that conviction, I borrowed from Arendt an alternative political perspective that later became the basis of a *virtù* theory of politics. Turning to

Nietzsche for help in making sense of Arendt's account of agency, I found more critical assistance. From him I learned that neutrality is a false idol, that no conception of politics or the self, no set of arrangements no matter how minimally conceived, can free itself of contestable values and beliefs, or stand apart from them. I develop an analogue to that argument in Chapter 4 when I argue, contra Arendt, that no regime is founded nor refounded without foundationalist supports.

The lesson that follows from Nietzsche's insight need not be the communitarian one. A *virtù* politics seeks out the rifts and fissures of foundational identities and constitutions; it does not consolidate them. The democratic politics of augmentation licensed by *virtù* politicizes the values and beliefs that enable its founding, and it calls up for contest the identities on which it rests. Rather than try to neutralize politics or separate it from substantive goods, it aims to prevent those goods from closing spaces of politics and attaining the foundational status to which they aspire. These spaces of politics are the spaces of alternative perspectives and forms of life. To explore them, to live them, to develop an ear for them is a form of political action because it disrupts the naturalizations (of subjectivity or the state) that other political theorists take as their starting points. This proliferation of political action effectively resists the state's organization of politics into approved spaces and formats; it decenters the state as the owner and licenser of politics. Democratic citizens must resist, not reconcile themselves to, the state's consolidations of its status as the locus of power as well as its corresponding reduction of politics to administration and of citizenship to a passive consumerism. Neither the consolidations nor the reductions are faits accomplis. The practices that secure them go on daily, as I point out with reference to Kantian respect, Rawlsian punishment, and communitarian identification; there are always spaces of alternative and resistance that remain to be explored, aggravated, and exposed in opposition to those who seek to close, efface, or soothe them.

Virtù does not exempt itself from its commitment to the proliferation of politics and self-overcoming. In Chapter 7, I renegotiate the virtue-*virtù* opposition, noting that, as it begins to sediment into place, its generative power is somewhat diminished. The problem is not simply that the theories examined here exceed and resist the simple classification of virtue or *virtù* even as they are enabled by it. It is that the oppositional structure of the virtue-*virtù* debate implies that there is a choice to be made between a politics of settlement and a politics of unsettlement, as if any politics could be one without the other. I conclude that virtue and *virtù* represent not two distinct options but two impulses of political life, the impulse to keep the contest going and the impulse to be finally freed of the burdens of contest. Both impulses are taken seriously by a democratic politics of augmentation, which strives to maintain the friction between virtue and *virtù* for the sake of the political space engendered by their struggle and endangered by the victory of either impulse over the other.

I reach these conclusions by way of my reading of Arendt's account of politics, but other contemporary political theorists arrive at similar conclusions by quite different routes. My arguments about the perpetuity of political contest converge at crucial points with the recent work of Stuart Hampshire (who gets there via Machiavelli), Sheldon Wolin (via Tocqueville as well as Arendt), Nancy Fraser (via Habermas), William Connolly (via Nietzsche and Foucault in tandem), Stanley Cavell (via Emerson), Michael Walzer (via Rousseau), Judith Butler (via Foucault and Derrida), Isaiah Berlin (via John Stuart Mill), Bernard Williams (via Berlin), and Richard Flathman (via Oakeshott, Wittgenstein, and Nietzsche).[5] Not all these theorists celebrate the perpetuity of contest—some grudgingly put up with it—and not all those listed here will be pleased to find themselves in this company. But all these theorists' arguments converge on one point: they are critical of attempts to still the unruly conflicts and contests of democratic politics for fear that the result must be violations of freedom, plurality, tolerance, individuality, or community.

The perpetuity of contest is not easy to celebrate. My own affirmation of it is animated, not by the benighted teleological belief that politically active lives are necessarily fuller or more meaningful than their alternatives, but by my conviction that the displacement of politics with law or administration engenders remainders that could disempower and perhaps even undermine democratic institutions and citizens. The U.S. Supreme Court's recent decision in *Planned Parenthood of Southeastern Pennsylvania v. Casey* supplied compelling new justifications for a woman's right to control her sexuality and reproductive freedom, but it also endorsed new restrictions on that right. When a woman's right to choose was first recognized in 1973 by a very different Court in *Roe v. Wade*, many citizens celebrated the Court's decision as the end of a battle. Those opposed to the decision, however, vowed to roll back *Roe v. Wade* and, nineteen years later, they have had great success.[6] The battle is being refought in the Court and in the state houses. Those who thought it was won in 1973 were surprised by this sequence of events. Many assumed that, once juridically recognized, the right to abort a pregnancy would never be returned to the space of political contest. In the past two decades they went on to fight other battles, doing relatively little to mobilize citizens and communities to protect and stabilize this new right, leaving pro-life organizations relatively free to repoliticize and redefine the issues. In response to the juridical settlement of a woman's right to choose, pro-lifers focused on the fetus and the family and on the relations of obligation and responsibility that tie women to them. Soon abortion became known as baby killing, pro-choice became antifamily, and pregnant single women became icons of danger whose wanton, (literally) unregulated sexuality threatens the safety and the identity of the American family. These identities and identifications are not stable. But in the absence of resistance to them, they could be stabilized. That realization has energized pro-choice citizens into action in the last few years, and the sites of the battle are proliferating.

These observations are by no means meant to imply that it would be better not to entrench a woman's right to terminate a pregnancy—that is a different debate, one that turns on considerations of political strategy and equal justice. My point is that there is a lesson to be learned from the experience of those who misread *Roe* as the end of a battle and later found themselves ill equipped and unprepared to stabilize and secure their still unstable rights when they were repoliticized and contested by their opponents. In their mistaken belief that the agon had been successfully shut down by law, pro-choice citizens ceded the agon to their opponents and found, years later, that the terms of the contest had shifted against them. Disempowered by their belief that the law had settled the issue without remainder, they failed to engage the concerns of moderate citizens who harbored doubts about the morality of abortion, leaving them and their doubts to be mobilized and radicalized by those who had no doubts about the practice's immorality and who were determined to see it outlawed again.[7]

To affirm the perpetuity of contest is not to celebrate a world without points of stabilization; it is to affirm the reality of perpetual contest, even within an ordered setting, and to identify the affirmative dimensions of contestation. It is to see that the always imperfect closure of political space tends to engender remainders and that, if those remainders are not engaged, they may return to haunt and destabilize the very closures that deny their existence. It is to treat rights and law as a part of political contest rather than as the instruments of its closure. It is to see that attempts to shut down the agon perpetually fail, that the best (or worst) they do is to displace politics onto other sites and topics, where the

struggle of identity and difference, resistance and closure, is then repeated.[8] These are the platforms of a *virtù* theory of politics.

Some will see in *virtù* a manly ethic. From the Latin *vir*, meaning
"man," *virtù* is, after all, a manly excellence, and those who sing
its praises, including Machiavelli and Nietzsche, often juxtapose its
strengths to a femininized virtue, women's weakness.[9] But *virtù* is not
forever bound to this opposition; there is no reason to think that its
disruptive powers leave these generative oppositions intact. Nor, indeed,
is there any reason to assume that *virtù* can be illustrated by only one
figure, a male and masculine figure, identifiable in terms of one univocal
sex/gender.

What if the subject of *virtù* is not the manly male warrior of ancient
Greece or Rome but the virago, a figure defined variously as a "turbulent
woman," a "whirlwind," a "woman of masculine strength or spirit," a
figure who, in herself, poses a limit to the continuing possibility of calling
those strengths and spirits masculine? What if *virtù*, with its sensitivity
to excess and remainders, turns out to be a force that disrupts and
unsettles such binary categories as masculine and feminine, pointing out
their inadequacies, their limits, their aporias? Perhaps this virago, this
masculine woman who is both human and a force of nature, is a more
appropriate figure for *virtù* than is the thoroughly identifiable, categorically settled and category settling masculine man of war.

The virago is, like Machiavelli's man of *virtù*, a warrior; but she is also,
like Machiavelli's *fortuna*, a turbulent force of nature, a whirlwind. The
virago is less thoroughly feminized than is Machiavelli's *fortuna*, but then
Machiavelli's man of *virtù* is less thoroughly masculinized than he is
often taken to be. Indeed, in spite of Machiavelli's reliance on the gendered opposition to structure his depiction of feminine *fortuna* and masculine *virtù*, the relation between the two turns out to be less adversarial
and oppositional than indebted and mimetic. The highest overall excellence of Machiavelli's man of *virtù* is his ability to be like *fortuna*, to be as
capricious, unpredictable, and wily as she. True manliness means the
capacity to cross-dress, to put on the apparel and wield the accoutre-
ments of the truest (because most false?) woman. *Virtù*, the capacity to
beat *fortuna* consistently and well, is the talent for beating her at her own
game. The trick is to outwoman *fortuna*, to be a better woman than she.
And only a man of *virtù* can do that. The talent of Machiavelli's man of
virtù is his capacity to cross uncrossable lines (between male and female,
man and nature), his willingness to take risks from which ordinary
humans withdraw.[10]

Aside from occasional ruminations like this one, I do not engage questions of gender and politics in a sustained way in this book. Issues of sexual and gender identity are most prominent in Chapter 4, where I discuss Arendt's public-private distinction, in Chapter 6, where I discuss *virtù* and virtue perspectives on homosexuality, and in Chapter 7, where I analyze the structural oppositions of Carol Gilligan's *In a Different Voice* alongside those of my own virtue-*virtù* opposition. In all chapters, how-ever, particularly those on Kant and Rawls but also, for the most part, those on Nietzsche and Arendt, I let stand those authors' confinement of their gaze and their pronouns to male subjects; and, when my prose mixes with theirs, I repeat the masculine nouns and pronouns that they privilege for the sake of a clarity whose reign, I know, often has conserva-tive effects. Issues surrounding the use of gendered language are political and undecidable; there is no right resolution of the problem, none that is unmarked by remainders. I was once persuaded by Sabina Lovibond's argument that the mere substitution of "she" for "he" is an assimilationist strategy, a dangerous concealment of the centuries of exclusion that continue to mark the disciplines of moral and political philosophy.[11] But I am more moved these days by a reluctance to perpetuate this exclusion, in spite of Lovibond's recasting of it as a strategy of resistance. Conse-quently, I use feminine pronouns and examples whenever possible, link-ing them to the agenda of subversion, disruption, and politicization that flows from *virtù*.

CHAPTER TWO

Kant and the Concept of Respect for Persons

One cold winter's day, a number of porcupines huddled together quite closely in order through their mutual warmth to prevent themselves from being frozen. But they soon felt the effect of their quills on one another, which made them again move apart. Now when the need for warmth once more brought them together, the drawback of the quills was repeated so that they were tossed between two evils, until they had discovered the proper distance from which they could best tolerate one another.

—Arthur Schopenhauer

2.0.

Many contemporary theorists treat Kant's concept of respect for persons as a standard that any theory must measure up to or take as its point of departure.[1] For these theorists, Kantian respect for persons expresses an admirable commitment to respect the integrity, rights, and individuality of individuated subjects. But, as I argue in this chapter, a close reading of Kant's theorization and justification of respect shows that, for the most part, Kantian respect is for the moral law, not for persons. At times, Kantian respect is for the morally worthy parts of persons, but never for persons tout court; and it is certainly never for those who are other, only for the possibility of their conversion to moral worthiness. As a result, Kantian respect turns out to operate only partly as the practice of respect for rights and integrity that is admired by so many. It has two other dimensions, respect for the moral law in persons and respect for the humanity in persons, that are less distancing than didactic and disciplinary. The practice of respect that is famous for elevating and enshrining man as an end unto himself turns out to consist also in the requirement that he order his behavior and his thoughts in conformity with certain moral ends.[2]

Similarly, Kant's legalistic politics turns out to be not merely regulative but productive. Kant looks to politics to ensure juridically that citizens treat each other as ends in the absence of a morally good will. But for him the state and its enforcement of positive law do not merely structure and weight incentives; they provide the necessary conditions for the development of individual autonomy and moral personality.[3] Kantian institutions are meant to secure the right victor in the self's perpetual struggle to be morally virtuous. The self's resistances to moral orderings might be seen as sites of politics, sites from which the remainders of the order of moral subjectivity might be engaged. But Kant depoliticizes these multiple resistances by organizing them into the dispositions and appetites of the merely contingent, inessential but always troublesome phenomenal self. The progress of the species—not respect for the individual person, the phenomenal self, or its felt resistances—is the ultimate justification for Kant's political orderings as well as the solace for those whose experience of the moral and political order is less than fulfilling and perhaps even violent.

Respect for the moral law, positive law, and persons is one complex strand of Kant's multilayered response to the destabilizing dissonances and ruptures caused by elements of the Enlightenment project. Kant himself seeks to further the Enlightenment agenda of rational scrutiny, reflection, and autonomy while harnessing the powers of reason to the pursuit of moral species progress. The disruptions of reason are obstacles to that progress (as, indeed, are the disruptions of a politics unharnessed by reason and its a priori principles of right). But, Kant insists, reason need not be a source of disruption and destabilization; if rightly used (particularly as licensed by the state and the discipline of philosophy), reason has the power to consolidate traditional practices and institutions rather than undermine them.[4] In the first *Critique* Kant appeals to reason to limit itself, but in his "Speculative Beginning of Human History" he turns to a familiar fable of beginning to rein in reason's excesses and to embolden us for subjectivity in the modern age.[5] I begin with Kant's fable of Eden because, like all fables of beginning, it is not really about a distant past. The stories fables tell about the founding of a form of life invariably serve as powerful illustrations of the now more subtle and sedimented but no less active processes and practices that constitute and maintain our present, daily.[6]

1. Beginnings

Kant's account of Eden features a single, self-sufficient man paired with a woman (who is necessary for the reproduction of the species but not for anything else, lest she compromise the self-sufficiency of man). There is *"only* a *single pair"* so that "war does not arise, as it would if men lived close to one another and were yet strangers," and so "that nature might not be accused of having erred regarding the appropriate organization for bringing about the supreme end of man's vocation, sociability, by allowing differences in lines of descent."[7] All of man's objective moral ends are prefigured in this originary state: self-sufficiency (later to be transfigured to autonomy), the continuation of the species through propagation, a state of peace (although this peace is not yet perpetual because it is prerational), and sociability. Prefigured, but not yet secured. These objective moral ends must await the ruptures of reason and its ensuing rapprochements.

Kant's moral and political philosophy as well as his philosophy of history are therapeutic responses to reason's traumatic disruption of man's natural existence, an event that sets man onto the course of history. In the first of four steps, reason's stirring disrupts man's immediate relation to his instincts and to the objects of nourishment he craves.[8] Bringing in "some sense other than those to which the instinct was tied— the sense of sight perhaps," reason leads man "to extend his knowledge of the sources of nourishment beyond the limits of instinct."[9] In this step, the possibility of error or confusion is first introduced. Distanced from his immediate, determined relation to his instincts (the "voice of God" within him) and from his immediate relationship to the objects around him, man is now capable of erring by relying on the "wrong" (i.e., uninstinctual) sense to guide him to nourishment or by seeking nourishment from inappropriate objects.

The new possibility of error signals another new possibility, that of free choice. Suddenly, "besides the particular objects of desire on which instinct had until now made [man] dependent, there opened up an infinitude of them, among which he could not choose, for he had no knowledge whatsoever, to base choice on." After taking an initial and "momentary delight" in this proliferation of possibilities, man quickly realizes that he faces an "abyss" and he is filled with "anxiety and unease." But there is no going back. Having "restlessly and irresistibly [driven] him to develop those capacities that lay within him," reason will "not allow him to return to that crude and simple state from which it had torn him."[10]

Reason's second intrusion structurally mirrors that of the first. In the second stage, reason insinuates itself between man and his next "most dominant" instinct, the instinct for sex. Man finds that "sexual attraction—which in animals rests on a passing, largely periodic impulse—is capable of being prolonged and even increased by the imagination." This change promises to enhance man's end of propagation because the imagination "pursues its affairs the more temperately, but at the same time with more obduracy and constancy, the more removed are the objects of the *senses*." But, as reason once again distances man from the objects of his satisfaction (even concealing some of them with the fig leaf), sites of pleasure proliferate and the possibility of error is introduced. Man is no longer certain that he is choosing appropriate sexual objects. With his passage "from mere animal desire eventually to love," he moves "from the feeling for the merely pleasant to the taste for beauty, at first only human beauty, but then also the beauty found in nature." Sensing, perhaps, that the end of propagation is endangered by this thoroughgoing eroticism, Kant quickly steps back from it and in the very next passage introduces, almost jarringly, the ideas of decency and respect.[11]

For Kant, human sociability and morality are founded on decency, "a propensity to influence others' respect for us by assuming good manners (by concealing whatever could arouse the low opinions of others), as the proper foundation of all true sociability." Decency's practice of concealment responds to reason's own disruptive concealments of the world from man by requiring that he step back from the temptingly proliferating effects of reason's disruptions of nature. At this stage, decency conceals all that is other to reason, including the instincts, drives, and inclinations that mark man as a natural (as opposed to a moral) being and arouse the low opinions of others. The severance of man from nature "was a small beginning," Kant says not a little wryly, "that was nonetheless epochal, since it gave an entirely new urge to man's way of thinking."[12]

This small beginning turns on a remarkable shift from an originary urge to self-display to conventional practices of concealment, a shift Kant traces in man's relation to language itself:

> While still alone, man must have been moved by the impulse to communicate—at first to make his existence known—to other living beings around him, especially those that make sounds that he could imitate and afterwards use as names. One still sees a similar effect of this impulse in children and thoughtless persons who disturb the thinking members of the commonwealth by rattling, shouting, whistling, and other noisy amusements (the same also occurs in religious devotions). For I can see no other motive for this except to make their existence known far and wide.[13]

Language, on this account, arises not out of a need to convey information but out of an existential impulse to announce one's existence (presumably

to gods and beasts). The impulse is later occluded as self-display gives
way to decency's concealments and existential announcements give way
to naming. Like a fig leaf, a name conceals or covers a thing and thereby
fixes it, making it a "something" rather than an "anything or nothing" and
stabilizing its identity.[14] In contrast to the spontaneity of the first linguistic act, naming is mimetic. Through mimesis and then naming, man
conceals and checks the meaninglessness of his (originary) utterance and
existence and responds to the abyss of freedom, to the endless proliferations and disseminations brought about by reason's concealment or withdrawal of the world from him.[15]

Reason's third step ruptures the temporal immediacy of Eden, with-
drawing from man not the present object (food or sex) but the present
moment. Now conscious of the future, man can "prepare himself in
advance for distant ends," but he finds himself once again faced with the
specter of proliferation. Suddenly there are many possible ends from
which to choose. This situation conforms "with his vocation" as a choosing agent but it marks the end of man's ability to "enjoy life's present
moment." To be conscious of the future is to be uncertain; it is to be
conscious of death.[16]

In this passage, the notion of an end has three distinct roles, each one
related to the idea of distance and each one given expression, as we see
below, in each of three strands of Kant's concept of respect for persons.
First, man has an end that is a vocation, a distant yet immanent teleological purpose. Second, in conformity with this vocation, man is uniquely
capable of positing and pursuing ends, goals, or projects. Finally, the
fulfillment of his vocation and the attainment of the particular ends he
seeks are rendered uncertain by man's new consciousness that his own
existence will end. His awareness of the future and of his mortality forces
him to come to terms both with his purposiveness as a man and with the
possible purposelessness of human existence. The latter possibility, "the
most inexhaustible source of cares and troubles," fills man "with fear"
and, for the first time in Kant's account, he responds violently to the
intrusion of reason. Craving the reassurance of the world that once spoke
to him univocally, he "rebuked and made a crime of the use of reason"[17]
(in the biblical account it is not man but God who does this).

There is some consolation for man, though it too is uncertain. Worse
still (or so Edenic man would have thought), the source of his consolation
is the same as that of his anxiety: the reason that forces man to face the
prospect of his own death also comforts him with the thought that he is a
member of a species with a redeeming vocation: to make "progress

toward perfection." This progress is discontinuous, not smoothly evolutionary but punctuated. It is, like the subject matter of Kant's fable of beginnings, a series of discrete events separated by gaps. But man's future, like his past, can be turned into a continuous and univocal narrative by way of the very mechanisms that enable Kant to write his speculative history. "Surely," Kant says, "it is permissible *to insert* speculations into the *progression* of a history in order to fill out gaps in the reports" (the gaps are in the *reports*).[18] This insertion—speculation—is carried out by the "imagination in the company of reason" and it produces an ordered, continuous narrative—hence a therapeutic narrative—of the past that makes sense of and gives purpose to a deeply alienating and aporetic condition.

Kant's account of reason's disruption of man's instinctive sexual behavior illustrates the role of speculation in transforming periodicity into historical continuity, punctuatedness into seamlessness, randomness into smooth evolution. Before reason's intrusion, sexual attraction in man, like that in animals, rested "on a passing, largely *periodic* impulse." In its withdrawal of sexual objects from man, reason made the identification of sexual objects a matter of speculation; thus the imagination was introduced to the experience of sexual attraction. Since the imagination "pursues its affairs with more obduracy and constancy, the more removed are the objects of the senses," human sexual attraction is no longer a periodic impulse.[19] Speculation, the imagination in the company of reason, transforms human sexuality from staccato, impulsive behavior into an unbroken practice (though it also leads to a disruptive proliferation of potential sites of erotic pleasure).[20]

Similarly, speculation bridges the distances between man and the world as well as the gaps between past and present, present and future. In this aspect of speculation, Kant sees consolation. Speculative history consoles man with the promise that one day he or others of his species will once again be at home in the world not as a natural creature but as moral, rational man. It assures him that the wound inflicted by reason's incision will be healed when he develops the capacities belonging to his "vocation as a moral species," thus ending "the conflict within himself as a member of both a moral species and a natural species." This achievement of a "second nature" is "the final goal of the human species' moral vocation." But it will take some time: "Only a perfect civil constitution (culture's ultimate aim) could end this conflict"; until then, man's "existence will as a rule be filled with vices and their results, the multiplicity of human miseries."[21]

Notwithstanding Kant's own faith in the future, these promises are not the most important comfort provided by speculation. More important is the redemption of narrative that speculative history itself delivers. Kant's promise of a meaningful future is lodged in a narrative of the past that turns an unbearable chaos of happenings and random events into a meaningful and coherent story that can be borne.[22] To read Kant's "Speculative Beginning of Human History" as a parable of the Enlightenment is to attribute the disenchantment of the world to the Enlightenment project of secularization. The subjection of everything to the relentless scrutiny of reason disrupted man's comfortable and overdetermined existence; deprived him of his traditional, univocal guarantees of order and meaning; left him uncertain, skeptical, abandoned, and fearful of mortality. But it also granted him the possibility of choice, the capacity to posit ends and live an autonomous life. These promises for a fulfilling future are energized by Kant's positing of a fictive past moment in which there was a perfect, even divine fit among subjects, their aspirations, and their situations. The uncertainties of socioeconomic, political, and cultural change are borne more easily as part of the story of a Fall. The narrative consoles. The only problem is that all events and all subjects must conform henceforth to the narrative lest it be destabilized. Henceforth, the experience of chaos, in the form of remainders, gaps or dissonances that resist incorporation into the grand narrative, will trigger the originary pattern of alienation this narrativization was supposed to heal.

The golden promise of choice and self-direction is the bastard offspring of reason's illicit intrusions into Eden. Consequently, Kant, unlike his first man in Eden (who might well be modeled on Rousseau), does not make a "crime of the use of reason." The Enlightenment's disruption of the world was a *misuse* of reason. Reason was not meant to undermine faith. Put to its proper use, and maintained daily, reason can deduce in the world an order that is reliable not because it is built on reason but because it is secured by the one object invulnerable to rational dissolution, the one object about which man need not speculate, an object not of cognition but of respect: the moral law.

2.2.   Respect for the Moral Law

As the "immediate determination of the will by the law and consciousness of this determination," respect provides Kant with an alternative source of the reassuring immediacy lost when reason disrupted man's immediate, instinctual relation to the world.[23] The immediacy of phenomenal instinct (the voice of God in man) is relocated in the immediacy of a rational respect (the voice of the moral law in man). Respect is the site of a rational rapprochement for those who have been dislocated and disaffected by reason's misuse.

Respect for the moral law, the law of laws, is a *moral* feeling, distinct from pathological feelings or inclinations in that it coincides with a rational experience—consciousness of the moral law. "Yet although reverence is a feeling, it is not a feeling *received* through outside influence, but one *self-produced* by a rational concept, and therefore specifically distinct from feelings of the first kind, all of which can be reduced to inclination or fear."[24] But the moral, rational feeling of respect is not simply a mood in which we regard the law. Respect brings the human consciousness of the moral law to fruition by acting "as an incentive to make this law itself a maxim." The feeling of respect moves us to will moral maxims. That is why Kant treats it as a distinctive form of practical awareness.[25]

The person who feels respect for the law experiences an awareness of himself as both a source of moral action and, simultaneously, a sensuous being, desiring the satisfaction of his inclinations. Consequently, to feel respect for the law is also to feel inadequate. Respect for the law humiliates us and yet moves us to act morally.[26] How does it do this? Why does it not simply paralyze us?

To answer this question, Kant introduces another element crucial to willing maxims in accordance with the moral law: an interest. The rational feeling of respect creates "an interest in obedience to the law and this we call the moral interest. And the capacity of taking such an interest in the law is really moral feeling."[27] All persons have this capacity, this moral feeling, insofar as they are, qua persons, conscious of the demands of morality. But what is this moral feeling? It can only be respect for the law. Respect for the law represents the *capacity* of persons to act morally and it also *produces* in those persons a moral interest that may enable them to realize this capacity.[28] The immediacy of respect turns out to be somewhat mediated, perhaps thereby secured, by this interest postulated by respect and also produced by it. To complicate matters further, Kant occasionally suggests that this interest is itself respect while arguing that the source of the interest is the practical law which "absolutely commands it and also actually produces it."[29] Either way, we are never invulnerable to the law's command.

Respect for the moral law is one of two kinds of incentive to perform one's duty. Kant's two kinds of incentive correspond to two kinds of duty, those of justice and those of virtue, and two kinds of legislation, juridical and ethical:

> If legislation makes an action a duty and at the same time makes this duty the incentive, it is ethical. If it . . . admits an incentive other than the Idea of duty itself, it is juridical. . . . Duties in accordance with juridical legislation can be only external duties because such legislation does not require that the Idea of this duty, which is internal, be of itself the ground determining the will of the agent. . . . ethical legislation also makes internal actions duties, but does not, however exclude external actions; rather it applies generally to everything that is a duty.[29]

Concerned only with external acts and not with the internal structure of subjectivity and the will, positive law can be enforced without violating its own presuppositions. Not so ethical legislation. Ethical legislation is self-legislation; it cannot be induced by fear or the promise of pleasure. Neither fear nor pleasure, both phenomenal inclinations, are identified with the self that legislates, the noumenal self. The test of an ethical action is not its outward conformity to the requirements of a law but the subject's internal conformity, the purity of his will, the unity of his will as an instrument of noumenal subjectivity. The subject's willing must be moved only by an *internal* sense of duty and motivated purely by respect or it forfeits the characteristic that makes it ethical.

A categorical moral law cannot look to inconstant and conditional inclinations and desires for motivation. It needs an incentive that is more commanding: "Only . . . something which does not serve my inclination, but outweighs it or at least leaves it entirely out of account in my choice—and therefore only bare law for its own sake, can be an object of reverence and therewith a command." Only the moral law commands us and only respect for the law brings us to will maxims in accordance with the law. With "nothing left able to determine the will except objectively the law and subjectively pure reverence for this practical law," the willing of moral maxims is secured as an unconditional and pure practice.[30] This is of the utmost importance to Kant, for whom "the true value of morality lies in the purity of its concept."[31] Oddly, this purity is enabled by respect, itself a paradoxically hybrid, rational, moral feeling—an incentive that does not induce but command, a medium through which imperfectly rational beings are made immediately aware of the moral law.

3. Reverence-Respect for Persons

Kant's complex practice of respect for persons operates daily to inscribe subjects into the moral categories and identities of the Kantian order. Continually refighting the Edenic battle to confine reason to its proper use while refurbishing morality's abstract incentives with examples, Kantian respect maintains the concealments on which enlightened reason depends and institutes among subjects the practical relations that virtue's closures require.

I organize Kant's varied and unsystematic remarks on respect for persons into three somewhat distinct but overlapping (and sometimes inconsistent) categories: reverence-respect (for the moral law in persons), teleological respect (for the humanity in persons), and liberal respect (for persons as ends in themselves). The first strand of Kant's concept of respect for persons, reverence-respect for persons, is respect for the moral law as it is manifested in the actions and self-legislation of others. Here the object of respect is not really persons but the law of laws: "The object of reverence is the law alone."[33] We reverence-respect persons when we witness the moral law at work in their activities, when their *example* awakens within us consciousness of the moral law.[34] This strand of respect is a moral feeling, not a practical duty. We do not owe it to all people, it is commanded and produced in us by some.

> To a humble plain man, in whom I perceive righteousness in a higher degree than I am conscious of in myself, *my mind bows whether I choose or not. . . .* Why? His example holds a law before me which strikes down my self-conceit when I compare my own conduct with it; that it is a law which can be obeyed. . . . *The law made visible* in an example always humbles my pride . . . *Respect is a tribute we cannot refuse to pay merit whether we will or not;* we can indeed outwardly withhold it, but we cannot help feeling it inwardly.[35]

The impossibility of refusal is the distinctive feature of reverence-respect for persons, as it was in Kant's account of respect for the moral law. Kant emphasizes the purity and goodness of the will as the center of his moral system, but the peak moral moment is this one, the one beyond willing, the tribute that *must* be paid, "whether we will or not."

This thing that can be neither refused nor willed is Kant's response to the originary refusal that moved his fable of beginning: "*Refusal* was the feat whereby man passed over from mere sensual to idealistic attractions, from mere animal desires to love."[36] It was (illicit) reason's refusal of the world, its withdrawal and concealment of the natural world from man, that disrupted his Eden and rendered him homeless, confused, anxious, and fearful. Man now seeks something that cannot be refused, something that commands. It cannot be an object of choice because his newly won freedom of choice terrifies Kant's first man in Eden. Instead, Kant offers him the comfort of a law of laws that is necessary, secure, and irresistible.

The law's force for man derives in part from its universality, but it is experienced most directly in the particularity of an example. Made visible in an example, the law bows the heads of those who witness it. The example empowers the law by making others conscious of it, but at the same time the law's power depends on its *not* being witnessed. The law's self-concealment, universality, and irresistibility all put it beyond the reach of politics and dispute. These are the conditions of the law's power. But they also limit the law's power. From a distance, the law is less able to engender the respect and immediacy Kant seeks. So he risks bringing the law closer, by way of an example. He risks idolatry.

Kant's treatment of particular moral actions or actors as exemplifications or personifications of the moral law violates a central tenet of his deontological ethic. The true essence of a Kantian moral act, the pure duty-bound willing of a moral maxim, is too internal to be made visible. Motives and intentions *cannot* be seen in the phenomenal realm. What example could illustrate—with certainty—the willing of universalizable maxims *out of a sense of duty?* And yet Kant permits reverence-respect to be aroused by outwardly moral actions, encouraging mimesis of what is already a mimetic act, the action of another in accordance with the moral law. In this capacity, though, reverence-respect—like idolatry—works only if we conceal the otherness in the object of worship. This is one of the services provided by the second strand of Kantian respect, teleological respect for persons.

2.4.   Teleological Respect for Persons

Teleological-respect is related to reverence-respect: man's teleological purpose is to will in accordance with the moral law and resist the determination of his inclinations to do otherwise. His purpose is to submit outwardly to that which he "cannot help feeling . . . inwardly," to reverence-respect for the law. But teleological respect differs from reverence-respect in that its object is not the moral law per se, it is the humanity in persons. According to Kant, man has "a duty of striving to raise himself from the crude state of his nature and from his animality and to realize ever more fully in himself the humanity by which he alone is capable of setting ends."[37] The practice of teleological respect contributes specifically to the endeavor to realize humanity in the self and in the species.

In this second teleological sense, respect has two facets: one is negative and forbids certain actions; the other is positive and involves an attitude toward others. The attitudinal aspect of teleological respect for persons is like esteem, but it differs from the ordinary sense of that term. Ordinarily, the objects of esteem are a person's talents or qualities. But teleological respect is accorded to others in its positive aspect when their actions are consonant with the humanity in them.[38] When they are not, when a person's actions subvert or abase his humanity, teleological respect is withdrawn.[39]

The human species lives in each individual person and each may, by acting in ways consonant with the humanity within him, contribute to the realization of the species' humanity. This means that teleological respect is contingent on the morality of actions. But, in contrast to reverence-respect, which is granted to the few people whose actions powerfully exemplify the moral law, teleological respect is granted to everyone, in virtue of their membership in the species, unless and until they give us reason to withdraw it. We respect the humanity in persons unless someone manifests disrespect for the humanity in himself.

> Humanity in his own person is the object of respect and he can demand this respect from every other man; but he must also do nothing by which he would forfeit this respect. . . . his insignificance as a natural man cannot detract from his consciousness of his dignity as a moral man, and he should not disavow his moral self-esteem regarding the latter; he should seek his end, which is itself a duty . . . always with the consciousness of his sublime moral disposition.[40]

A person who forfeits our teleological respect for him is deprived of our positive appraisal of him as a moral actor and human being. At times, as in his essay on education, Kant implies that the deprivation may be didactic. "The withdrawal of respect is the only fit punishment for lying." Here Kant does not mean reverence-respect, for it is not in the character of reverence-respect to be withdrawn. It is evoked in us, commmanded and produced in us, even in spite of ourselves; it is not at our command. And he cannot mean liberal respect, for he does not recommend that we violate the rights of the teller of the lie. He suggests that "if a child tells a lie, a look of contempt is punishment enough." The only respect whose withdrawal would amount to giving the child a look of contempt is teleological respect in its positive aspect. And it is not just the child who is so treated. "Lying makes a man the object of common contempt, and is a means of robbing him of the respect for the trust in himself that every man should have."[41]

In response to a person's failure to respect the humanity in himself, we may (and perhaps even ought to) withdraw our (positive) attitude of teleological respect for a person, but we remain obligated to accord him teleological respect in its negative aspect: no matter what he does, we may not violate the negative duties of teleological respect for persons in our conduct toward him. Certain actions are categorically forbidden by Kant's duties of virtue.

According to Kant, the violation of the duties to refrain from pride, calumny, and mockery diminishes the moral status of the object of our derision in the eyes of others. By making another the object of ridicule we effectively deny the humanity in his person. We hamper his subsequent attempts to fulfill himself as a moral being and we make it difficult for him to accord the humanity within himself his teleological respect, in both its aspects. Moreover, the denigration of humanity in a single individual "diminishes respect for humanity as such," undercutting the teleological impulse in all persons. For these two reasons, we may censure vice, but "we ought not deny all moral worth to the immoral man, for this supposes, inconsistently with the idea of man, that he can never improve." (Presumably, showing contempt for the teller of a lie is a constructive instrument for the censure of vice, whereas ridiculing him amounts to a denial of all moral worth in him.)[42]

The individual always retains his potential to be a moral being. Regardless of the circumstances of our withdrawal of teleological respect for him, he may regain it at a later date, unless he practices bestiality for which the punishment is expulsion from civil society.[43]

In his discussion of objective duties to oneself, Kant outlines the duties (negative and positive) of teleological respect. Negative duties are "limiting." Directed to moral self-preservation, their principle is "live according to nature . . . that is, preserve yourself in the perfection of your nature." Suicide, carnal self-defilement, avarice, false humanity, and lying all contradict this principle. The first three are "unnatural vices" that violate the "humanity in one's own person" and turn man into an "unnatural thing, i.e. a loathsome object." As with calumny, mockery, and pride, we have a negative duty to refrain from these practices for the sake of the humanity in ourselves and others, as well as, in Mary Gregor's words, an "accessory obligation of striving to promote the moral well-being of others through the primarily negative means at our disposal."[44]

Our positive duties to ourselves, by contrast, are widening, not limiting. Their goal is moral self-perfection. Their principle is "make yourself more perfect than mere nature made you."[45] Those who violate these duties will lose the teleological respect (in its positive dimension) of others. But the negative duties of teleological respect to others, the duties to avoid false humanity and lying, calumny, mockery, and pride, hold always. The withdrawal of the attitude of teleological respect is not license to degrade humanity in others. That would degrade humanity in ourselves. When we withdraw teleological respect, we withdraw our approval of another (or ourselves) as a teleological being. This sense of teleological respect (best described as positive and attitudinal) entails the appraisal and approval of the moral character of persons.

Kant mentions this positive, attitudinal dimension of teleological respect in a remark on friendship. Morally, a friend has a duty to point out his friend's faults. Correction is a duty of love. But it puts the chastised friend in fear of losing "something of his friend's respect."[46] What does Kant mean here by respect? The chastised friend does not fear that his friend will no longer respect the distance between them. He fears, rather, that his friend has come to disapprove of him, to doubt the purposiveness with which he is directed to his own teleological fulfillment. These are *faults* that are being corrected, after all.

The same sort of fear makes one subject reluctant to confide in another. Were the confidences not mutual, "his candidness would lower him in the respect, the estimation of the other." Against Kant's backdrop of decency and its concealments, the confidence is necessarily a confession. The friend who cannot contain himself destabilizes the dynamic of friendship. To confide—to confess—inhuman impulses, impurity, or bestiality is to make further friendship impossible. This is why "each friend is generously concerned with sparing the other his burden and bearing it all by himself, even concealing it altogether from his friend." Keeping one's ill-fittedness to oneself is a true act of friendship, for Kant. The friend yearns for communication and proximity but he indulges that yearning at his peril. Kantian friendship, which Kant values precisely as a privileged site of communication, preserves itself with guarded silence and distance.[47]

To lose a friend's respect is to lose the friendship. In both cases (of the chastised, corrected friend and the one who confides too much), Kant implies that the loss of respect may be didactic, as it is when he counsels contempt for the teller of a lie.[48] But this is not its justification. The withdrawal of teleological respect is a rejection, a partial expulsion from the society of manners and decency. Its justification is the safeguarding of the practice of friendship and the ideal of humanity. Both, as Kant conceives of them, are too fragile to survive confrontations with the otherness in and among selves.

Kant seldom uses the term "respect" in this teleological sense.[49] It surfaces when he talks about friends taking the risk of confiding in each other, as well as when he discusses the withdrawal of respect from a person who violates the humanity in himself.[50] Teleological self-respect (and the self-control, concealment, and discipline it implies) is what the members of Kant's community look for in others; it is the basis of their inclusion or exclusion of others from their moral and juridical arrangements.

2, 5.   Liberal Respect for Persons

According to Kant, it is "inconsistent with the idea of man" to suppose that an immoral man "can never improve." But there *are* some men who by their deeds make themselves "unworthy" of their humanity.[51] To them, we do not accord reverence-respect and we may even withdraw our teleological respect. But we may not refuse them liberal respect. Liberal respect is the acknowledgment we give to the distance between individuals. It involves taking others into account when willing maxims and acknowledging their existence as a constraint on our choice of which maxims to will. A person need do nothing to deserve this brand of respect. He need only exist—and refrain from bestiality. I call this aspect of Kant's concept of respect "liberal respect" because of the classical liberal trappings that surround it. It requires that men relate to each other from a distance,[52] as equals,[53] and as bearers of rights.[54]

Respect for rights signals a regard for the person as an end in himself: "A violation of the rights of man intends to use the person of others merely as a means without taking into consideration that, as rational beings they ought always at the same time to be rated as ends."[55] We think of this claim—that we ought to rate people at the same time as ends—as the basis of Kant's concept of respect. But what does it mean? Given the heterogeneity of Kantian respect, the injunction to treat persons always also as ends shifts depending on which perspective we view it from: teleological respect or liberal respect?

Under teleological respect, the stress is on regarding others as ends-in-themselves. To accord teleological respect to a person is to acknowledge his conduct of himself in accordance with his natural and moral ends. Should this person deviate from those ends, we withdraw our teleological respect but continue to accord him liberal respect. "I cannot deny all respect to even the immoral man as a man; I cannot withdraw at least the respect that belongs to him in his quality as a man."[56] Under liberal respect, the stress is not on (positively) regarding others as ends but on (negatively) not using others as mere means. That is why Kant's description of his principle of humanity as an end-in-itself sometimes sounds very much like the liberal value of negative liberty. Kant describes the principle as "the supreme limiting condition of every man's freedom of action," and he connects it to the duty of respect: "The duty of free respect to others is really only a negative one (of not exalting oneself above others) and is thus analogous to the juridical duty of not encroaching on another's possessions."[57] Not to exalt oneself above others means taking others into account as one's equals when choosing which maxims to will. Willing a maxim that does not take account of the equality of others violates their rights.[58] As Gregor rightly points out, Kant's duties of respect (so understood) "extend the relations of freedom and equality beyond the sphere of external compulsion into that of attitude of will and limit not merely external actions, but also, in a sense, our ends themselves."[59]

Understood in this way, as a principle of liberal respect that constrains not only acting but also willing, the second categorical imperative (CI_2) ends up looking much like the first (CI_1), just as Kant claimed it should. Liberal respect disallows the willing of maxims that would impinge on others' willing maxims of their own. This means that, to be consistent with the liberal principle of persons as ends-in-themselves (CI_2), our maxims must be universalizable (CI_1). As H. J. Paton puts it, it is "Kant's view that to treat others as ends-in-themselves is to treat them in such a way that their rational wills can be in agreement with ours and that they must be able to contain within themselves the end of our action towards them."[60]

But CI_1 and CI_2 are not indistinguishable. Kant gives distinctly different arguments for them. The former imposes a logical test through which we must will our maxims; the test imposed by the latter is teleological. Gregor explains it best when she argues that, as regards CI$_2$, Kant

> is not thinking of logical consistency as the criterion of moral action. The freedom from contradiction which he requires in a universalized maxim is, rather, a teleological consistency between our maxim and our objective rational ends. Thus in Kant's own account of suicide, it is not the self-defeating character of the maxim that makes it immoral. It is rather the fact that, in acting on a maxim of arbitrarily destroying our capacity for free or moral action, we are in contradiction with our objective end as free or moral agents, and so in contradiction with ourselves.[61]

Certain maxims fail CI$_1$'s test of universalizability because of their self-contradictory character. CI$_2$, considered as a principle of liberal-respect, has a similar character of "do not unto others," but the test it imposes is not a logical one. The maxims it forbids are not those that would contradict themselves if universalized but those that would contradict the ability of others (and ourselves) to will maxims in their (and our) own right.

Kant's independent arguments for liberal respect and teleological respect should not be allowed to obscure the fact that both are grounded in reverence-respect. Without practical awareness of the moral law, we would not understand ourselves to be obligated to respect persons in these two other senses.[62] Without practical awareness of the moral law, we would be less in need of self-concealment (we would have less to conceal), and so we would have less of a stake in practices of respect. Together these three distinguishable practices of respect work to support and maintain the forms of moral subjectivity Kant identifies as man's proper, natural, and moral end.

2.6.   Setting the Conditions for Moral Improvement

To violate the duties of teleological respect is to act immorally. It is also immoral to violate the duties of liberal respect, but it is not only immoral to do so: in Kant's republic it is also illegal. Whereas teleological respect is strictly an ethical duty, liberal respect is both an ethical and a juridical duty. As a juridical duty, it may be enforced by positive law, justifiably, because its nonviolation is a necessary (though not sufficient) condition of the development of autonomy in Kantian citizens.

Because Kant sees the political-legal order as an instrument for the realization of moral ends, he believes that we have a moral duty to enter civil society: "Natural right allows us to say of men living in a lawless condition that they ought to abandon it." Those unwilling to do so may be coerced. The coercion is legitimate even if those living outside the law have done nothing to injure members of the legal order. It is legitimate because it defends Kantian citizens against the specter of lawlessness: "Man (or an individual people) in a mere state of nature robs me of any such security and injures me by virtue of this very state in which he coexists with me. He may not have injured me actively (*facto*) but he does injure me by the very lawlessness of his state (*statu iniusto*), for he is a permanent threat to me, and I can require him either to enter into a common lawful state along with me or to move away from my vicinity."[63]

The role of law in civil society is to ensure that the actions of citizens conform with what is morally required even in the absence of moral motivation. This is how "the problem of justice can be solved even for a "nation of devils." The juridical enforcement of liberal respect for persons (respect for rights) disallows actions that interfere with the ability of others to will maxims and act in their own right as free, equal, and rational beings. Positive law ensures that relationships between persons in civil society are conducted in accordance with juridical duties whether or not the citizens will morally that it be so. Thus, Kant says, "the depravity of human nature . . . is largely *concealed* by governmental constraints in law-governed civil society," and this concealment serves the moral ends of politics: It

> not only gives the whole *a veneer of morality*, by putting an end to outbreaks of lawless proclivities, it genuinely makes it much easier for the moral capacities of men to develop into an immediate respect for right. For each individual believes of himself that he would by all means maintain the sanctity of the concept of right and obey it faithfully, if only he could be certain that all the others would do likewise, and the government in part guarantees this for him; thus a great step is taken towards morality (although this is still not the same as a moral step), towards a state where the concept of duty is recognized for its own sake, irrespective of any possible gain in return.[64]

The juridical state solves the free-rider problem, securing nonmoral incentives for cooperation through the force of positive law and thereby setting in place one of the necessary conditions for the moral improvement of the species. All three strands of respect join in the condition-setting project by reinforcing the "veneer of morality" secured by governmental constraints. All three discourage self-disclosure and intimacy while promoting self-concealment and containment, hiding from view any resistances to the Kantian project and using strategies of appraisal and isolation to inscribe selves into the moral order, daily.

But how is this possible? How can it be, given Kant's distinction between the phenomenal and noumenal realms, that the legal protection of rights and the practice of respect for persons (in the phenomenal realm) contribute to the development of autonomy in persons (in the noumenal realm)? As George Armstrong Kelly put the problem, "it should be impossible," in Kant's view, "for citizenship or public law-abidingness to make men moral. . . . a false juncture would be made between the realms of autonomous and heteronomous causation."[65] The phenomenal realm, the realm of chance and fortune, is supposed to have no relevance to the agent's willing of moral maxims, hence indeed their quality as moral and the will's quality as pure. But Kant makes one important concession. In the *Doctrine of Virtue* he allows that

> adversity, pain, and want are great temptations to transgress one's duty. So it might seem that prosperity, strength, health, and well-being in general, which check the influence of these, could also be considered obligatory ends which make up the duty of promoting *one's own* happiness, and not merely the happiness of others.—But then the end is not the agent's happiness but his morality, and happiness is merely a means for removing obstacles to his morality—a *permissible* means, since no one has a right to demand that I sacrifice my own ends if these are not immoral. To seek prosperity for its own sake is no direct duty, but it can well be an *indirect duty: The duty of warding off poverty as a great temptation to vice* [my emphasis]. But then it is not my happiness but the preservation of my moral integrity that is my end and also my duty.[66]

As we saw earlier, Kant holds that we have a duty to seek our own moral perfection and an obligation to promote the moral well-being of others through negative means, that is, through the nonviolation of the negative duties of teleological respect. Although we also have a duty to promote the happiness of others, we can do nothing positive to promote their moral perfection; this is a task that must be self-imposed (albeit with the support and pressure of the attitude of teleological respect, applied with care). We have no duty to seek our own happiness; no such duty is necessary because "by a tendency of his nature man inevitably wants and seeks his own happiness."[67] But in the passage quoted above Kant concedes that seeking one's own happiness (notably in prosperity) may be a means to the attainment of one's own perfection. When the battle be-tween respect for the law and the inclinations takes place in conditions of adversity, pain, and want, the inclinations are more likely to win out. In adverse conditions, it is more difficult to act as duty requires. And, as Kant says, "whatever diminishes the obstacles to an activity furthers this activity itself."[68]

Kant's concession that happiness and perfection may be related casts new light on the duty to promote the happiness of others. Perhaps it requires us to help others pursue their own perfection. If adversity, pain, and want are obstacles to morality, then their removal may be a permissi-ble means through which to pursue our perfection and to aid others in the pursuit of theirs. Thus, perhaps the obligation to promote the moral well-being of others is not limited to the nonviolation of the duties of teleological respect after all. The practice of promoting the moral well-being of others may have more positive, and more active dimensions, even if they are—technically—restricted to condition setting.[69]

Kant's commitment to condition setting accounts further for his claim that we have a duty to enter civil society. In Kant's civil society, condi-tions of adversity are lessened. The state solves the free-rider problem, giving much needed reassurance to everyone and making cooperation possible. The state's provision of equality, rights, and liberty under law ensures the security and privacy of its citizens and sets the conditions that enable them to pursue their natural happiness and moral perfec-tion.[70] But in lessening the violence and adversity of the state of nature the juridical state exercises a violence of its own, a violence that is the product of the state's organization and concentration of power.

In "The Right of Punishment and the Right of Pardon," Kant advo-cates the "equality of punishments . . . in accordance with the strict law of retribution," but he points out that, if the number of murderers involved in a single crime is very great, the sovereign may depart from what justice "wills in accordance with universal laws of *a priori* origin." In such an "emergency," the sovereign has "the power to act as judge himself" and "to pass a sentence which imposes a penalty other than death on the criminals." Kant says that the sovereign should consider this option because the "state will not wish to blunt the people's feelings by a spectacle of mass slaughter."[71] But is that what the state is concerned about: that the people's feelings will be *blunted* by the spectacle of slaugh-ter? Or is the sovereign advised to depart from the strict law of retribu-tion because the people's feelings may be *aroused* by this powerful con-frontation with state violence? Their arousal would be destabilizing. It might lead some to question or challenge Kant's a priori laws and the requirement of strict retribution. More important, it might lead some to interrogate the role of the sovereign or the practice of punishment in the state. The biggest problem posed by violence may be its enormous power to politicize. Is that why Kant attends to it with such care, while suggesting that the sovereign do the same?

The same sorts of concerns about violence and its politicizing and destabilizing potential may inform Kant's concession that the "supreme power" may make "laws which are primarily directed towards happiness." Is it wariness of the destabilizing power of economic violence that leads Kant to allow governmental concern for citizen welfare to serve as a "means of securing the rightful state," even though he generally rejects the possibility that phenomenal conditions can affect noumenal ends?[72]

His distinction between the phenomenal and noumenal realms notwithstanding, Kant sees the establishment of the rightful state as the most important condition of man's moral development. Without the stability of the state's institutions, the security of its ethical and juridical practices, (and the violence of its maintenance), the species would have little hope of ever redeeming itself. These requirements suggest that Kantian autonomy, the individual condition of unconditional self-governance, is highly heteronomous, a fragile condition, enormously dependent on external care, intersubjective community practices, juridical support, and stable phenomenal conditions.[73]

2.7.   Kant's Virtue Theory of Politics

Some of Kant's best insights regarding the self call attention to the fundamental ambivalence that marks subjectivity, the otherness haunting the practices of respect and concealment that are the necessary means to the ends Kant values, the self's perpetual failure to discipline itself according to the dictates of virtue, its incapacity to close the circle of its subjectivity and call it a fait accompli. Riven not only by the phenomenal-noumenal distinction and its attendant conflicts of desire and will, the Kantian self is also marked by a characteristic "unsocial sociability," by a "tendency to come together [with others] in society, coupled, however, with a continual resistance that constantly threatens to break this society up." The solution is a "perfectly just civil constitution" in which "freedom under external laws would be combined to the greatest possible extent with irresistible force."[74] In Kant's politics, external laws do the work of his law of laws in morals: both are irresistible, one backed up by the external force of state violence, the other by the internal force and command of reverence. In each sphere, the unsocial (or too social) or recalcitrant aspects of human character or actions are shaped by the irresistible force of law.

The irresistibility of moral and positive law is most forcefully felt in the absence of phenomenal violence; hence Kant's concerns about punishment and hunger or juridical and economic violence. Hence, too, his desire to secure domestic as well as international peace and stability. It is only in conditions of peace that "those capacities which make our species worthy of respect can be properly developed."[75] But the process of development is slow. Although Kant sometimes promises that the species will one day achieve moral perfection, the promise is for a distant future and it applies to the species, not to individuals.

Individuals struggle endlessly, in Kant's world, to fashion themselves into virtuous, respect-worthy subjects.[76] The ideal of virtue cannot be met by any man, but it provides the standard by which individual, cultural, and political orderings are judged nonetheless. Reasoning from the standpoint of virtue, Kant sees the tumult of moral and political struggle as a necessary evil that Fallen men must bear. He sees no promise in the self's resistance to the ordering of subjectivity, no dimension of struggle that is worthy of affirmation (apart from its extrinsic goal of marking the species' projected progress toward virtue and the end of struggle).

From the perspective of *virtù*, however, the self's resistance to the requirements of moral virtue and subjectivity is cause not for mourning but for celebration. There is vitality in a self that exceeds all orderings. Its excess denaturalizes existing arrangements and signals the possibility of alternative ethical and political ideals. Nietzsche looks to *virtù* to identify these spaces of alternative, envisioning the displacement of virtue with new, individuating, ethical and aesthetic practices of *virtù*. Hannah Arendt values the disturbances Kant seeks to quiet for the sake of the virtuosic politics they generate. Without these spaces of resistance and resistibility, there could be no action, no self-display, no self-enactment, no *virtù*; there would be only legal, juridical, bureaucratic administration or despotism, behavior, self-concealment, and virtue.

Kant does not assume or insist that his conception of moral subjectivity and political order fits and expresses the self without remainder. But he does assume an expressive correspondence between his moral-political order and the noumenal self. That assumption grounds his refusal to allow his own ideal of moral virtue to be affected by or responsive to phenomenal resistances to it. Had Kant allowed the experience of rifts in subjectivity to inform his politics, had he politicized the ambivalence of unsocial sociability (rather than just regulating it), had he affirmed the struggle of subjectivity instead of putting up with it, he might have developed a more political vision. Instead, he responds to each rift with a strategy of closure: in response to reason's disruptions of Eden, he divides reason into Jekyll and Hyde parts, right use and misuse, denouncing reason's disruptive aspect as an imposter from which reason can be rescued without loss—as if reason's powers of consolidation could survive in the absence of its powers of dissolution.

Similarly, Kant divides the dynamic impulse of unsocial sociability into two distinct urges, mapping them onto public-private, politics-culture distinctions that he never critically analyzes. He turns to positive law to occlude the gap between moral and natural man by securing moral outcomes in the absence of moral motivation. And he trusts that politics, rightly used, will support and maintain positive law in this effort; misused, politics interrogates and renders problematic the bases of moral and political order. Finally, he depends on fables to make the world into a more secure home for man and to give him the faith he needs to participate in the collective and perpetual project of developing virtue in the species. The fables tell man that he is an end in himself, but, along the way, means and end are inverted. The construction of the home becomes the end, and man—the Kantian subject—a means to it.[77]

Like all fables, Kant's seek to construct a "we," a community to whom the fable is addressed, by whom the fable is told and retold. The construction of the "we" goes on at several levels, even at the level of authorship. Kant writes his fable of Eden together with his readers, asking for their approval and consent as he proceeds: "Surely it is permissible . . ." His fable teaches us that we are all members of one family, descended from a single couple and therefore capable of a perpetual peace that is not threatened by strangers or otherness. The lesson of Kant's fable is that we need to pursue our shared end of culture; but this end does not merely express a preexisting community identity, it creates identities into which subjects are constituted. Perhaps that is why Kant ends his fable with an appeal to a duty to hope, an "inborn duty of influencing posterity in such a way that it will make constant progress (and I must thus assume that progress is possible)." Without "the prospect of future improvements," we would be "confronted by the sorry spectacle not only of those evils which befall mankind from natural causes, but also of those which men inflict upon one another."[78] In Kant's view, there is only one set of options: either men are capable of modifying their conduct according to principles of right or they are condemned to an irredeemably violent existence: "If there is nothing which commands immediate respect through reason, such as the basic rights of man, no influence can prevail upon man's arbitrary will and restrain his freedom. But if both benevolence and right speak out in loud tones, human nature will not prove too debased to listen to their voices with respect."[79] It is Kant's construction of these options, as oppositional and exhaustive, that Nietzsche and later Arendt call into question.

Nietzsche develops his own fables to offset Kant's. One of their lessons is that Kant is right to attribute man's alienation from the world to reason. But there is no *misuse* of reason here. For Nietzsche, this is what reason does, qua reason. Its powers of consolidation are integrally connected to its powers of dissolution. Reason creates whole universes of meaning, rejecting that which resists its categorization and demanding that the world accommodate its requirements of order and calculability. It presents itself as irresistible because right and is then driven to conceal that which is manifestly resistant to its demands. From the perspective of *virtù*, Nietzsche challenges man to reason differently, to overcome his originary terrors and face the fact that his need for closure and meaning engenders violence and isolation instead of the peace and friendship he seeks, to find within himself the capacity to reclaim (in transvalued form) the present moment and the self-sufficiency whose loss Kant both mourns and secures.

CHAPTER THREE

Nietzsche and the Recovery
of Responsibility

Not riddle enough to scare human love from it, not solution enough to put to
sleep human wisdom:—a humanly good thing was the world to me today, of
which such bad things are said.

—Zarathustra

Although famous for his aspiration to go "beyond good and evil," Nietzsche seeks a transvaluation of values, not an abandonment of them. He
criticizes traditional moral values for their unethical qualities—their
dishonesties and cruelties enrage him—but he does not reject them tout
court. He recovers each of the traditional virtues, restructuring and
recasting them so that they might take their place in a new table of values
that is, in Nietzsche's estimation, more honest and less cruel than its
predecessor, more generous to life.

Three Kinds of Recovery

I characterize Nietzsche's project as one of recovery because the term
evokes three of the project's salient features. First, Nietzsche hopes that
his project might move the human species (or some of its members) out of
sickness and into recovery. By unmasking the values that have made the
human animal sick," Nietzsche hopes to usher in a period of convales-
cence and perhaps even make way for the possibility of rebirth.[1] Our
values have "become disvalued and false," Nietzsche says, and that "can
be very painful, but then comes a consolation: such pains are birth-
pangs. The butterfly wants to get out of its cocoon, it tears at it, it breaks
it open: then it is blinded and confused by the unfamiliar light, the realm
of freedom."[2]

The second sense of recovery supports and animates the project of the first. Nietzsche recovers the origins of values that we now take to be universal, transcendent, and true in order to show that they are in fact conditional and partial, developed out of struggles with alternative ethics and forms of life that have since been lost, silenced, or concealed.[3] In *The Genealogy of Morals*, for example, Nietzsche recovers the silenced and forgotten morality of the lords (a presocratic ethic of good and bad), contrasts it with the slave morality of good and evil, and traces the processes by which the slaves' values vanquished those of the lords. The recovery is not nostalgic. Nietzsche's recoveries propel his readers forward, *beyond* good and evil, not backward to a time before it. When an imaginary interlocutor (in another text) says about Nietzsche, "Bad! Bad! Look—isn't he going backward?" Nietzsche responds: "Yes, but you misunderstand him if you complain of it. He is going backward like someone who is about to take a great leap."[4]

In an earlier essay, "On Truth and Lies in an Extra-Moral Sense," Nietzsche adopts the same approach, speculatively recovering the origins of language to show that the suppression of differences and the establishment of false equivalences through metaphor are indispensable to its claim to truth. Like slave morality, language claims to correspond to things as they are, to give them "adequate expression," but "it is only by means of forgetfulness that man can ever reach the point of fancying himself to possess a 'truth'" of this sort. Specifically, man forgets that language originates in the experience of a twitch, a "nerve stimulus," that is then transferred into an image. The transfer is a metaphor. Then "the image . . . is imitated in a sound: second metaphor." In short, language is two metaphors away, not from an independent reality, but from a neurological twitch that is mistaken as a response to an external, "real" event in the world. Nietzsche concludes that "we possess nothing but metaphors for things—metaphors which correspond in no way to the original entities."[5]

Both recoveries, of the origins of language and of the rival morality of the lords, attempt to harness the radical and transformative powers of memory. Like Kant's "Speculative Beginnings of Human History," these are fables with a point. Unlike Kant's "Speculative Beginnings," their point is not to calm and heal the effects of an originary disruption but to disrupt a set of linguistic, conceptual, and moral settlements. Nietzsche's purpose, at this stage, is not to construct a "we" but to deconstruct existing ones; hence his reliance on genealogy. Genealogy does not simply recover forgotten pasts. Suspicious of would-be unities, it seeks out the gaps and complexities that testify to their imperfect construction. Its premise is that "everything that enters consciousness as 'unity' is already tremendously complex: we always have only a semblance of unity."[6] Its aim is to highlight the processes—the rites of power, pain, and knowledge—that maintain the appearance of unity, daily.

Why daily? Language equalizes things that are inherently unequal, concealing and silencing unruly differences in order to organize its world around constructs of the same.[7] But concealed and silenced differences are not thereby obviated. They continue to have effects in the world. They surface as the (often inscrutable) resistances or obstacles to the human project of making sense of the world. And we respond to them by trying to cure or extirpate their manifestations since, like "all suppressed truths," they "become poisonous."[8]

Atoms, the will, things in themselves—none is (antecedently) true; all are interpretations, impositional projections.[9] If it can be said that the world has any total character, Nietzsche says it must be that it "is in all eternity chaos—in the sense not of a lack of necessity but of a lack of order, arrangement, form, beauty, wisdom and whatever other names there are for our aesthetic anthropomorphisms."[10] To attribute particular features, qualities, or moods to the world is to attempt to fix and order a world characterized above all by an impulse to change, although moving in no particular direction, an impulse Nietzsche identifies with life itself, sometimes calling it will to power.[11]

God, virtue, the ego, and the subject are not given; they are interpretative creations, fictions. To insist on their givenness (or rightness or expressiveness) is necessarily to conceal their varied, violent, haphazard, and tenuously constructed origins. This concealment is a kind of original sin, an initial wrongdoing that occasions the rule of morality henceforth. Nietzsche says, "How little moral would the world appear without forgetfulness! A poet could say that God has placed forgetfulness as a doorkeeper on the threshold of the temple of human dignity."[12] Forgetting is hard to overcome because once a morality is formed it "enters consciousness as a law." It then "becomes venerable, unassailable, holy, true; it is part of its development that its origin should be forgotten—that is a sign that it has become master."[13] Like words, moral concepts sediment quickly into place. Genealogical critique loosens those sedimentations, to recover and remember (at least momentarily) a morality's origins until morality is no longer master: at that point, it becomes "interesting."[14]

This brings us to the third sense of recovery, to "cover again." Nietzsche's genealogical recoveries show that all language, all moral values, indeed all systems of valuation are palimpsests of interpretation. But traditional moral values are not only not true, they are also no longer viable. Indeed, their self-defeating character is the motive force behind Nietzsche's genealogical recoveries. "Morality itself," he notes, "in the form of honesty, compels us to deny morality."[15] The recognition that our values lack the essential quality that is supposed to be their stabilizing force enables us to reclaim them as our own constructs (not given nor received) and perhaps even to *re-cover* them, to add another layer to the palimpsest and create new values that are more viable and less impositional than the old ones. "He who hath grown wise concerning old origins," Nietzsche says, "lo, he will at last seek after the fountains of the future and new origins."[16]

Wisdom and recognition come slowly, however, for nihilism—the acknowledgment that traditional values are hollow—proceeds subtly. So Nietzsche tries to hurry it along by announcing the death of God. That God is dead is not earth-shattering news. The death had already been announced by Hegel. But the consequences of the death are legion. "Christianity is a system, a consistently thought out and *complete* view of things. If one breaks out of it a fundamental idea, the belief in God, one thereby breaks the whole thing to pieces."[17] And yet the remnants of theology lurk everywhere: "God is dead; but given the way of men there may still be caves for thousands of years in which his shadow will be shown—And we—we still have to vanquish his shadow, too."[18] Nietzsche locates the remnants of theology in the sedimentations of language and its grammar, in the devotion to science, in the Enlightenment faith in reason, in the Kantian project of constructing or justifying a world governed and directed by reason or right, in the transformation of morality into laws of nature that govern the physical world. These remnants persist because the "overturning of opinions does not immediately follow upon the overturning of institutions: the novel opinions continue, rather, to live on for a long time in the deserted and by now uncomfortable house of their predecessors, and even keep it in good condition because they have nowhere else to live."[19]

We must seek out all the new ideas that find the houses of their predecessors habitable (and make them into homes). "Here no terms are permissible: here one has to eradicate, annihilate, wage war." Without faith, our understanding of our physical, moral, and even linguistic world must collapse. If much of the rubble is still standing, it is because we have been fearful to embrace the consequences of the death of God;

they are enormous. "One interpretation has collapsed but because it was considered *the* interpretation it now seems as if there were no meaning at all in existence, as if everything were in vain."[20]

This "as if" marks Nietzsche's belief in the generative power of a nihilism that is a transitional stage that prepares the way for self-overcoming.[21] Nietzsche endorses this nihilism in its most abyssal destruction without investing its negativity with an absolute character. He does not yield to the temptation to believe in nothingness as we once believed in God. He valorizes nihilism because he believes that "extreme positions are not succeeded by moderate ones but by extreme positions of the opposite kind." And so he declares war on Christianity and its remnants, rejecting "every compromise position with respect to it," forcing "a war against it" and against the morality of good and evil. This is a creative destruction, however, for "from such abysses, from such severe sickness, also from the sickness of severe suspicion, one returns newborn . . . with merrier senses, with a second dangerous innocence in joy, more childlike and yet a hundred times subtler than one has ever been before." The nihilism Nietzsche affirms rightly occasions anguish, but it is also cause for rejoicing. Its generative powers and effects teach the practice of re-covery, of building anew.[22]

Nietzsche's rhetoric is apocalyptic in discussing nihilism, but the building he envisions is not ex nihilo. He himself re-covers many standard moral virtues, including courage, moderation, compassion, self-discipline, truthfulness, benevolence, love, respect, magnanimity, and responsibility. All have already been re-covered numerous times, taken up by Christianity from Aristotle and refurbished, and then taken over again by Enlightenment thinkers. Nietzsche re-covers them again, turning them from reactions of weakness and resentment into expressions of strength and abundance of power.[23] He also re-covers virtue as *virtù*, again identifying the former with weakness, the latter with strength.[24] I touch on many of these re-coveries in the course of my reading of Nietzsche's recovery of responsibility, but I take responsibility as my central focus and point of departure.

The Genealogical Recovery of Responsibility

On The Genealogy of Morals, Nietzsche's central text on responsibility and his own "speculative beginning of human history,"[25] tells the story of the Fall of the noble lords who once ruled the earth with a dinosaur-like ease, simplicity, and naturalness that Nietzsche envies and admires. Nietz-sche's lords soon disappear, not because of any particular original sin per se, but because of the cunning of some snakelike characters—the herd—who introduce into the lordly life complexities that these simple, power-ful creatures can neither engage nor overcome.

Nietzsche mourns the passing of the lords but does not yearn nostalgi-cally for their return. Although he admires their power, he also seems to think them a rather boring species. The herd that manages the lords' extinction is less powerful than its beastly adversaries but also more interesting in part because it manages cleverly to defeat the more power-ful lords but also because its practices establish the necessary conditions for the emergence of yet a third form of subjectivity that overcomes the first two: Nietzsche's sovereign individual. This creature, through hard work and long discipline, attains a lordlike form of life, succeeding (where the lords failed) in establishing for himself an existence indepen-dent of the herd's encroachments.

For Nietzsche, herd morality is an expression of ressentiment: ressen-timent of the weak for the strong, of the weak for their condition of weakness, for the arbitrariness of the world, for the human inability to control the circumstances of life; ressentiment for time's unyielding determination to march on. We are too weak to accept nature's con-tingency, to endorse that contingency as a challenge that might humble us but might also do us honor if we responded to it honorably, that is, out of strength instead of weakness. Acting out of weakness rather than strength, we seek to domesticate nature and all that is unknown to us. We divest ourselves of importance by placing a divine being (or reason or nature or progress) at the center of the world, a being whose job it is to render our world meaningful if not always knowable. Paradoxically, we at the same time manifest enormous hubris as we pridefully place our-selves at the center of this onto-theological universe, insisting that we are God's creations, indeed, his preferred creations, unlike and superior to the animals whose pelts we appropriate for our clothing. God, we be-lieve, lives for us, loving us, watching us and judging us, *all* of us, constantly. Nietzsche points out this paradox, noting the extent to which "these forms of depersonalization in fact give the person a tremendous importance."[26]

In authoring this domesticated world for ourselves, we authorize our own domestication. In refusing the world we refuse ourselves. Our moral values, herd values, do not spur us on to greatness, they enshrine mediocrity, that which is a prerequisite for herd membership. We become perfect instruments, obedient, unthoughtful, and fearful. We constrain our exercises of power and creation in the world in order to ensure our safe preservation.

Responsibility is one of the instruments we use to control the contingency we fear; it, in turn, controls and domesticates us. Nietzsche illustrates the process with a parable:

> That lambs dislike birds of prey does not seem strange: only it gives no ground for reproaching these birds of prey for bearing off little lambs. And if the lambs say among themselves: "these birds of prey are evil; and whoever is least like a bird of prey but rather its opposite, a lamb—would he not be good?" there is no reason to find fault with this institution of an ideal, except perhaps that the birds of prey might view it a little ironically and say "*we* don't dislike them at all these good little lambs; we even love them; nothing is more tasty than a tender lamb."[27]

This institution of an ideal is simply the first step. What follows is the demand that "strength should not express itself as strength," that these birds of prey could do otherwise and are to blame for preying on little lambs. This demand, Nietzsche says, is as "absurd as to demand of weakness that it *should* express itself as strength," for it relies on the myth of free agency. It posits an actor prior to action, "a 'being' behind the doing." But, Nietzsche insists, no such being exists. It is

> only owing to the seduction of language (and of the fundamental errors of reason that are petrified in it) which conceives and misconceives all effects as conditioned by something that causes effects, by a 'subject'. . . . popular morality also separates strength from expressions of strength as if there were a neutral substratum behind the strong man which was *free* to express strength or not to do so. But there is no such substratum; there is no "being" behind doing, effecting, becoming; "the doer" is merely a fiction added to the deed—the deed is everything.[28]

We translate our grammatical need for a subject into a belief that a being exists behind the doing. Our belief in the givenness of subjectivity naturalizes the grammatical subject and provides a foundational ground for our belief in free will. Nietzsche challenges this belief with the claim that "the 'subject' is not something given, it is something added and invented and projected behind what there is."[29] He renders this belief problematic by reminding us of its purpose, of why it is so important to us, of its role in the later development of an ethic of responsible subjectivity that meets the herd's particular need to have someone to blame for their misfortunes.

At this early stage of the *Genealogy*, however, the purpose of the myth of free will as told in the fable is to make the birds of prey accountable.—accountable but not yet responsible. The road to responsibility is a long one; it is the road to interiorization. It begins with the creation of memory through rites and rituals of pain: "Ah reason, seriousness, mastery over the affects, the whole somber thing called reflection, all these prerogatives and showpieces of man: how dearly they have been bought! How much blood and cruelty lie at the bottom of all 'good things'." Although "good things" is in scare quotes here, Nietzsche does believe that there is in fact a measure of goodness in these things. He does not celebrate the project of making men "calculable" but he does note that the process also produces "the ripest fruit," the sovereign individual. The latter is a creature possessed of the "right to make promises" and the "right to affirm oneself." These rights and powers Nietzsche values highly. He is impressed by the new sophisticated capacities of memory and promising (especially by contrast with the lords' easy indifference) even as he is outraged by the processes of pain and torture that produce and maintain them.[30]

The violence does not stop here. It continues with the next step in the process, the unfortunate development of the bad conscience, the consciousness of guilt. Relying on the etymological connection between *Schuld* (guilt) and *Schulden* (debts), Nietzsche argues that the idea that " 'the criminal deserves punishment *because* he could have acted differently'—is in fact an extremely late and subtle form of human judgment and inference." In its early stage, punishment was a way of repaying debts, it "was *not* imposed *because* one held the doer responsible for his deed, thus *not* on the presupposition that only the guilty should be punished."[31]

The next stage of the *Genealogy* completes and perfects the construction of the interiorized subject in the name of *ressentiment*. The agent of this final stage is the ascetic priest who ministers to the herd. In his hands the concepts of duty and guilt are moralized. The herd turns to the priest for comfort from its suffering. But it is not worldly suffering the herd cannot bear, it is the meaninglessness of suffering, its pure contingency. "For every sufferer instinctively seeks a cause for his suffering; more exactly, an agent; still more specifically a *guilty* agent who is susceptible to suffering." The sickly sheep seek a blameworthy agent and the ascetic priest provides it. He alters the direction of ressentiment and turns it inward: it is they themselves who are to blame and henceforth they must understand suffering as punishment. This gives meaning to their suffering but it also transforms man, "the sick animal," into a "sinner," a responsible subject who is incessantly self-punishing. Since suffering and discontent are permanent features of human existence, "the term of punishment is [also] unending"; and man's suffering is increased, not diminished.[32]

The standards of purity and goodness set by the ascetic priest can be met by no man. (If they could be, man's contingent suffering would again be inexplicable.) If he "compared himself only with other men . . . he would see he was only bearing the general burden of human dissatisfaction and imperfection." But instead he is plagued always by guilt and inadequacy for he "compares himself with a being which alone is capable of those actions called unegoistic and lives continually in the consciousness of a selfless mode of thought, with God; it is because he looks into this brilliant mirror that his own nature seems to him so dismal, so uncommonly distorted."[33] Holding himself deeply responsible for his failure to live up to the ideal, and blind to the violence and subjugation inherent in his attempts to discipline himself according to the priestly dictates, man experiences the resistances within himself as offenses against nature, culture, and god. Because each attempt to enforce this self-discipline engenders new resistances, atonement as a fait accompli is impossible:

> In this psychical cruelty there resides a madness of the will which is absolutely unexampled: the *will* of man to find himself guilty and reprehensible to a degree that can never be atoned for; his *will* to think himself punished without any possibility of the punishment becoming equal to the guilt . . . his *will* to erect an ideal—that of the holy god—and in the face of it to feel the palpable certainty of his own absolute unworthiness.[34]

The attribution of responsibility is the reactive strategy of those too weak to live with contingency, of those who resent what happens to them, of those who wish things could have been otherwise and turn this wish into a doctrine—that of free will, a doctrine that seeks to master contingency by enshrining the belief that things could indeed have happened differently, if only we had willed it so.

Nietzsche's account might be taken as a response to Kant, although it is also much more. In Kant's "Speculative Beginning of Human History," responsibility or blameworthiness arises directly out of man's confrontation with the possibility that his world is meaningless and contingent. Indeed, Kant goes so far as to hold man responsible for having brought about that confrontation. He is responsible for his misuse of reason; and he is responsible because he misused reason. That misuse brings him to the edge of an abyss and to a recognition, an unbearable recognition, of his own mortality and contingency. Kant responds to this confrontation by making man responsible henceforth for the right use of reason and for its development in himself and in the species. This responsibility is meant to make life more bearable. Perhaps it does. But it also makes life more heavy and burdensome because it demands that man conceal from himself and from others those ineliminable parts of himself that evidence, by their very ineliminability, the fruitlessness of the project that is man's only consolation.

Responsibility is meant to mark man as an end in himself but instead it makes man and life itself into a means. The end is a belief in species progress. The end is consolation and redemption. And this, for Nietzsche, is truly an end. It marks the death of any sort of human creativity, affirmation, or vitality. Kant, in the very act of privileging man and making him the center of existence, disempowers him and makes him into a common, mediocre being.

Nietzsche would agree with Kant's observation that "from such warped wood as man is made, nothing straight can be fashioned." But for Nietzsche this is a reason to give up on the ideal of straightness. The ideal fosters self-loathing. For Kant, that self-loathing is a positive thing—"If we violate" our duty, "we feel the consequences directly, and appear despicable and culpable in our own eyes"[35]—a testimony to the power of the idea of duty and the extent to which men are responsible subjects. For Nietzsche, however, the propensity of the herd's ideal of responsibility to foster self-loathing in subjects who are told that they are irremediably crooked but ought nonetheless to become straight is a reason to challenge the Kantian ethic of duty and responsibility and to see the "bad conscience" it produces as "an illness" (albeit in the sense that pregnancy is an illness).[36]

The Re-covery of Responsibility: Against Remorse

Nietzsche's critique of responsible subjectivity is scathing. And if we read only the *Genealogy*, we might turn its last pages convinced that Nietzsche will have nothing to do with this category, that he would have us reject it finally and completely. But he does not reject it finally and completely; he affirms it. He notes that the responsible subject, "the inwardly unjust, guilt-conscious man," is not the "*antithesis*" but the "*necessary preliminary*" of the "wise, innocent (conscious of innocence) man" to whom his project is dedicated. He condemns the illness produced by the herd's ideal, "man's suffering *of man, of himself*," but then he immediately attenuates his position, adding that "the existence on earth of an animal soul turned against itself, taking sides against itself, was something so new, profound, unheard of, enigmatic, contradictory, *and pregnant with a future* that the aspect of the earth was essentially altered." Indeed, for all of his talk about the blood and pain and torture involved in its construction and maintenance, Nietzsche has enormous admiration for memory: he esteems above all the ability to stand by one's word, to promise, even above the easy power of the lords.[37]

What is the point, then, of this scathing critique of responsible subjectivity? In the *Genealogy*, Nietzsche's point is that none of these achievements is natural, that none can be had except at great cost, and, further, that they *can* be maintained as part of the systematic ethic of ressentiment that initially gave rise to them but that they ought, instead, to be lifted out of that context and redeemed, grafted onto an alternative ethic in which pain, self-discipline, and responsibility have their place but not as instruments of ressentiment, not as catalysts of self-loathing.

Thus, although it comes as something of a surprise, Nietzsche goes on to describe the philosophers of the future whom he admires as "responsible for themselves," as possessed of "the will to self-responsibility." Moreover, he says that when we go beyond herd morality we will "determine worth and rank by the amount and variety of that which an individual could carry within himself, by the *distance* his responsibility could span."[38]

What does Nietzsche mean by the responsibility he endorses as an excellence? Curiously, to be responsible in his sense is to recognize the impossibility of *moral* responsibility, to acknowledge the high costs of its maintenance and understand that the doctrine of free will is a fiction, that "no one is accountable for existing at all, for being constituted as he is, or for living in the circumstance and surrounding in which he lives. Indeed one is necessary, one is a piece of fate."[39] To be responsible in Nietzsche's re-covered sense is to overcome the need to make sense of misfortune by linking it to blameworthy agents, to move beyond the self-destructive ressentiment of moral responsibility to the point where one is capable of affirming the past, not passively and fatalistically but creatively and redemptively.

The key to this reading comes in several passages, each entitled

"Against Remorse." In *The Gay Science*, Nietzsche says, "A thinker sees his own actions as experiments and questions—as attempts to find out something. To be annoyed or feel remorse because something goes wrong—that he leaves to those who act because they have received orders and who have to reckon with a beating when his lordship is not satisfied with the result."[40] Remorse is the slave's learned response to his lord's dissatisfaction with him. As remorse is internalized and transformed into a moral feeling, the lord's beating is rendered unnecessary: the remorseful subject beats himself when things go wrong. Nietzsche criticizes him for this, for his inability "to have done with the experience" (the very inability his lord sought to cultivate in him): The "re-opening of old wounds, this wallowing in self contempt and contrition is one more illness, out of which no 'salvation of the soul' can arise but only a new form of soul sickness." Actions do go awry, Nietzsche concedes, even those of lordlike men. But the "'bite' of conscience" is a "hindrance to recovery." What response is appropriate, then? "One must," says Nietzsche in *The Will to Power*, "try to counterbalance it all by new activities, in order to escape from the sickness of self-torture as quickly as possible."[41] In short, we are to leap once more into the breach.

This is what Nietzsche's lords do. They are not immune to ressentiment, although it appears in them less often than "in the weak and impotent". But when the noble lords experience it, ressentiment "consummates and exhausts itself in an immediate reaction, and therefore does not *poison*." It is characteristic of a noble personality that one is "incapable of taking one's enemies, one's accidents, even one's misdeeds seriously for very long—that is the sign of strong, full natures in whom there is an excess of the power to form, to mold, to recuperate and to forget."[42] Those possessed of strong, full natures do not dwell on the past. Their strength is their capacity to live in the present. Their power sends them onward to the next event, the next challenge, the next puzzle.

Nietzsche's rejection of remorse should not be mistaken for a valorization of all deeds. Many deeds are less than laudable, but Nietzsche believes that no amount of remorse can change that.[43] He rejects remorse because it locks us into cycles of guilt, vengeance, violence, and self-loathing rather than point us beyond them. He wants to move beyond remorse, but in his quest to do so he does not counsel us simply to shrug off past deeds and events as if they were nothing to us. As we see in the next sections, Nietzsche's own approach is more subtle than that. He himself engages the past creatively and artistically, perpetually viewing it through new and multiple perspectives, seeking out ways of being in the present and future that might redeem the past and transform it. Nietzsche rejects remorse, but he does not reject the past along with it nor does he adopt a carefree and indifferent attitude toward any and all actions. His rejection of remorse is part of a broader, positive ethic in which the self seeks new, more functional ways to relate to itself and its past.[44]

Nietzsche envisions a self that continually renegotiates its relation to the past that constitutes it. The renegotiation is continual because the self adds to its past daily. Every day, it faces new opportunities for ressentiment and remorse; every day, it faces anew the challenge to overcome them. This is "how one becomes what one is,"[45] through the complicated process of adaptation, affirmation, and transformation Nietzsche calls responsibility. By positioning his new responsibility against remorse, Nietzsche clears the way for the next stage of the argument in which his thought of eternal recurrence plays a central role: the re-covery of responsibility as a positive ethic.

The Re-covery of Responsibility: Eternal Recurrence

Nietzsche's readers interpret eternal recurrence variously: as cosmology, physics or metaphysics, hypothesis, utopia, dystopia, perspective, truth; as a way of redeeming the past or as a guide to action in the future. Rather than arbitrate among these, let me add to the list another possibility that draws on elements in some of these other readings while seeking to improve on them by situating eternal recurrence squarely in the midst of Nietzsche's analyses of ressentiment, responsibility, and the self as a work of art.

Eternal recurrence—described in *Thus Spake Zarathustra* as the heaviest thought, the thought that everything recurs ("this identical selfsame life" from the most important even to the smallest detail)—is a thought that only those free of ressentiment can bear to think.[46] The first time Zarathustra confronts the thought, he cannot stand it. He cannot bear to think of "the eternal return also of the smallest man!—that was my disgust at all existence!"[47] It is in thinking the thought of eternal recurrence that Zarathustra finds that he has not yet achieved the abundance and self-sufficiency to which he aspires. Eternal recurrence tests him: is he prepared to affirm his existence? or does he still harbor within himself clusters of ressentiment that he has yet to confront and overcome? Zarathustra himself does not know the answer to these questions, until he thinks the thought of eternal recurrence. Thinking that thought enables him to locate the things he cannot bear (the smallest man), to identify the moments of existence he would rather avenge than affirm.

Nietzsche argues that the only way to get past passive nihilism is to relentlessly uncover the remnants and shadows of god still lurking in our language and values, and to relentlessly seek out the remnants and shadows of ressentiment still lurking within ourselves. Eternal recurrence helps him in his project by providing a surefire test for ressentiment. Those in whom the thought engenders despair are those who still harbor ressentiment for something in the past, for something within themselves.

Kant poses this test for himself several times, and he fails it brilliantly and consistently. In "Theory and Practice" he asks whether there are grounds to believe that the human "race will always progress and improve, so that the evils of the past and present will *vanish* in the future good?" If only the answer were yes, he says, "we could at least admire the human species for its constant advance towards the good; otherwise we should have to hate or despise it."[48] A drama of mere repetition unredeemed by the promise of progress or a goal is unbearably Sisyphean.

But, even on Kant's account, the human condition of struggle is unbearable not for the individual actors who are caught up in it but for those who, like god, observe the spectacle from the point of view of reason: "This empty activity of backward and forward motion, with good and evil constantly alternating, would mean that all the interplay of members of our species on earth ought merely to be regarded as a farce. And in the eyes of reason, this cannot give any higher a value to mankind than to the other animal species."[49] Human existence appears farcical (in Kant's sense) when held to the standard of reason set by Kant and when viewed from the outside by a spectator with a divine, rational perspective. According to Nietzsche, these are reasons to reconsider the perspective Kant adopts. Nietzsche's thought of eternal recurrence directs our attention away from the perspective of (Kantian) reason and toward the perspective of action and its actors; it tries to satisfy not the reactive needs of ressentiment but the active need to affirm human existence.

The source of ressentiment, Nietzsche argues in *Zarathustra*, is the stubborn irreversibility of time's "It was." The "It was" puts the will "in chains." It is "the Will's teeth-gnashing and lonesomest tribulation." Faced with it, the will is "impotent," a "malicious spectator of all that is past." The will's inability to will backward fills it with rage and leads it to take "revenge on whatever doth not, like it, feel rage and ill-humor."[50]

Those with the power to will the eternal recurrence of the same show they are free of ressentiment and the will to revenge by being able to "redeem what is past, and to transform every 'It was' into 'Thus would I have it!'" Man's ability to do this makes him bearable. Nietzsche says, "How could I endure to be a man if man were not also the composer, and riddle-reader, and redeemer of chance!"[51] The vengeful will that resents the "It was" must be overcome by the creative will, a will capable of affirming the "It was" with the greatest affirmation possible, the will that it should all recur eternally as the same.

But there is a problem with Nietzsche's account. If man can redeem the "It was" and transform it into a "Thus I would have it," then he is not thereby simply accepting or affirming the past. If he can redeem the "It was" by willing the eternal recurrence of the same, then the will is not, after all, an impotent spectator of the past. He does will, precisely when the will is supposed to be impotent. By willing the eternal recurrence of the same, he does change the past, powerfully and artistically. The problem appears to be intractable, until we attend to "the moment" in Nietzsche's account.

In *The Gay Science*, Nietzsche offers a different formulation of the thought of eternal recurrence, "the greatest weight." He asks us to imagine that a demon appears into our "loneliest loneliness" and says to us:

> This life as you now live it and have lived it, you will have to live once more and innumerable times more; and there will be nothing new in it, but every pain and every joy and every thought and sigh and everything unutterably small or great in your life will have to return to you, all in the same succession and sequence—even this spider and this moonlight between the trees, and even this moment and I myself. The eternal hourglass of existence is turned upside down again and again, and you with it, speck of dust!

In response, Nietzsche asks, "Would you not throw yourself down and gnash your teeth and curse the demon who spoke thus? Or have you once experienced a tremendous moment when you would have answered him: 'You are a god and never have I heard anything more divine'."[52] A tremendous moment could raise a man above his ressentiment; it could make him indifferent to things he once raged against and able to will their eternal return for the sake of a moment so glorious that it makes everything else—every pain, humiliation, and injury—worthwhile. This affirmation, the celebration of the eternal return of the same, is not a mere willing; it is produced by an action or an experience so overwhelming and abundant that ressentiment itself is overcome.

The image of teeth gnashing so prominent here occurs also in *Zarathu-*

stra, where it stands as a metaphor for the will's rage against time's "It was."[53] In *The Gay Science*, the image anchors Nietzsche's contrast of two attitudes toward the past: vengeful rage and affirmation. Affirmation is possible only in the "tremendous moment," only during the present moment. Vengeful rage is so fastened on the past that it makes redemptive action in the present impossible. It paralyzes our creative capacities. Nietzsche's thought of eternal recurrence tries to reorient us away from our preoccupation with the past toward the present, away from spectatorship to action, away from paralysis to movement. Only if we shift our emphasis away from the remorseful contemplation of the past will we be empowered to go on. Only through new, creative, and powerful activities, not through remorse, or guilt, or god, can we achieve this reorientation. Only from *within* the moment, a tremendous moment, could we ever will the eternal recurrence of the same.

When Nietzsche says that in the tremendous moment of the present the demon appears to us as a god and the thought of eternal recurrence as divine, he reclaims the figure of god from Kant. He does not ask a rational spectator if the spectacle of endless human striving is bearable; he poses the challenge to the actor who experiences a tremendous moment. The spectacle is made bearable by a moment that is thoroughly present, the very moment that was withdrawn from Kant's man in Eden when his (misused) reason fastened his attention on the future and on his mortality. Nietzsche recovers that present moment, seeking in *it* a site of redemption, without reference to some transhistorical meaning or a faith in future progress. The "sole fundamental fact," Nietzsche argues, is that "the motion of the world . . . does not aim at a final state." In eternal recurrence, Nietzsche seeks "a conception of the world that takes this fact into account. Becoming must be explained without recourse to final intentions; becoming must appear justified at every moment (or incapable of being evaluated; which amounts to the same thing); the present must absolutely not be justified by reference to a future; nor the past by reference to the present."[54]

When willing the eternal recurrence of the same, the object of the will is not the past per se. The "It was" is transformed not by the willing of the thought but by that which enables us to will the thought, the experience of a tremendous moment before which the remnants of ressentiment melt away. The thought, in its character as a test, helps us identify the resistances that prevent us from willing the eternal return of the same. But it also changes us. Those who think the thought, even if they fail its test, even if they have never experienced a moment tremen-

dous enough to overcome their ressentiment, may find themselves transformed by their confrontation with this possibility. If so, they may come
to appreciate another dimension of the thought of eternal recurrence: its
character as a guide to action.

The guidance function of the thought is most apparent in *The Gay
Science*'s formulation of it, with its striking echo to Kant's first formulation of the categorical imperative: "The question in each and every thing
'Do you desire this once more and innumerable times more?' would lie
upon your actions as the greatest weight."[55] Here eternal recurrence is an
ethical perspective that tests the self's relation to the actions it is about to
perform, not to those already past. Will the action it contemplates enable
the self to answer this question resoundingly in the affirmative? Or will
it be one more link in a chain of ressentiment? Is there any chance that
it might bring about a tremendous moment? Or will it mire the self
even more deeply into the cycle of vengeance Nietzsche seeks to overcome?[56]

To overlook the centrality of the moment in Nietzsche's account is to
run the risk of underestimating the importance of acting and of willing to
this drama.[57] Hannah Arendt and Ronald Beiner both make this mistake.
Arendt more or less correctly perceives that Nietzsche's notion of eternal
recurrence is "not a theory, not a doctrine, not even a hypothesis, but a
mere thought-experiment." And she understands that eternal recurrence
involves "the overcoming of vengeance." But she believes that this overcoming "is a merely mental exercise" and so she argues that Nietzsche
ends up repudiating the will:

> The Will's impotence persuades men to prefer looking backward, remem-
> bering and thinking, because, to the backward glance, everything that is
> *appears* to be necessary. The repudiation of willing liberates man from a
> responsibility that would be unbearable, if nothing that was done could be
> undone. In any case, it was probably the Will's clash with the past that
> made Nietzsche experiment with Eternal Recurrence.[58]

As Ronald Beiner points out, however, Arendt is moved to reflect on the
human faculties of willing and judging by the same problematic that
moves Nietzsche to experiment with eternal recurrence: "How can 'an
angry spectator' of the past [of time's 'It was'] be turned into a satisfied
spectator?" In short, for both Nietzsche and Arendt, "the meaninglessness of temporal succession (and therefore of all Being, regarded as a
temporal succession) is the hard truth that must be faced."[59]

According to Beiner, "Arendt initially sought a solution to the problem of 'the moment' in the nature of acting and thus in some sense in willing," but "her ultimate solution reposes in reflective judgment." Likewise, Beiner argues, "Nietzsche initially sought a solution to the problem of meaning (or nihilism, the devaluation of the highest values) in the will" but "his ultimate solution leads away from the will."[60] But Beiner over-emphasizes Arendt's reliance on judging: he dismisses too quickly Arendt's understanding of willing and acting as human responses to the problem of meaning. And this is equally true of Beiner's treatment of Nietzsche.

Influenced by Arendt's reading of Nietzsche, Beiner argues that Nietzsche ultimately seeks a solution to the problem of meaning not in willing but in thinking. Indeed, Beiner ends up collapsing the two and describes Nietzsche's "solution," eternal recurrence, as something like the will to think. "For Nietzsche," Beiner argues, "the will, the iron resolve, to *think* this problem [of 'the meaninglessness of temporal succession'] is itself its own solution. Those who can bear to *think* this problem in all its starkness will be the new creators, the redeemers of Western decadence."[61]

There is some merit to this reading, but it is important to note that for Nietzsche eternal recurrence is less a solution than it is one of several contingent responses to the problem of meaninglessness. It is less a solution than it is part of a broad and varied process of self-overcoming. Moreover, Beiner's rendering discounts the transformative and active dimensions of eternal recurrence; Beiner overlooks the fact that the thinking of the thought of eternal recurrence actually empowers and even guides those able to bear its weight. In *The Gay Science*, Nietzsche says that the weight of the thought may "crush" some of us: those of us incapable of willing and performing actions that we could endorse in this most affirmative way will be paralyzed by the thought. But Nietzsche also says that others will be changed by the thought: henceforth, their choices in willing and acting will be informed by the test of eternal recurrence. They will aim through their actions to bring about for themselves a tremendous moment, a moment in which all of the past is affirmed, however momentarily, and the will to vengeance is overcome. This willful, active dimension of eternal recurrence is problematically obscured in Beiner's, and in Arendt's, readings of Nietzsche.

Arendt argues that, for Nietzsche, "what is needful is not to change the world or men but to change their way of 'evaluating' it, their way, in other words, of thinking and reflecting about it." What she does not see is that Nietzsche seeks a change in ways of thinking because he believes that such a change would radically affect not just men's perceptions of the world but what they actually do in the world. Indeed, it is noteworthy that, in defence of her claim that Nietzsche is hostile to willing, Arendt relies on an incomplete quotation from *The Will to Power*. According to her, Nietzsche "did not stop with the discovery of the Will's *mental omnipotence*. He embarked on a construction of the given world that would make sense, be a fitting abode for a creature whose 'strength of will [is great enough] to do without meanings in things . . . [who] can endure to live in a meaningless world'."[62] Eternal recurrence, Arendt claims, affirms this meaninglessness. The activity of willing is quieted to the point of "stillness" and "nothing is left but the 'wish to be a Yes-sayer', to bless everything there is for being, 'to bless and say Amen.'"[63]

There is no mention in Arendt's account of the role willing plays in bringing about the moment in and through which eternal recurrence appears not as a curse but as a divine blessing. Nor is there any mention of the last phrase of the passage on which Arendt relies here, a phrase Nietzsche himself highlights. The complete passage reads as follows: "It is a measure of the degree of strength of will to what extent one can do without meanings in things, to what extent one can endure to live in a meaningless world *because one organizes a small portion of it oneself.*"[64] Nietzsche does not ask that man have the strength of will to do without meaning, but that he do without meanings *in* things, that he, in short, not attribute an inherent, given meaningfulness to things as things-in-themselves. As the last phrase of the passage makes clear, if man is capable of doing this, it is not because he can live without meaning, or because he passively, stoically, affirms everything as is, but because he is strong enough to be content with a meaningfulness that originates with him, with his own organization of a small portion of a meaningless world. And this, as we see in Chapter 4, is not terribly different from the task Arendt herself assigns to politics.

Both Nietzsche and Arendt seek alternative, nonresentful, responses to the human condition, to the daunting contingency of the human world. For Arendt, politics is the site of transformation; it is the new response-ability, an activity in which actors find themselves beyond ressentiment, capable of powerful affirmations because, somehow, their actions successfully and grandly organize a small portion of an otherwise meaningless world. For Nietzsche, the transformative device and response is eternal recurrence. Eternal recurrence is the opposite of the reaction of the weak and powerless, the opposite of the moral practices of responsibility, remorse, and ressentiment. It is a new kind of responsibility, the old one wrested from the hands of those who wielded it as a weapon, re-covered and turned into an expression of man's affirmation of the world and himself as they are, as pieces of contingency that often defy our attempts to overcome them but sometimes become splendid, if momentary, testaments to human creativity and power.

Alternative Responsibilities: The Self as a Work of Art

In its transformative character, eternal recurrence is part of an exercise of self-affirmation and self-construction. It is an act of artistry, recovery, and self-fashioning. This is Nietzsche's response to responsible subjectivity: to conceive of the self as a work of art.

The point of art is to praise, to "glorify," to "select," to "highlight." Art "is the great stimulus to life." Art alone is honest. If everything is illusion, indeed falsification, at least "art treats *illusion as illusion:* therefore it does not wish to deceive; it is *true."*[65] To treat *ourselves* as a work of art is no easy task, however. It requires great self-discipline. But not the self-discipline of Christianity, which "combats the passions with excision in every sense of the word: its practice, its 'cure' is *castration.* It never asks 'How can one spiritualize, beautify, deify a desire?' It has at all times laid the emphasis of its discipline on extirpation. . . . But to attack the passions at their roots means to attack life at its roots: The practice of the Church is *hostile to life."*[66] Nietzsche re-covers self-discipline from the church, describing a process analogous to the one that made music possible as a separate art. According to him, music became a separate art through a process that had to "immobilize [but not excise] a number of senses, above all the muscular sense . . . so that man no longer straightaway imitates and represents bodily everything he feels."[67] This thoroughgoing imitation is the original Dionysian condition, a condition too chaotic for man to embrace as is, a condition too full of life, a condition inviting a valorization through a disciplining.

The process of self-discipline endorsed by Nietzsche is, like this one, a creative process, a process of self-affirmation. Through self-discipline, one is able to " 'give style' to one's character" and "attain satisfaction" with oneself. This self-discipline is for those with strength because only "strong and domineering natures" can "enjoy their finest gaiety in such constraint and perfection under a law of their own." Those of weak character, "without power over themselves, . . . hate the constraint of style," perhaps because there is no formula for stylization:

It is practiced by those who survey all the strengths and weaknesses of their nature and then fit them into an artistic plan until every one of them appears as art and reason and even weaknesses delight the eye. Here a large mass of second nature has been added; there a piece of original nature has been removed—both times through long practice and daily work at it. Here the ugly that could not be removed is concealed; there it has been reinterpreted and made sublime. Much that is vague and resisted shaping has been saved and exploited for distant views; it is meant to beckon toward the fair and immeasurable. In the end, when the work is finished, it becomes evident how the constraint of a single taste governed and formed everything large and small. Whether this taste was good or bad is less important than one might suppose, if only it was a single taste![68]

To give style to oneself is to sign oneself, to develop a signature, an individuality, by working with, reshaping, and exploring the possibilities contained in and presented by raw materials that we did not choose. We free ourselves of the rage against contingency by beautifying, deifying, sometimes concealing, and thereby unifying until we are satisfied with ourselves, until we have recovered ourselves by, in effect, re-covering ourselves. Until we are able, like Zarathustra, to say at once in a single breath: "I am who I must be. I call myself Zarathustra."[69]

By giving up the demand that we, in our particularity, fit the requirements of the general category of subjectivity, we free ourselves from the "will of man to find himself guilty and reprehensible to a degree that can never be atoned for."[70] Nietzsche's re-covered self-discipline liberates us from the rage against contingency *because* it operates according to a principle of selectivity, because it is governed by a single taste, and because its object is particular. As Kant points out in his *Critique of Judgement*, and as Nietzsche seems to agree, the problem of contingency only arises, as a problem, when we try to know the world objectively.[71] The process of objective knowing subsumes particulars under general categories—concepts—that relegate the particular to the realm of the unknowable or contingent: they suppress difference. The problem of the particular, of the contingent or different, disappears if we give up on this project of explanation via subsumption. And we can do this through art.

According to Kant, the object of art is the particular, which art seeks to unify and to communicate. Because of its fundamental particularity, however, art is inimitable, and this is a problem for Kant, who worries that artistic genius (possibly the model for Nietzsche's creative artist) produces "original nonsense."[72] Not so for Nietzsche, who celebrates the incommunicability of art. Of *virtù*, the talent of artistic self (re)production and creativity, Nietzsche says happily: "It does not communicate itself; it does not propagandize." Virtue, on the other hand, Nietzsche identifies with mimicry.[73]

Rather than oppose virtue to art, Kant analogizes the beautiful and the moral, perhaps because the analogy enables him to withdraw from the abyss of the (possibly and terrifyingly incommunicable) beautiful.[74] Nietzsche, however, sees in the beautiful (as Kant would call it), in art, an alternative to the impositional constructions of morality, just as he sees in his re-covered self-discipline an alternative to the self-discipline of the moralists. Nietzsche's re-covered self-discipline valorizes the particularity and multiplicity that make the self resistant to the formation of moral, responsible subjectivity. His disciplined artist sees his unruly, multiple, and particular self as the source of a singular vitality and richness he distinctively shapes. He does not seek total self-mastery (and he does not experience the vengefulness that comes with that quest) because he understands Zarathustra's observation that "one must still have chaos in one, to give birth to a dancing star."[75] Neither does he expect total submission. He knows that his canvas is not passive and that artistry is interactive. He is responsive to the self as he shapes it.

By contrast, the self-discipline of the moralists is a resentful self-denial, symptomatic of an ineliminable dissatisfaction with the self. The subject is a creature of self-loathing. His attempts to discipline himself according to the dictates of rationality, subjectivity, goodness, or virtue continually and inevitably engender resistances within himself and, because he assumes the construction is natural, virtuous, or good, these resistances appear to him to be offenses against reason, nature, or god. As such, they testify to his irremediable inadequacy and abnormality and they feed and foster a readiness for revenge. The artist, unlike the moralist, is not made "bad and gloomy" by the "sight of what is ugly" for he does not hold himself up to some unattainable and general standard. He sees the wisdom in Zarathustra's advice: "Be not virtuous beyond your powers and seek nothing from yourselves opposed to probability."[76] He approaches himself artistically, stylizing that which he cannot affirm in himself as is through a process of discipline that requires not only strength and abundance of power but also great patience. He is like an architect, representing

neither a Dionysian nor an Apollinian condition: here it is the mighty act of will, the will which moves mountains, the intoxication of the strong will, which demands artistic expression. . . . Pride, victory over weight and gravity, the will to power, seek to render themselves visible in a building; architecture is a kind of rhetoric of power, now persuasive, even cajoling in form, now bluntly imperious. The highest feeling of power and security finds expression in that which possesses grand style.[77]

This grand style is the artist's standard. And the thought of eternal recurrence may help him attain it. Eternal recurrence provides the artist not only with the ultimate affirmation of his work but also with an important tool of self-creation. Thinking the thought enables him to locate those things for which he still harbors resentment. Even the sedimented resentments that form part of the self's "second nature" can be called up for refashioning.[78] The artist's reworking of his first and second natures shows him to be possessed of "the will to self-responsibility" and to be motivated by the desire to achieve that "worth and rank" awarded according to the "distance his responsibility could span."[79] How much of his past can he redeem with his artistry? How many episodes and remnants can he beautify with his signature? Does he possess the abundance of power, the strength, self-discipline, love of beauty, and joy necessary to pass the tests of Nietzschean responsibility?

The old responsibility bound subjects together into a community in which each member was liable to be judged by others and depended on others for forgiveness. Nietzsche's re-covered responsibility replaces this network of interdependence with a kind of self-magnanimity and apartness, severing not only the resentful ties that bind the subject to his past but also the ties that bind the subject to his fellows. The new responsibility is an attractive alternative to the cycle of self-loathing as Nietzsche depicts it. But is it not an alternative for Nietzsche's overman—for a being who lives separate from others, uncommunicative, self-sufficient, and indifferent to others, a being whose exercises of power frighten even some of Nietzsche's more sympathetic readers?[80] What is the bearing of Nietzsche's re-covered responsibility for those who do not live as overmen, for those who live among others while seeking to overcome ressentiment?

By way of response to these questions, I want to suggest two related, more nuanced readings of the overman. First, even the overman is not as self-sufficient, apart, and complete as he is often taken to be. How can the overman be a fait accompli? He must renegotiate his relationship to himself and his past, daily. Constituted by language and other human (all too human) practices and institutions, the overman is forever faced with the challenge of self-overcoming, continually confronted with new opportunities for ressentiment and rage. The point is made by Zarathustra when he says, "I am who I must be; I call myself Zarathustra." The phrase crystallizes the perpetuity of the struggle that grips those who are who they must be while at the same time striving to name themselves as they will. Nietzsche's overman never arrives at a safe resting place because his past is always being altered by his present and future and because he is always reshaping himself accordingly. He may well possess the abundance that enables him to respond to challenges with magnanimity rather than with ressentiment, but respond he must.

Put another way, perhaps the overman is always in struggle because he is never totally in control of a self; that is, perhaps he is not a distinct being apart from others but a personification of the parts of the self that resist the impositional formation of responsible subjectivity. This second possible response to the questions raised above radicalizes and democratizes Nietzsche's figure of the overman, refiguring it as a part of the self, of all selves, in ways suggested by Nietzsche's own texts.[81] On this reading, Nietzsche's figure of a resistant and unmasterable being is seen to exist within each of us. Through the figure of the overman, Nietzsche addresses the resistances within us, valorizing them, and thereby rendering more problematic the claim that subjectivity is natural, given, or expressive. This reading takes Nietzsche's genealogy of responsible subjectivity as an invitation to think of the self as an original multiplicity, a nonunified whole of microselves that includes, among others, the overman. We might think of each of these selves as a participant in a distinct language game.[82] One of these language games is the traditional practice of responsibility, and that practice attaches itself to one of these microselves, the subject (personified by Nietzsche's figure of the herd). Another is Nietzsche's re-covered responsibility, which attaches itself to another microself, the overman.

By unmasking the practice of moral responsibility, Nietzsche articulates that which the practice insists must be inarticulable—the otherness within the self that resists the discipline of moral responsibility—and calls it the overman. He offers that otherness a legitimate avenue of expression instead of silencing it by branding it abnormal, unnatural, or irresponsible. He valorizes it and its resistance to formation into responsible subjectivity, hoping to ease the propensity of the traditional practice of responsibility to produce a destructive cycle of self-loathing and vengeance. He relaxes the demand that subjects fit into a mold of natural subjectivity. He shows how the practice of moral responsibility punishes and conceals those parts of the self and those selves that are resistant to the production of subjectivity, and how its production of uniform, reliable, calculable, individual subjects constantly diminishes alternative possibilities of individuality, spontaneity, and responsibility.[83] Eternal recurrence is an instrument of one of these alternatives: the self as a work of art. *Virtù*, recovered by Nietzsche from virtue, is one of its excellences.

Nietzsche's Re-covery of Virtue as *Virtù*

Virtù is the ethical perspective sometimes adopted by Nietzsche in his effort to unmask the cruelties of the morality of virtue. It is also one of the names he gives to a set of ethical and organizing dispositions with the power to displace moral virtue. Nietzsche's most lengthy discussion of his own conception of virtue as *virtù* comes in *The Will to Power*. There he sets out to "defend virtue against the preachers of virtue [for] they are its worst enemies." They err in teaching "virtue as an ideal *for everyone*," thereby taking "from virtue the charm of rareness, exceptionalness and unaverageness—its aristocratic magic." Nietzschean virtue is everything the virtue of the preachers is not. It does not unite men or bespeak their commonality. "It is unprofitable, imprudent, it isolates." It individuates. In so doing, "it rouses enmity toward order, toward the lies that are concealed in every order, institution, actuality."[84] *Virtù* rouses enmity toward order because its individuation of particular selves calls critical attention to the processes that produce most selves into ordered, responsible subjects. The lies it thereby exposes are the ones that justify the herd's ordering of selves into its institutional arrangements, the lies that posit commonalities where there is difference, expressiveness where there is resistance, community where there is individuality. Since the world is not designed to fit the herd's needs, its linguistic, political, and moral constructions engender resistances in the world and in the self; these resistances are concealed and suppressed by those who insist that their system expresses, realizes, or fits the world for which it is designed. Nietzsche, declaring that "the will to system is a lack of integrity,"[85] looks to *virtù* to expose those concealed resistances, to cultivate, style, transform, and redeem them through alternative constructions of the self that are artistic, affirmative, and personal.

Nietzsche re-covers virtue as *virtù* for an ethic that seeks not the order of system but that of artistry, not organized systematicity but "small portions" of stability, not belonging and community but self-sufficiency and "self-restoration,"[86] not formulaic guidance but personal direction. Against Kant, Nietzsche says,

> A virtue has to be *our* invention, *our* most personal defense and necessity:— in any other sense it is merely a condition of *danger*. What does not condition our life *harms* it: a virtue merely from a feeling of respect for the concept "virtue" as Kant desired it is harmful. . . . The profoundest laws of preservation and growth demand the reverse of this: That each one of us should devise *his own* virtue, *his own* categorical imperative.[87]

The virtue Nietzsche prefers has the following features:

> I recognize virtue in that (1) it does not desire to be recognized; (2) it does not presuppose virtue everywhere, but precisely something else; (3) it does not suffer from the absence of virtue, but on the contrary regards this as the distancing relationship on the basis of which there is something to honor in virtue; it does not communicate itself; (4) it does not propagandize — (5) it permits no one to judge it, because it is always virtue for itself; (6) it does all that is generally forbidden: virtue, as I understand it, is the real *vetitum* within all herd legislation; (7) in short, it is virtue in the style of the Renaissance, *virtù*, moraline-free virtue.[88]

Virtù is the real *vetitum* (the fundamental forbidden) of herd legislation because it marks the refusal or the incapacity to participate in the practice of responsible subjectivity. It refuses the herd's claim on one's self, it is uncommunicative, it stands apart from the herd's morality game insofar as standing apart is possible.[89] This "apartness" problematizes the herd's form of life since the fundamental claim and aspiration of herd morality is its universality: the values of the herd address and apply to everyone; that is the lesson the little lambs sought to teach the birds who preyed on them.

The real *vetitum* of herd morality is represented by the "powerful men" who "have become impossible" and "harmful and forbidden" under herd morality, the irresponsible, strong men whom the herd (through its practice of responsibility) brings "close to that type of which the criminal is the perfection."[90] As these powerful men are criminalized, so are the parts of the self they personify, the parts of the self that resist and exceed the constructions of responsible subjectivity. Nietzschean *virtù* is the virtue loyal to those forbidden parts of the self, those overman parts that are moral virtue's real *vetitum*.

Nietzschean *virtù* refuses the herd's will to system and celebrates the necessary failure of its attempts to mold the world in its image according to its imaginings because those failures make art and wisdom possible.[91] It responds artistically to the self's contingency by disciplining it not according to the dictates of responsible subjectivity but, rather, according to the style and taste dictated by each particular, individual self. In Nietzsche's view as in Machiavelli's, the man possessed of *virtù* responds to the inherent contingency of the world by creating something of lasting value or beauty, a testament to the individuality of the creator and to his creative power.

Like Machiavelli, Nietzsche sees *virtù* as an instrument of self-fashioning that does not interiorize the values of others; *virtù* is an "exteriorization of virtue,"[92] manifesting a concern with one's appearance in the world, not with the purity of one's soul and the promise of eternal salvation.[93] And, like Machiavelli, Nietzsche sees in *virtù* an ability to live with uncertainty. For Machiavelli, the architect of the tradition's more famous re-covery of *virtù*, the prince who possesses *virtù* is able to act suddenly, spontaneously, gloriously, and adaptively in anticipation of and in response to *fortuna*, his malicious, seductive, and worthy adversary in a political world that is contingent, unstable, unreliable, unpredictable, and unsystematic. Those who would seek political success in this world must emulate its qualities and make themselves adaptable to any contingency through the cultivation of *virtù*.[94] Otherwise, their regimes will surely fall victim to *fortuna*.

Those unwilling or unable to see the variability of *fortuna* live in a world of illusion symbolized by the armed fortress. "The fortress," Wolin argues, "in all of its seeming solidity, dramatized the false hope that there could be points of fixity, an unchanging basis of political and military security, in a restless world."[95] The hope is false because, as Machiavelli says, men may only "second *fortune*," they "cannot oppose her; they may develop her designs, but they cannot defeat them."[96]

Taking the symbol of the armed fortress one step farther, we might say that those who cultivate virtue seek to make *themselves* into a fortress. To their chagrin, they find themselves still unable to master or control events and, worse yet, now also unable even to adapt to changes around them. Immobile in a world constantly in motion, they cannot maintain themselves or grow. The point is taken up by Nietzsche when he argues that the man who obeys the dictates of the moralists "stands in a fixed position with a gesture that wards off, armed against himself, with sharp and mistrustful eyes—the eternal guardian of his castle, since he has turned himself into a castle." Although "he can achieve *greatness* this way," Nietzsche notes that he is "cut off from the most beautiful fortuities of his soul. Also from all further *instruction*."[97]

Both Nietzsche and Machiavelli seek in *virtù* a manly alternative to what they describe as the feminizing, enfeebling and immobilizing virtue of Christianity.[98] But Nietzschean *virtù* departs from that of Machiavelli in one important respect. *Virtù* for Machiavelli is a political excellence, connected with the greatest of all worldly rewards, glory. The ruler possessed of *virtù* wins glory for himself by founding and maintaining a lasting regime, best of all a republic.[99] Machiavelli criticizes virtue because its otherworldliness turns men away from the grandest of human worldly endeavors and sabotages the enterprise of politics. Nietzsche, however, does not share Machiavelli's enthusiasm for politics. *Virtù* in his view is an individual excellence in the service, not of founding a republic, but of the strategic disruption of the impositional orderings of the herd and of the alternative construction of the self as a work of art.

Those who have noticed this difference have been less than charitable to Nietzsche. Noting that "Machiavelli of course was no Nietzschean, nor Nietzsche a Machiavellian," Mark Hulliung argues that "there is a distinction of the most profound significance between the will-to-power of the great community against other communities and the will-to-power of the great individual against the community." And John Figgis claims that Nietzsche's "*Übermensch* is but Machiavelli's man of *virtù* stripped of those public ends which make even Cesare Borgia less odious."[100] Intent on castigating Nietzsche, neither asks the obvious questions: why does Nietzsche re-cover *virtù* from Machiavelli and yet ignore its connection to political thought and action? why does he not set his account of *virtù* in an account of institutions? These questions are seldom posed because it is simply assumed that Nietzsche has no patience for politics, no interest in institutions, no fascination with the public realm. But these assumptions are mistaken. In fact, Nietzsche has a real impatience with "misarchism," the "hatred of rule or government."[101] And he has a deep reverence for institutions (of particular kinds) as well as an abiding interest in the way they function to produce and maintain a variety of forms of life and excellence, one of which is *virtù*.

Nietzsche's Reverence for Institutions

In an early essay, "Homer's Contest," Nietzsche celebrates the ancient Greek agon, citing it as evidence for his claim that "the Greek genius tolerated" and "justified" the "terrible presence" of great passions like cruelty and struggle. The Greeks' attitude toward the great passions distinguishes the "coloring" of their "individual ethical concepts" from our own:

> The whole of Greek antiquity thinks differently from us about hatred [discord] and envy, and judges with Hesiod, who in the one place calls one Eris [strife] evil—namely, the one that leads men into hostile fights of annihilation against one another—while praising another Eris as good— the one that, as jealousy, hatred, and envy, spurs men to activity: not to the

activity of fights of annihilation but to the activity of fights which are *contests*. The Greek is envious, and he does not consider this quality a blemish but the gift of a *beneficent* god head. What a gulf of ethical judgment lies between us and him!

Nietzsche endorses the second Eris and he celebrates the Greeks' commitment to the contest as well as their belief that "the contest is necessary to preserve the health of the state." Without the contest, Nietzsche explains, "without envy, jealousy, and ambition in the contest, the Hellenic city, like the Hellenic man, degenerates. He becomes evil and cruel; he becomes vengeful and godless."[102]

According to Nietzsche, it was for the sake of the contest that the Greeks practiced ostracism. In contrast to most commentators, who see ostracism as proof of the Greek demos' intolerance of excellence, Nietzsche sees the practice as evidence of the Greek commitment to the promotion of excellence. The agon's contests challenge actors to test themselves, to discover their talents and develop their strengths. Ostracism protects this institutional promotion of excellence. It banishes those strong enough to dominate the agon in order to keep the agon open. "Why should no one be the best?" Nietzsche asks rhetorically: "Because then the contest would come to an end and the eternal source of life for the Hellenic state would be endangered. . . . Originally [ostracism] is not a safety valve but a means of stimulation: the individual who towers above the rest is eliminated so that the contest of forces may reawaken."[103]

Similarly, Machiavelli endorses republicanism because of its unique commitment to the preservation of contest. "Human desires are insatiable," he warns. They cannot be extirpated but they can be held in a creative and productive tension. Those critical of Rome's internal dissension, in particular of "the quarrels of the Senate and the people of Rome," Machiavelli says, "were probably more impressed by the cries and the noise which these disturbances occasioned in public places, than by the good effect which they produced."[104]

What good effects? In every republic, including Rome, the struggle of the nobles and the people results in "all the laws that are favorable to liberty." Were it not for their fear of being dominated by the nobles, the people would withdraw from politics, forego the freedom of political action, and forsake *virtù* to dedicate themselves wholly to their mundane, private pursuits. And were it not for the people's active, political resistance to them, the nobles would put an end to all liberty, public and private, and impose a tyrannical rule on the republic. Because the nobles in a republic are always moved by their ambition to dominate the people, and the people moved always by their desire to secure their liberty, their struggle is perpetual. The perpetuity of their struggle, and the institutional obstacles to its resolution, prevent any one party from dominating and closing the public space of law, liberty, and *virtù*. Machiavelli's republic, like Nietzsche's Greek agon, "desires, as *protection* against the genius, another genius."[105]

From Machiavelli's perspective, then, the tumult of the republic signals not disorder but good health and vibrant energy. The republic's "agitations" caused no "exiles nor any violence prejudicial to the general good" and they empowered the republic: "To have removed the cause of trouble from Rome would have been to deprive her of her power of expansion."[106] Consequently, the Roman republic did what "every free state ought" to do when it afforded "the people the opportunity of giving vent, so to say, to their ambition."[107] In particular, Machiavelli admires Rome's faculty of accusation, which allowed "the excitement of the ill-humors that agitate a state [to] have a way prescribed *by law* for venting itself."[108] If a republic's energies are not expended in war, they turn inward. If legitimate, institutional avenues of expression are not available, instincts and ambitions will seek other avenues of expression, and the result will be destabilizing conspiracies and the eventual overthrow of the regime.[109] In short, what Nietzsche says of individuals—"All instincts that do not discharge themselves outwardly *turn inward*"[110]— Machiavelli finds to be true of republics.

Nietzsche follows Machiavelli in looking to law as a potential solution for the perpetual disorder that threatens the condition of human community (a condition that he says we tend to underrate). According to Nietzsche, law was initially instituted by "active, strong, spontaneous, aggressive" men "to impose measure and bounds upon the excesses of the reactive pathos and to compel it to come to terms."[111] The problem with the reactive pathos is that it is incapable of limiting its own excesses because its will to vengeance and ressentiment are inherently boundless.[112] Institutions of law can, and initially did, provide a community with the discipline that a sense of limit and measure brings.[113]

But not all institutions of law serve to diminish or dilute ressentiment. On the contrary, law is easily turned into an instrument of the will to vengeance and Nietzsche knows this. His point here—made against Duhring, in particular—is that there is no necessary relationship between law and ressentiment, that the institution of law can be a powerful and vital expression of the will to power, and that law is compatible with a form of life devoted not to self-entrenchment and maintenance but to self-overcoming. Nietzsche makes the point by distinguishing two kinds of law, one active, the other reactive, both devoted to the project of ordering a contingent world as part of an attempt to maintain a community and its form of life: "A legal order thought of as sovereign and universal, not as a means in the struggle between power complexes but as a means of preventing all struggle in general . . . would be a principle *hostile to life*, an agent of the dissolution and destruction of man, an attempt to assassinate the future of man, a sign of weariness, a secret path to nothingness." Nietzsche prefers the sort of law that operates as a means in a struggle and not as a weapon against all struggle: "Legal conditions can never be other than *exceptional conditions* since they constitute a partial restriction of the will of life which is bent upon power, and are subordinate to its total goal as a single means: namely as a means of creating *greater* units of power."[114] This is an agonistic conception of law, a conception of law for a vital order dedicated to the preservation of the contest. Here, law is necessarily partial: it knows and practices the self-discipline of self-limitation. For the sake of a broader agonistic struggle, it rejects the reassurance of an expressivist ground, understands itself as an imposition, and resists the temptation to become the uncontested genius that dominates the agon without measure nor limit. Its self-restraint makes it appropriate for a theorist who prefers institutions that are humble, chary of the will to system, and willing to chasten their own ambitions. This is, after all, a conception of law and institutions whose aspiration is deeply paradoxical: to *promote* Nietzschean *virtù* even as it insists on rousing enmity toward "every order, institution, actuality."

Nietzsche's brief endorsements of the agon and of particular kinds of legal and institutional order are compatible with many of his scattered remarks about the problem of founding, organizing, and maintaining communities of knowledge or power. Taken together, they make clear his commitment to maintain institutionally a measure of stability, a measured stability, while at the same time refraining from too thoroughly domesticating the contingent world and selves that condition these communities. That we impose our own ordering on the world and ourselves is not, in itself, objectionable to Nietzsche.[115] He knows that these impositions are our way of making the world habitable and he admires and endorses our capacity to do this: "In order for a particular species to maintain itself and increase its power, its conception of reality must comprehend enough of the calculable and constant for it to base a scheme of behavior on it."[116] The thought of a life without calculability, without some measure of constancy, horrifies Nietzsche. He says in *The Gay Science* that he hates "*enduring* habits" such as "constant association with the same people, a permanent domicile, or unique good health," but in the very next passage he insists that a life entirely devoid of habits, a life that would demand perpetual improvisation would be "most intolerable . . . the terrible par excellence." That, Nietzsche says, "would be my exile and my Siberia."[117] The life of which Zarathustra speaks, "this life which must ever surpass itself," must also situate and maintain itself, and often it will and ought to do so institutionally.

These remarks could be treated as raw material out of which one might critically reconstruct an account of Nietzschean institutions. But this is not my task. Suffice it to note that there is a reverence for institutions present in Nietzsche's work and that it is an important (and underrated) strand of Nietzsche's thinking. And suffice it then to ask: why does Nietzsche himself not follow up on any of these elements in his own thinking? why does he not pursue a political theory in a more sustained if not systematic manner? why does this *virtù* theorist stop short of developing a *virtù* theory of politics?

I think the answer lies in Nietzsche's belief (which he shares with Machiavelli) that politics, once a grand enterprise, is one of the casualties of modernity and its preoccupation with acquisition, safety, and salvation. Machiavelli held fast to the belief that the Roman political experience could be recovered, arguing that those who thought the imitation of noble actions impossible were under the false impression that "heaven, the sun, the elements, and men had changed the order of their motions and power, and were different from what they were in ancient times."[118] But Nietzsche strongly disagrees on this point. Human beings have changed. Indeed, from Nietzsche's perspective, Machiavelli's attempt to revive his ideal of Roman republicanism is not only naive but nostalgic, resentful of the changes time has brought. And these changes are not to be underestimated. Modern political thought and practice, in Nietzsche's view, instantiate the very attitudes he seeks to overcome. Under the hegemony of asceticism, politics is the new forum for the expression of ressentiment, the latest instrument of vengeance in a world in which whenever people gather together the conditions of herdliness begin to set in. Politics in modernity has been all too successful in its project of containment, control, and disempowerment. We cannot go back.

Under modern institutional conditions, political participation and action cannot promote the excellences of *virtù* because they aim precisely to uproot them. In the production of modern man, "another human type is disadvantaged more and more and finally made impossible; above all, the great '*architects*'." What Nietzsche admires in the architect is a kind of stalwartness, an individual calculability and reliability quite different from the herd's predictability. In the absence of the stalwart character, "a society in the old sense of that word . . . *cannot* be built anymore. . . . everything is lacking, above all the material. *All of us are no longer material for a society*."[119] The once grand projects of building societies and political institutions are, like the architect and his "grand style," casualties of modernity. Not until the responsible subject of modernity is overcome will there again appear men possessed of the responsibility, freedom, and *virtù* necessary for a vital politics that is not nostalgic, resentful, or vengeful. Nietzsche does not say much about what this politics will look like, but what he does say is disturbing. The "great politics" of the future will be aristocratic, the herd dominated and the earth shaken by the few overmen whom Nietzsche describes variously as philosophers, commanders, legislators, and masters.

Nietzsche's connection of great politics with the overman is less disturbing than provocative, however, if we continue to read the overman as a personification of the parts of the self that are resistant to the formation of responsible subjectivity. In this way, we can build on the politicizing impulses of Nietzsche's recoveries of responsible subjectivity without endorsing his vision of "great" politics as such (there is, in any case, no necessary connection between the two). This approach suggests that there may even be a *virtù* theory of politics here, perhaps a politics of resistance that "rouses enmity toward every order" by interrogating every formation of subjectivity, every claim to expressivist success, every displacement of power and politics. Rather than reconstruct this Nietzschean alternative, I turn next to focus on a political theorist who explicitly devotes herself to the construction of a *virtù* theory of politics that draws its inspiration from both Nietzsche and Machiavelli: Hannah Arendt.

Arendt and Nietzsche speak virtually in a single voice as they bemoan the modern disappearance of politics and the ancient reverence for institutions, attributing the degeneration in part to the modern preoccupation with a misbegotten ideal of freedom that leads to the mistaken identification of authority with tyranny. Nietzsche explains that

> For institutions to exist there must exist the kind of will, instinct, imperative which is anti-liberal to the point of malice: the will to tradition, to authority, to centuries long *responsibility*, to *solidarity* between succeeding

generations backwards and forwards *ad infinitum*. If this will is present, there is established something such as the *Imperium Romanum*.

But, he continues, this will is no longer present:

> The entire West has lost these instincts out of which institutions grow, out of which the future grows. Perhaps nothing goes so much against the grain of its "modern spirit" as this. One lives for today, one lives very fast—one lives very *irresponsibly;* it is precisely *this* which one calls "freedom." That which makes institutions institutions is despised, hated, rejected: whenever the word authority is so much as heard one believes oneself in danger of a new slavery.[120]

Arendt echoes the sentiment: "Behind the liberal identification of totalitarianism with authoritarianism, and the concomitant inclination to see 'totalitarian' trends in every authoritarian limitation of freedom, lies an older confusion of authority with tyranny, and of legitimate power with violence." Indeed, she argues, "the rise of totalitarianism . . . makes us doubt not only the coincidence of politics and freedom but their very compatibility. We are inclined to believe that freedom begins where politics ends." The "liberal credo" has been widely adopted: " 'The less politics the more freedom.' "[121]

Like Nietzsche, Arendt believes that the dominant ethoi of modernity are expansionist, that there is very little space left, if any, in which to experiment with new, creative alternatives. But, unlike Nietzsche, she issues a call to politics, even as she documents its demise. She proposes a politics for modernity, a politics in which *virtù* is central. She looks to politics to provide the occasion and the stage for *virtù* and individuality. And she seeks in politics a public affirmation of and response to worldly contingency. Whereas for Nietzsche great politics can proceed only after the repersonalization of man is complete, for Arendt great politics is the medium through which that very goal is achieved. In short, Arendt, unlike Nietzsche, shares Machiavelli's faith in the transformative power of politics.[122]

CHAPTER FOUR

Arendt's Accounts of Action and Authority

Action is eloquence; Speak that I may see thee.
—Ben Jonson

Utterance have I become altogether.
—Zarathustra

The possibility of new beginnings and rebirth is as important to Arendt as it is to Nietzsche. She lodges the possibility partly in her own account of an original, originating beginning, that of the American revolution and founding. Like Kant's "Speculative Beginnings" and Nietzsche's *Genealogy*, Arendt's account of the origins of the American republic and the practice of political authority that maintains it is a mythical and fabulist construction. In it, the aspirations of Kant's and Nietzsche's fables are combined. Like Kant's fable, hers begins with an event that makes history possible, creating "the condition for remembrance"[1] and enabling the constitution of a "we," in this case the "we" of political community and action. Like Nietzsche's fable, hers proceeds by unmasking the greatest obstacle to the project, the hegemony of a depersonalizing, deindividuating, normalizing condition similar to the herd's: the "rise of the social," according to Arendt, is largely responsible for the displacement and domestication of political spaces in modernity.

Arendt theorizes political authority as part of a broader conception of politics and political action that gives pride of place to virtuosity as self-display and to *virtù* as, in effect, enmity toward (too much) order. Like Nietzsche, she worries that the ordering of the self into a moral, well-behaved subject diminishes its propensity to act creatively and spontaneously. And, like Nietzsche, she knows that some institutions are more likely than others to occasion action, that only some sets of arrangements will manifest the institutional respect for contingency that is one of the necessary conditions of virtuosic action. Finally, less like Nietzsche, Arendt thinks that the preservation of creative action and the founding of authoritative institutions are more important than ever in the postfoundational age of modernity. She departs from Nietzsche in her insistence that virtuosic action is never isolated, that it is always "in concert," in some way a part of a political community's self-constitution, always involved in a dynamic of institutional founding and refounding.

I look to Arendt's vision of politics, first to her account of action and then to her account of political authority in particular, to give more substance and contestability to a *virtù* theory of politics. I begin with her treatments of action, identity, and the self, tracing her theorization of action as sui generis, her treatment of identity as a product not the precondition of action, and her (Nietzschean) reading of the self as a multiple creature that resists and exceeds the constructions of autonomy, agency, and responsible subjectivity. These commitments are central to Arendt's account of how lasting identities or republics can be founded without "foundationalism" and of why, indeed, they must be. What emerges in the course of this account is her compelling belief, not only that a politics can operate without the seamless foundations virtue theorists insist are the necessary condition of politics, but that a democratic politics must do so. Foundational foundings, Arendt argues, invariably close political spaces and engender coercive and exclusionary political practices.

Working with her Nietzschean conception of the self as multiplicity and of identity as a hard won and not always well-fitting product of action, Arendt theorizes politics as an always unfinished business, committed simultaneously and perpetually to the settlement and unsettlement of identities, both personal and institutional. These features of her view buttress her commitment to a nonfoundational politics of (re)founding and suggest that hers is not the expressive politics of community, dialogue, deliberation or consensus that some of her readers mistake it to be.[2] It is a *virtù* theory of politics, an activist, democratic politics of contest, resistance, and amendment.

Action, Identity, and the Self

Both Arendt and Nietzsche attempt to resurrect action and actors from the insignificance and danger to which traditional philosophy and morality have consigned them. Both see the development of the moral, responsible subject—a real subject that is chronologically and ontologically prior to the appearance of his action—as symptomatic of the moralists' destructive and ultimately nihilistic need to control behavior and tame virtuosity. Both agree that the deprivileging of action is a threat not only to virtuosity but to diversity, plurality, freedom, and individuality as well as to meaning itself. And both respond by decentering the subject of morality and behavior, challenging the popular belief in a rational, free-willing, choosing, intending agent, in charge of itself and its actions in order to reassert a primacy of action over actor.

Arendt's theorization of action echoes Nietzsche's claim that the search for a doer diminishes the power of action by seeking a cause for action where there is none, where there is only "the feeling of strength, tension, resistance, [and] muscular feeling."[3] Our belief in a doing subject, Nietzsche explains, is

> only owing to the seduction of language (and of the fundamental errors of reason that are petrified in it) which conceives and misconceives all effects as conditioned by something that causes effects, by a "subject." . . . popular morality also separates strength from expressions of strength as if there were a neutral substratum behind the strong man which was *free* to express strength or not to do so. But there is no such substratum; there is no 'being' behind doing, effecting, becoming; "the doer" is merely a fiction added to the deed—the deed is everything.[4]

Arendt agrees with Nietzsche that there is no essential self, no given unity awaiting discovery or realization. There is no being behind the doing. But she departs from Nietzsche in focusing exclusively on the political actor. She allows the herd its victory in the private realm, resisting only its usurpation of the spaces of *political* action in the contingent public realm. Only in the public realm of action, on Arendt's account, is it the case that there is no doer, that the deed is everything.

Unlike private realm behavior, political action does not derive its meaning from the intentions, motives, or goals of actors. Intentions, motives, goals, indeed agency itself are all *causes* of action, symptoms of behavior; to turn to them is to instrumentalize action, to treat it as an effect, a symptom, or an expression of a prior, privileged source of meaning. No action is unattended by intentions, motives, and goals, but each action "is free to the extent that it is able to transcend" them,[5] that is, to the extent that it produces or gives birth to the actor or performer rather than merely express his antecedent character, to the extent that it creates "new relations and realities" rather than consolidate old ones.

Freedom is not a subject-centered condition. Arendt criticizes those who (like Nietzsche's lambs) take freedom out of the contingent world of action, attach it to the subject, and internalize it by attributing it to the will. "The philosophical tradition . . . distorted the very idea of freedom . . . by transposing it from its original field, the realm of politics and human affairs in general, to an inward domain, the will, where it would be open to self-inspection." Turned into an "inner feeling" with no "worldly tangible reality," freedom is privatized and is left "by definition politically irrelevant," transformed from an expression of active power to the capacity to control one's action, to choose inaction. Arendt resists this transformation: "To be free and to act are the same."[6]

Only in the public realm of action are we capable of joining together with others to bring "something into being which did not exist before."[7] The creativity of action means that it cannot be judged by already established standards, such as those that are identified by Arendt with "behavior" and by Nietzsche with "popular morality." To judge action according to standards external to it, standards derived "from some supposedly higher faculty or from experiences outside action's own reach," would be effectively and decisively to compromise action's uniqueness:

> Unlike human behavior—which the Greeks, like all civilized people judged according to "moral standards," taking into account motives and intentions on the one hand and aims and consequences on the other— action can be judged only by the criterion of greatness, because it is in its nature to break through the commonly accepted and reach into the extraordinary where whatever is true in common and everyday life no longer applies because everything that exists is unique and *sui generis*.[8]

Moral standards are illicit in the realm of action because, as condensations of previous settlements, they diminish action. If the deed is everything, then it cannot be judged or captured by general rules and categories; they can only succeed in masking or undermining the innovative and initiating power of action. The problem with general rules is that they "can be taught and learned until they grow into habits that can be replaced by other habits and rules"; the problem is that they are inherently linked, in Arendt's view, to behavior, which is rule-governed, imitable, and never truly innovative. Political judgment (unlike moral judgment) "is the faculty to judge particulars with*out* subsuming them under general rules."[9]

Identity is one of the new realities generated by action and resistant to judgment by general (moral) rules. Prior to or apart from action, the self

is fragmented, discontinuous, indistinct, and most certainly uninterest-
ing. A life-sustaining, psychologically determined, trivial, and imitable
biological creature in the private realm, this self attains identity—becomes a "who"—by acting in the public realm in concert with others. In
so doing, it forsakes "what" it is, the roles and features that define (and
even determine) it in the private realm, the "qualities, gifts, talents and
shortcomings, which [it] may display or hide," and the intentions, motives, and goals that characterize its agency.[10]

The psychological and biological self of the private realm is confined
there: "Feelings, passions and emotions can no more become part and
parcel of the [public] world of appearances than can our inner organs."
These features of the private self are, like our inner organs, "never
unique." As Arendt says of the biological self: "If this inside were to
appear, we would all look alike." When this inside does appear, in the
form of demands made publicly on behalf of the urgent needs of the
hungry or poor body, then the one individuating capacity humans possess is silenced: there can be no speech, no action, no freedom, unless and
until the violently pressing, indeed irresistible needs of the body are
satisfied.[11]

Arendt sometimes implies that the reason to act is situated in a need to
escape the body and be freed, episodically, from its urgency and irresistibility; at other times she focuses on the need to escape the commonality of our biological existence, which is exaggerated in modernity
as the social develops into a strongly conformist set of arrangements with
"innumerable and various rules, all of which tend to 'normalize' its
members, to make them behave, to exclude spontaneous action or outstanding achievement."[12] Here, the reason to act is situated in action's
unique, individuating, (antidotal but still sui generis) power, and in the
self's agonal passion for distinction and outstanding achievement.

For the sake of "who" they might become, Arendt's actors risk the
dangers of the radically contingent public realm where anything can
happen, where the consequences of action are "boundless," uncontrollable, irreversible, and unpredictable, where "not life but the world is at
stake."[13] Arendt's actors are never self-sovereign. Driven by the despotism of their bodies (and their psychologies) in the private realm, they are
never really in control of what they do in the public realm either. This is
why, as actors, they must be courageous. Action springs up ex nihilo, it is
spontaneous, novel, creative, and, perhaps most disturbing, always self-
surprising: "It is more than likely that the 'who' which appears so clearly
and unmistakably to others, remains hidden from the person himself."[14]

Through innovative action and speech, Arendt's actors manifest freedom and "show who they are, reveal actively their unique personal identities and thus make their appearance in the human world."[15] The actors' momentary engagements in action in the public realm win them an identity that is lodged forever in the stories told of their heroic performances by the spectators who witness them: "With word and deed we insert ourselves into the human world and this insertion is like a second birth."[16] The metaphor of rebirth, a constant theme throughout Arendt's work, is related to her claim that our "capacity for beginning is rooted in *natality*."[17] Once new in a world that preceded us, we can be the vehicles of the introduction of novelty into the world. But we can be reborn only if we sever the umbilical cord that ties us to the womb of our biological and natural existence.

Arendt presents the bifurcations between the determinism of the natural body (in the private realm) and the freedom of the acting self (in the public realm) as attributes of individual selves, but they actually operate to distinguish some selves from others in the ancient Greece that is her beloved model. Here the experience of action is available to very few. The routine and the urgency of the body are implicitly identified in *The Human Condition*, as they were explicitly in ancient Greece, with women and slaves (but also with children, laborers, and all non-Greek residents of the polis), the laboring subjects who tend to the body and its needs in the private realm where "bodily functions and material concerns should be hidden."[18] These inhabitants of the private realm are passively subject to the demands their bodies and nature make on them and to the orders dictated to them by the master of the household to which they belong as property. As victims of both the tiresomely predictable, repetitious, and cyclical processes of nature and the despotism of the household, they are determined, incapable of the freedom Arendt identifies with action in the public realm. Free citizens, by contrast, can tend to their private needs in the private realm (or, more likely, have them tended to), but they can then leave these necessitarian, life-sustaining concerns behind to enter the public realm of freedom, speech, and action. Indeed, their ability to leave these concerns behind is the mark of their capacity to act: in politics, after all, "not life but the world is at stake."

This passage, made episodically by free citizens from the private to the public realm, indicates that the chasm between the two realms is not nonnegotiable.[19] But this is true only for citizens, only for those who are not essentially identified with their condition of embodiment, for those who can be other than only and passively embodied beings. This is, in effect, the criterion for their citizenship. For others, whose very nature prevents them from ever becoming citizens because their identity *is* their embodiment (and this is the criterion for their barbarism), there is no negotiating the public-private impasse.

This problematic feature of political action is certainly one that Arendt attributes to the polis, but is it right to attribute it to Arendt herself? She does often speak as if her private realm and its activities of labor and work were to be identified with particular classes of people, or bodies, or women in particular. But, as Hanna Pitkin points out, at other times the private realm and its activities of labor and work seem to represent "particular *attitude[s]* against which the public realm must be guarded." Since Arendt's real worry about labor and work is that they require and engender particular mentalities that hinder or destroy action, Pitkin suggests that "perhaps a 'laborer' is to be identified not by his manner of producing nor by his poverty but by his 'process'-oriented outlook; perhaps he is driven by necessity not objectively, but because he *regards* himself as driven, incapable of action."[20]

Or, better, perhaps it is the laboring mentality that is excluded from political action, a mentality that is taken to be characteristic of laboring as an activity but which may or may not be characteristic of the thinking of any particular laborer, a mentality that is certainly not taken to signal a laboring nature or essence that is expressed when the laborer labors. There is no being behind this doing. The same analysis applies to work. On this account, then, no determinate class of persons is excluded from political action. Instead, politics is protected from a variety of mentalities, attitudes, dispositions, and approaches all of which constitute *all* selves and subjects to some extent and all of which are incompatible with the understandings of action Arendt valorizes.[21]

By now, it is increasingly clear that the self of *The Human Condition* is not simply bifurcated; the laboring, working, and acting self is the site of several struggles: between its private and public self, that is, between its slavish mentality and its yearning for freedom, its risk-aversiveness and its courageous competitiveness, and among the three different, incompatible and rival mentalities of labor, work, and action in the *vita activa* alone. Elsewhere, it is animated (and conflicted) by other mentalities as well, for example, by the attitudes presupposed and engendered by intimate or solitary pursuits and by the three distinct, incompatible, and reflexive mental faculties Arendt describes in *The Life of the Mind*.

For the first time, in *The Life of the Mind*, Arendt explicitly says that "there is difference in identity." Committed to the view that the life of the mind is structured by three distinct and rival mental faculties—thinking, willing, and judging—she criticizes the "implicit monism" of philosophers who claim that "behind the obvious plurality of man's faculties and abilities, there must exist a oneness." Her dismissal of this view of the self recalls Nietzsche's suggestion in *The Will To Power* that "the assumption of one single subject is perhaps unnecessary; perhaps it is just as permissible to assume a multiplicity of subjects, whose interaction and struggle is the basis of our thought and our consciousness—in general? . . . My hypothesis: the subject as multiplicity."[22]

The subject as multiplicity is the self of *The Life of the Mind*, a plurality whose parties, in the absence of any hierarchical ordering, often engage in a struggle for dominion. The inner conflicts experienced by this self are among each of the three mental faculties but also within them; each mental activity is "reflexive," recoiling "back upon itself." This reflexivity is strongest in "the willing ego," where the "I-will is inevitably countered by an I-nill." Indeed, in the conflict between willing and nilling the victor never completely vanquishes its opponent. "There remains this inner resistance."[23] This self is not, ever, one. It is itself the site of an agonistic struggle of which Arendt approves because, like Nietzsche, she sees the self's multiplicity as the source of its power and energy, as one of the conditions of action.

In *The Human Condition*, Arendt argues that plurality, which "has the twofold character of equality and distinction," is the "condition *sine qua non* for . . . the public realm." There, plurality is an ineliminable feature of intersubjective human existence not to be denied; in *The Life of the Mind*, our inner multiplicity, composed of three equal and distinct (and reflexive) faculties, is an ineliminable feature of ourselves, not a weakness to be mastered. Attempts to overcome plurality or multiplicity, Arendt warns, will result in "the abolition of the public realm itself" and the "arbitrary domination of all others" or in "the exchange of the real world for an imaginary one where these others would simply not exist."[24] The preconditions for action would disappear along with the space for otherness.

Arendt rejects autonomy as a value on precisely these grounds. She sees in it "a mastery which relies on domination of one's self and rule over others." It imposes a false unity and univocity on a self that is actually fragmented and multiple apart from action. The identity Arendt celebrates has nothing to do with self-knowledge, unified agency, or autonomy. The actor's story and identity are, in an important sense, not his, for the "essence of who somebody is" cannot be "reified" by himself. In the public realm, action falls into an "already existing web of human relationships" where it is affected by "innumerable conflicting wills and intentions" and "almost never achieves its purpose." The disclosure of 'who' we are, therefore, "can almost never be achieved as wilful purpose as though one possessed and could dispose of this 'who,' in the same manner he has and can dispose of his qualities [his 'what'ness]."[25] In the public realm of appearances, we are what we appear to be. The spectators who witness our performance have a privileged vantage point or perspective from which to discern or judge "who" we are. And there is no predicting who that will turn out to be. Consequently, man cannot "rely upon himself" nor "have complete faith in himself (which is the same thing)."[26]

Arendt celebrates the contingency of the public realm (contingency "is the price human beings pay for freedom"), but she knows that human beings cannot live together without some stabilizing measures. Her realm of action has resources of its own to meet this need: promising and forgiving mitigate the contingency of human affairs while respecting the multiplicity of the self and the plurality of the public realm of action. They are action's two "moral precepts," the only ones compatible with action's sui generis character, "the only ones that are not applied to action from the outside." Both "arise . . . directly out of the will to live together with others in the mode of acting and speaking, and thus they are like control mechanisms built into the very faculty to start new and unending processes." Both serve "to counter the enormous risks of action," without depriving action of its exhilaration and generative power, of its risk and excess.[27]

Acting through Speech: Promising and Forgiveness

Promising and forgiving are not only mechanisms that constrain action. They are two of Arendt's favorite examples of action: each consists in the unique combination of "word and deed" that Arendt celebrates as action.[28] Each is a performative utterance, a speech act that in the act of being spoken brings "something new into being that did not exist before" and creates "new relations and realities."[29] But each is also curious. Arendt theorizes a promising that does not postulate promisers and a kind of forgiving that does without the attribution of responsibility. She expects promising and forgiving to form sites of stability that, in their partiality, respect the contingency of the public realm (as well as the determinism of the private).

Promising enables us to "set up in the ocean of uncertainty, which the future is by definition, islands of security without which not even continuity, let alone durability of any kind, would be possible in the relations between men." It is important that these sites of security maintain themselves as islands (as *partial* land mass) because the "moment promises lose their character as isolated islands of certainty in an ocean of uncertainty . . . they lose their binding power and the whole enterprise becomes self-defeating." This is why Arendt's practice of promising does not postulate promisers. The contingency and uncertainty she values include "man's inability to rely upon himself or to have complete faith in himself (which is the same thing)," and promisers are subjects who are reliable and well able to guarantee who they will be tomorrow independently of any stability created by promising.[30]

Arendt looks to promising as a source of stability because, unlike the totalizing strategies of self-mastery or autonomy, promising creates limited and isolated areas of stability in the in-between of the public realm. These performatives do not require the excessive and comprehensive ordering of the self that the ideals of autonomy and coherence demand. Only the fragile stabilities of promising are consistent with the freedom that is action and with Arendt's view of the self as a site of struggle. Here is the "danger and advantage" recommended by Arendt's politics, that we must "leave the unpredictability of human affairs and the unreliability of men as they are."[31]

It is because of this danger, unreliability, and unpredictability—and because action is in a further "predicament of irreversibility"—that forgiveness has an important place in Arendt's politics. One is "unable to undo what one has done though one did not, and could not, have known what he was doing."[32] The only way out of this predicament, Arendt argues, is through "forgiving, dismissing, in order to make it possible for life to go on by constantly releasing men from what they have done unknowingly."[33]

According to Arendt, "forgiveness is the only reaction which does not merely re-act but acts anew and unexpectedly, unconditioned by the act which provoked it and therefore freeing from its consequences both the one who forgives and the one who is forgiven." But Arendt seems to overestimate the power of forgiveness; the act of forgiving has consequences of its own that she does not consider. The parties involved become enmeshed in a relationship of inequality that is inconsistent with Arendt's account of action, a relationship in which one party is the generous "one who forgives" and the other, the indebted and grateful "one who is forgiven." The point is made by Nietzsche, who argues that forgiveness does not release the parties from the consequences of a trespass, it subtly binds them to them. "No deed can be undone by being regretted no more than by being 'forgiven' or 'atoned for.' One would have to be a theologian to believe in a power that annuls guilt: we immoralists prefer not to believe in 'guilt'."[34] On Nietzsche's account, forgiveness is not an antidote to the will to vengeance, it is one of its instruments.

Oddly enough, Arendt turns out to be in complete agreement with Nietzsche's critique. On closer inspection, her practice of forgiveness is quite distinct from the moral practice Nietzsche condemns. Indeed, she too rejects the moral practice because she too sees it as vengeful. In its place, she theorizes forgiveness as a process of "constant mutual release," a process of "dismissing" that "is the exact opposite of vengeance." The process is meant to counteract vengeance, which Arendt, like Nietzsche, describes as reactive, a "form of re-acting against an original trespassing, whereby far from putting an end to the consequences of the first misdeed, everybody remains bound to the process."[35]

Arendt's theorization of forgiveness recalls not the imperatives of the moralists but the indifference of Nietzsche's lords and their lordly practice of dismissing. In contrast to the weak, the truly strong have no need of forgiveness, Nietzsche argues. Indifferent to trespasses, they dismiss them without ceremony in what might well be called a process of constant mutual release: "It is a sign of strong, rich temperaments that they cannot for long take seriously their enemies, their misfortunes, their misdeeds; for such characters have in them an excess of plastic curative power, and also a power of oblivion." They are "unable to forgive" because they have "forgotten."[36]

Arendt recovers forgiveness in the hope that she can harness this "plastic curative power" for her radically contingent realm of action. She envisions a forgiveness that creates new realities and relations by liberating actors from the cycle of vengeance; hence the absence of responsibility from her account. Her focus on promising and forgiveness pays tribute to Nietzsche; he himself singled out these practices in the first two essays of the *Genealogy*, celebrating the power and greatness of the practice of dismissing that Arendt calls forgiveness, while also admiring the discipline and nobility of the promising that she celebrates as heroic. Forgiving, as dismissing, is the great natural capacity of the lords whose power affords them a magnanimity and indifference beyond the reach of others. And promising, as a form of binding oneself for the future, is the great achievement of the self-disciplined and sovereign individual. Both are prized by Nietzsche and both are recovered by Arendt.

But Arendt's tribute is cautious and not without reservations. The forgiving and promising Nietzsche prizes are individual endeavors: the promisor binds himself in time, he commits himself to some future action but not to other persons. And the dismissing of the lords is a shrug of indifference that in no way constitutes an ongoing relationship between them and others; on the contrary, it is meant to ward off precisely that. By contrast, the forgiving and promising admired by Arendt constitute lasting political communities; promising binds some to others, in time, and forgiving empowers those bonds to survive. Arendt theorizes a promising and forgiveness for the sake of an action in concert and a politics of founding that Nietzsche thought could not (and should not) take place in the inhospitable conditions of modernity. This is why Arendt recovers forgiveness instead of following Nietzsche's lead and jettisoning it to replace it with "dismissing." Dismissing is for lords; Arendt, like Nietzsche in some moods, finds "man" a more interesting creature.

The Postulates of Action

The characterization of Arendtian action as performative fits nicely with her insistence that action is a combination of word and deed. But it poses some problems for her equally central claim that action is a "beginning" with "nothing to hold on to . . . as though it came out of nowhere in either time or space."[37] Surely Arendt's action must have something to hold on to. How can her performatives function without a public subscription to an authoritative discursive practice? Even a promising that is performative postulates a community of promisers, a group of people who may hold different values and beliefs but who nonetheless share, at the very least, understandings of what it means to make a promise and of what one must do in order for one's performance to be recognizable as a promise (or a founding, a declaration, a forgiving). In short, promising, even on Arendt's account, is a practice.[38]

And yet Arendt gives no account of the conditions of the practice. She only tells us why promising is of paramount importance to those committed to the activity of politics in modernity. Nietzsche too sees the practice of promising as important, but that does not prevent him from investigating the postulates of promising, nor does it stop him from seeing the pain, violence, and blood that contribute to its productions. He addresses the problem directly: "To breed an animal with the right to make promises—is not this the paradoxical task that nature has set itself in the case of man? Is it not the real problem regarding man?"[39]

The process by which this "problem" has been "resolved" historically is the object of Nietzsche's scathing criticism in the second essay of the *Genealogy*. According to Nietzsche, performatives like Arendt's are built on acts of violence that contribute to the construction of the modern, responsible, and promising subject. Arendt might be seen to be responding to this problem indirectly, by giving an account of promising that she believes is less demanding and coercive, and less bloody, than the historical practice of which Nietzsche is so critical. But she does not respond directly to the problems posed by Nietzsche, and that is because she does not share Nietzsche's ambivalence toward the construction of promisers and the practice of promising. She does not see promising as a practice that is necessarily built on a base of violence.[40] Indeed, for her, promising is the "highest human faculty" and so she sees only its enabling character. She even denies Nietzsche's own ambivalence, claiming with approval that "he saw in the faculty of promises (the 'memory of the will' as he called it) the very distinction which marks off human from animal life," ignoring the fact that, in the phrase to which she refers, Nietzsche says the problem is "how to breed an *animal* with the right to make promises."[41]

Arendt also fails to address the fact that, if *her* practice of promising is to do the work she expects of it, it must be highly sophisticated, even ritualized. As such, it would belie the moment of contingency that is characteristic of her politics. Indeed, there is an apparent paradox here: Arendtian action, which includes the act of promising, is terribly risky because it takes place in a contingent world where its meaning and consequences are always underdetermined if not indeterminate. And yet Arendtian promising is supposed to *counter* "the enormous risks of action," to serve as a "control mechanism" by establishing little islands of stability in the radical contingency of the public realm. The problem is that, if promising is to be a source of reassurance and stability, the operation of the practice and the meaning of particular promises must be relatively unproblematic. If that is the case, then action as promising cannot occur ex nihilo and will not be as risky, as contingent and unpredictable, as Arendt says it is.[42] On the other hand, if action is that contingent, then promising will not by itself be able provide the stability Arendt expects it to: the source of stability is coming from somewhere else, possibly from something external to action's purely performative speech act.[43]

It might be objected that this paradox is not Arendt's but my own, the inevitable result of my having applied the constructs of J. L. Austin, a theorist concerned primarily with ordinary circumstances, to the work of Arendt, a theorist devoted above all to the extraordinary.[44] This way of framing the problem, however, turns on an opposition between the ordinary and the extraordinary that is challenged by Jacques Derrida in "Signature, Event, Context" when he suggests that Austin's theorization of the ordinary necessarily involves him in a theorization of the extraordinary. Derrida's treatment of Austin is useful in this context partly because it is strikingly analogous to my own claim that Arendt's theorization of the extraordinary ought necessarily to commit her (as it did Nietzsche) to a theorization of the ordinary. With this analogy in mind, I turn now to examine more closely Derrida's critical celebration of Austin and his theorization of performative utterance.

Stabilizing Performatives: Arendt, Austin, and Derrida

Derrida celebrates Austin's focus on performative utterance because it highlights certain features of language that escape notice when the focus is on the "classical assertion," the constative utterance. Distinct from a constative, a performative, Derrida explains, "produces or *transforms* a situation, it operates," and "this constitutes its internal structure, its manifest function or destination." Performative utterances draw our attention to the other-than-referential character of language, to its extra-communicative power, to its creation, in effect, of "new relations and realities," to its constitution of speaking subjects who are not quite present to themselves, not quite in control of the language games in which they are both players and playthings. Performative utterances are not cognitive statements; they are events. This is why they defy analysis "from the authority of the *value of truth* . . . at least in its classical form, substituting for it the value of force, of difference of force (*illocutionary* or *perlocutionary* force)." This move from the value of truth to that of force, Derrida notes with approval, seems "to beckon toward Nietzsche."[45] It also echoes Arendt's account in which action is judged by the standard of greatness, not by standards of morality or truth.

Thus far, Derrida argues, it seems that "Austin has exploded the concept of communication as a purely semiotic, linguistic or symbolic concept." From Derrida's perspective, this would be the great merit of Austin's account and it is certainly the aspiration with which Austin's famous lectures begin. But Austin retreats from the radicality of his innovation and develops a theory of speech acts that seeks to domesticate the unreliable "value of force" that stands at its center through the reassuring security of the "value of context."[46]

Contextualism provides Austin's performatives with the conditions of their success; these include "the values of 'conventionality', 'correctness', and 'completeness'." Derrida argues that each contributes, ultimately, to the value that governs them all, that "of an exhaustively definable context, of a free consciousness present for the totality of the operation, of an absolutely full meaning that is master of itself: the teleological jurisdiction of a total field whose *intention* remains the organizing center." The problem for Derrida is that this denies the insights with which Austin's account of performativity began: the creative power and the differentiated force of performatives are reined in by an "exhaustively determinable context [that] implies teleologically that no *remainder* escapes the present totalization." Austin's account, which Derrida celebrates because it begins with a performative that is a *doing*, ends up positing a *being* behind the doing, in this instance an intentionalism and contextualism that govern speech acts and see to it that there "is no 'dissemination' escaping the horizon of the unity of meaning."[47]

This "univocality of the statement," Derrida continues, turns out to be Austin's "philosophical 'ideal'." To attain it, he employs a "remarkable" procedure:

> It consists in recognizing that the possibility of the negative (here, the *infelicities*) is certainly a structural possibility, that failure is an essential risk in the operations under consideration; and then, with an almost simultaneous gesture made in the name of a kind of ideal regulation, an exclusion of this risk as an accidental, exterior one that teaches us nothing about the language phenomenon under consideration.[48]

Derrida's concern is with Austin's limitation of his analysis to performative utterances "issued in ordinary circumstances." How should we read Austin's decision to exclude from consideration the various abnormalities, like infelicities and performatives that are "used not *seriously*," while at the same time acknowledging the fact that "*every* utterance is open" to "the possibility" of these risks? In what, Derrida asks, can this openness consist (what can it signify?) given Austin's exteriorization of risk, his effective conversion of infelicity from a structural possibility to an unfortunate accident that is now construed as the "other" of performativity, and even of language itself? The consequences of this conversion, its implications and effects, are graphically depicted by Derrida:

Does the generality of the risk admitted by Austin *surround* language like a kind of *ditch*, a place of external perdition into which locution might never venture, that it might avoid by remaining at home, in itself, sheltered by its essence or *telos*? Or indeed is this risk, on the contrary, its internal and positive condition of possibility? this outside its inside? The very force and law of its emergence? In this last case what would an "ordinary" language defined by the law of language signify? Is it that in excluding the general theory [of infelicities] Austin, who nevertheless pretends to describe the facts and events of ordinary language, makes us accept as ordinary a teleological and ethical determination?[49]

On this reading, the problem with Austin's exclusion of risk is that it deprives performatives of their "very force and law." But what does this mean? What does it mean to say that "this risk" is language's "internal and positive condition of possibility?" It means that performativity, as such, postulates a "necessary possibility" of infelicity, without which performatives lose the very characteristics that distinguish them from the constative utterances to which they are juxtaposed by Austin. Most important, it means that, once the possibility of dissemination, risk, and infelicity has been excluded, the performative loses its character as an event, as a speech *act*.

Derrida's point echoes one of Arendt's major concerns in her theorization of action: on her account as on Derrida's, the possibility of infelicity is a structurally necessary possibility of action (hence Arendt's insistence that contingency is a necessary condition of action). Speech action would be something else if it could not go awry—if promises could *not* be mistaken, if performatives could not be infelicitous; if these misfortunes could not befall them, *we would not need to say them.* Life would be, literally, uneventful if context and intentions were successful in producing the total, exhaustive context of simple ordinariness to which Austin (at times) aspires on their behalf. If speech action was only felicitous, we would be in a realm of process and predictability where calculation, but not action, would be the appropriate modus operandi. We would be in Arendt's private realm, inactive and relatively silent.

We might say that by excluding risk and infelicity from his analysis, by turning to intentions and context to safeguard performatives from risk, infelicity, and dissemination, Austin effectively converts the performative into something very like the constative utterance whose hegemony he initially tries to escape. To the "doing" of performativity, he adds a "being." To the happening of the event, he appends a secure, even ritual, predictability. As Austin's lectures proceed, performative utterances become more and more like their constative counterparts, initially their stipulated opposites.[50] The now more sophisticated performative begins to operate as a vehicle: it, too, transports a content, an intention, a mood, a subject that exists prior to the event or speech act, a subject that stands apart from the act and is present to itself, autonomous, self-knowing and intending, even well-intentioned. This slide from the exhilarating difference of performativity into constation leads Derrida to describe Austin as implicated in a kind of unwitting collaboration with the very "philosophical tradition with which he would like to have so few ties."[51]

Derrida's point is not that the features of performativity singled out by Austin have no effects. His point is not to deny the "relative specificity of the effects of consciousness, of the effects of speech," or to claim in opposition to Austin "that there is no effect of the performative, no effect of ordinary language, no effect of presence and of speech acts." But he does insist, contra Austin, that "these effects do not exclude what is generally opposed to them term by term, but on the contrary presuppose it in dissymmetrical fashion, as the general space of their possibility." The issue at hand is not the question of whether or not performatives work; they often do. The issue is *why* they work. According to Derrida, when performatives work it is not in spite of but in part because of (1) "everything that might quickly be summarized under the problematic heading of 'the arbitrariness of the sign';" and (2) "the fact that something possible—a possible risk—is always possible, is somehow a necessary possibility." Likewise, according to Arendt, when action works, it is not in spite of but partly because of the risk, infelicity, and dissemination that are action's characteristic features.[52]

By now the comparisons to be drawn between Derrida's Austin and Arendt begin to emerge. Both, undoubtedly, celebrate performativity— for example, promising—as a unique and eventful form of speaking and acting. But whereas Arendt tries to theorize a promising that does not presuppose the prior, self-knowing subject, Austin's theorization lodges itself precisely in that subjectivity and in the intentionalism that goes with it. This is one of the strategies that allows Austin to convert performativity from an event into an instance of ordinary language. As Derrida points out, however, if Austin's practice of promising appears ordinary, that is because he has stabilized it and made it safe. Austin protects his performatives from risk, infelicity, and indeterminacy by keeping them at home, by harboring them in the comforting security of an overdetermined context that guarantees their success.[53] On Arendt's account, by contrast, promising is anything but ordinary; it is heroic and risky. Arendt's goal is to highlight the *extra*ordinary character of promising, its uniqueness and creative power. Promising occurs precisely in a realm where Arendt's actors are *not* at home; there is no security, no overdetermined context to domesticate promising; on the contrary, the mise-en-scène of Arendt's performative action is the radically contingent public realm where anything might happen, where the consequences of action are boundless, unpredictable, unintended, and often unknown to the actors themselves.

Arendt's emphasis on the extraordinariness of action, however, leaves her unable to account for how promising *works*. That is, whereas Austin seems to be incapable of accounting (structurally) for the failure of promises, Arendt seems to be, conversely, incapable of accounting for their success. Unlike Derrida, who is careful not to *deny* the effects of consciousness, of ordinary language, and of presence, Arendt seems to do precisely this: her practice of promising works, as action, only to the extent that it accomplishes something above and beyond the expression of a subject's intentions, motives, or goals, to the extent that it emerges ex nihilo, unconditioned by the very (ordinary) circumstances that enable Austin's performatives to succeed. Indeed, Arendt's exclusion of the ordinary from her account of action leaves her open to the same sort of criticism Derrida levels at Austin for excluding the extraordinary from his.

For Derrida, Austin's contextualism and intentionalism are part of a broader effort to shelter language from risk by giving it a "home" and keeping it there, where it is "sheltered by its essence or *telos*." According to Derrida, Austin makes language at home by effectively denying that risk and infelicity are structurally necessary possibilities of language, by treating them as merely circumstantial and then banishing them to the exterior realm of the extraordinary, the exceptional. Arendt makes the same sort of move and the point of Derrida's critique therefore applies equally well to her. She too distinguishes ordinary language from its extraordinary features: ordinary language is the private realm's mode of communication. Distinct from the sort of language Arendt valorizes as "speech" and "action," private realm discourse is strictly communicative and narrowly referential, so narrowly referential that it need not even be spoken. Here "speech plays a subordinate role, as a means of communication or a mere accompaniment to something that could also be achieved in silence." Since the point of language in the private realm is "to communicate immediate identical needs and wants," the body can handle the task without speech: "signs and sounds," Arendt says, "would be enough."[54]

Lodged in the same opposition of ordinary versus extraordinary discourse as Austin's, Arendt's account reverses Austin's valuation and privileges not the ordinary but the extraordinary, celebrating the latter's exceptional and rule-resistant character.[55] Rather than banish the extraordinary to some "place of external perdition" for the sake of the safety of normal speech, Arendt gives pride of place to extraordinary speech acts.[56] Thus, her political speech acts are, paradoxically, terribly risky and dangerous and yet also, like Austin's performatives, remarkably safe. Arendtian action has a place to call home, a place where it is secure (at least conceptually) from the ever-present but now exteriorized threats represented by the realm of the household, the realm of the home: the threats of violence, process, ordinariness, presence and repetition, of the urgent, irresistible needs of the body, of the mute, referential communication of "immediate identical needs and wants." The paradox is elusive because the home Arendt ingeniously provides for her political performatives is not safe and secure; it is dangerous, uncertain, and infelicitous. In a reversal of Austin's "remarkable" procedure, Arendt protects politics from its alterities precisely by asserting a strong connection between performatives and the necessary possibility of infelicity and risk. In so doing, however, she, no less than Austin, posits a home for language, a place where, as Derrida says, it is "sheltered by its essence or *telos.*"

Arendt's appeal to teleology, unlike Austin's, is explicit: our ability to promise is not merely important, it is the "highest human faculty." To promise is to exercise our capacity for beginning, our faculty of action, and this "faculty of action is ontologically rooted in the fact of natality." These appeals are meant to stabilize the realm of the extraordinary, to lodge Arendtian action in an expressive moment of self-realization and telos. But they are not enough. If Arendt's performatives are to work in the way she expects them to, if they are to contribute to the creation of "worldly permanence and reliability," then she has to account for their stabilizing power and their durability with something more than the stories told by spectators, though also (given her commitment to the contingency of action) with something less than Austin's contextualism and intentionalism.[57]

And she does. As it turns out, Arendt's performatives are not, strictly speaking, *speech* acts; they are acts of writing. Indeed, Arendt's third examples of political action, the American Declaration of Independence and the Constitution, are perfect ("the perfect way for an action to appear in words") because they are written: "Since we deal here with the written, and not the spoken word, we are confronted with one of the rare moments in history when the power of action is great enough to erect its own monument."[58]

If we take this passage seriously, if we take writing to be the perfection of Arendtian action, and speech to be its poor mimetic or derivative cousin, then many of the apparent oddities of Arendt's account of action begin to make more sense. These same oddities are, on Derrida's account, characteristic features of *all* language, best seen through the lens of writing: "One writes in order to communicate to those who are absent. The absence of the sender, of the receiver, from the mark that he abandons, and which cuts itself off from him and continues to produce effects independently of his presence and of the present actuality of his intentions, indeed even after his death, his absence . . . belongs to the structure of all writing—and . . . of all language in general."[59] Here, in this short passage, we have all the characteristic features of Arendt's account of action, gathered together under the heading of "absence": Orphaned by its author, exceeding his authorizations, action is context defiant ("a written sign carries with it a force that breaks with its context"[60]), resistant to intentionalist interpretation and control, boundless in its possible effects, and free from the determination of motives and goals. "Somebody began it and is its subject," writes Arendt, "in the twofold sense of the word, namely, its actor and sufferer, but nobody is its author."[61] Arendtian action, like Derridian writing, disseminates; it posits no being behind the doing, no antecedently stable self present and transparent to itself autonomously authoring the terms of its own existence.[62] The self that writes is stabilized as an actor by various supports and disciplines, one of which is writing itself.

What Derrida says of language or writing in general holds well for Arendt's account of political action, her characterization of it as speech action notwithstanding: the features of both can be better seen through the lens of writing than speech because speech fosters the misleading illusion of presence. Writing, by contrast, illustrates the "force of rupture" that both Derrida and Arendt characterize as an "event." But writing also fosters an illusion, that of permanence. Derrida unmasks that illusion partly by exposing the iterability, the necessary possibility of (imperfect) repetition and citation, that lies at the heart of writing and of language in general.[63] Arendt in effect unmasks the same illusion when she points out that amendment and augmentation are structurally necessary possibilities of her most cherished actions, the written documents of the American revolution and founding. The written Declaration of Independence and the Constitution combine permanence with augmentation in a way that enables them to create some "worldly permanence" while at the same time respecting the contingency of the radically unpredictable and uncontrollable public realm. This is the basic premise of Arendt's endorsement of these founding documents, and it provides the point of departure for her theorization of a practice of political authority for modernity.

Acting through Writing: Founding the New American Republic

As Arendt conceives of it, the problem of politics in modernity is largely attributable to the rise of secularism and to the corresponding dearth in modernity of commonly held and publicly powerful instruments of legitimation such as political authority.[64] These elements lead many of her readers to treat Arendt as a nostalgic or essentialist theorist of authority for whom political authority is (or was) a uniquely ancient and Roman experience that disappears as part of "the modern loss of tradition and the weakening of religious beliefs."[65] But Arendt does not simply mourn the disappearance of political authority in modernity; she also celebrates it. And, in the spirit of celebration, she constructs a replacement for it: through her fabulist rendering of the American revolution and founding, she offers a powerful account of a practice of authority *for* modernity.

Arendt is ambivalent about the disappearance of authority in modernity. On the one hand, it marks the restoration of the world to humanity, the recovery of human worldliness, and new possibilities of innovative political action.[66] On the other hand, it leaves the modern world bereft of the very things that once secured the foundation and longevity of the Roman republic: tradition, religion, and authority. Without the resources of authority, it seems as if the task of founding and maintaining lasting institutions is, as Nietzsche often thought, impossible. Arendt poses the problem, quoting Rousseau:

> "The great problem of politics, which I compare to the problem of squaring the circle in geometry . . . [is]: How to find a form of government which puts the law above man." Theoretically [Arendt adds], Rousseau's problem closely resembles Sieyes's vicious circle: Those who get together to constitute a new government are themselves unconstitutional, that is, they

have no authority to do what they set out to achieve. The vicious circle in legitimating is present not in ordinary lawmaking, but in laying down the fundamental law. . . . The trouble was—to quote Rousseau once more— that to put the law above man and thus to establish the validity of man-made laws, *il faudrait des dieux*, "one would actually need gods."[67]

For Arendt, then, the problem of politics in modernity is, how do we establish lasting foundations without appealing to gods, a foundationalist ground, or an absolute? Can we conceive of institutions possessed of authority without deriving that authority from some law of laws, from some extrapolitical source? In short, is it possible to have a politics of foundation in a world devoid of traditional (foundational) guarantees of stability, legitimacy, and authority?

According to Arendt, the American revolutionaries and founders stumbled on a solution, but they did not know what they had achieved. Arendt glorifies them for their great innovations, their courage, their vision. But she faults them for being inadequately conscious and con-fident of themselves as innovators. Their revolution took them by sur-prise: "What they had thought was a restoration, the retrieving of their ancient liberties, turned into a revolution and . . . ended with a declara-tion of independence. But the movement which led to revolution was not revolutionary except by inadvertence." Somewhat frightened, they sought to mitigate the radical contingency of the revolution by speaking the language of restoration that was indeed true to their original inten-tions in rebellion. Ultimately, though, it became clear to them that restoration was not the whole goal. Their experience of public freedom in the revolutionary process made them value political action and par-ticipation, the act of coming together in deliberation, debate, and deci-sion. Free political action is seductive.[68]

Thus, they were moved to complete their revolutionary task, seeking in the end not merely liberation but the reconstitution of the political realm in order to enable the citizenry of the new republic to experience the happiness of public freedom and political action. Now conscious that this new goal, which they had not deliberately chosen, was radically new, they both reveled in their good fortune to be a part of this world historical event and sought comfort from its weightiness. They turned to theory, to the science of politics, for aid in their "task, the creation of new power." And "they turned to history," pedantically documenting re-publican constitutions of all sorts, driven, Arendt argues, not by the need to learn how to "safeguard . . . civil liberties—a subject on which they certainly knew more than any previous republic," but by the need to learn about "the constitution of power."[69]

Insofar as this turn to antiquity constituted a search for pedagogic examples, Arendt approves of it. Like Machiavelli, she believes that historical stories and fables are invaluable in providing the inspiration necessary to embolden ourselves for action: "Without the classical examples shining through the centuries, none of the men of the revolutions on either side of the Atlantic would have possessed the courage for what then turned out to be unprecedented action."[70]

The turn to antiquity, however, constituted not only a search for pedagogic examples; it also constituted a search for a beginning to anchor the newly constituted republic: "Politically speaking," the American revolutionaries were right to believe they had to derive "the stability and authority of any given body politic from its beginning." The problem was that "they could not conceive of a beginning except as something which must have occurred in a distant past."[71] In this respect then, the turn to antiquity was in quest of reassurance that the innovation of the revolution was not radical but derivative. But the reassurance was false, for their action *was* unprecedented. Hence its greatness.

The quest for reassurance marked a lack of faith on the part of the revolutionaries in their own action. This lack of faith led them also to attempt to ground their reconstitution of the political realm in an "absolute," a law of laws that they trusted to serve as "the source of validity of their laws and the fountain of legitimacy for the new government." The result was a paradox: "It was precisely the revolutions, their crisis and emergency, which drove the very 'enlightened' men of the eighteenth century to plead for some religious sanction at the very moment when they were about to emancipate the secular realm from the influences of the churches and to separate politics and religion once and for all."[72]

This quest for an absolute in which to ground and legitimate the reconstitution of the political realm is, according to Arendt, deeply misguided. Absolutes occlude the contingency that is the quintessential feature of the public realm, the feature in virtue of which political freedom and human innovation are possible. Moreover, they deprivilege the very human achievement of reconstitution and founding, making it dependent on something external to the human world. And that external something, whether it be god, natural law, or self-evident truth, is untenable in the modern era. Natural law needs "divine sanction to become binding for men," and "the authority of self-evident truth . . . still bears clear signs of divine origin," whereas in modernity "the loss of religious sanction for the political realm is a matter of accomplished fact."[73]

But there is a more fundamental issue at stake here. Even if appeals to an absolute could still sway us, even if religious sanction was still viable for the political realm, appeals to an absolute as a ground of politics, in Arendt's view, would be illicit. For an absolute is

> a truth that needs no agreement since, because of its self-evidence, it compels without argumentative demonstration or political persuasion. By virtue of being self-evident, these truths are pre-rational—they inform reason but are not its product—and since their self-evidence puts them beyond disclosure and argument, they are in a sense no less compelling than "despotic power" and no less absolute than the revealed truths of religion or the axiomatic verities of mathematics.[74]

In politics, the appeal to an absolute is illicit because of its constative character. The uniquely political action, on Arendt's account, is not the constative but the performative utterance, a speech act that in itself brings "something into being which did not exist before";[75] hence Arendt's claim that the "grandeur" of the Declaration of Independence consists not "so much in its being 'an argument in support of an action' as in its being *the perfect way for an action to appear in words*."[76] Its perfection inheres in its pure performativity and also, as we saw earlier, in its written manifestation.

In spite of Arendt's celebratory tone, she is forced to admit that the Declaration of Independence does not consistently maintain the performative posture she admires. The preamble to the Declaration contains two appeals to a "transcendent source of authority for the laws of the new body politic," an appeal to "nature's god" and an appeal to self-evident truths. What is interesting, though, about the appeal to self-evident truths is that the sentence "we hold these truths to be self-evident" is partly performative in character. These famous words, Arendt argues, "combine in a historically unique manner the basis of agreement between those who have embarked upon revolution ['We hold'], an agreement necessarily relative because related to those who enter it, with an abso-lute ['self-evident']" that signals not agreement but compulsion.[77]

The statement's performative quality Arendt attributes to Jefferson's dim awareness that it was a fallacy to believe that irresistible laws were "of the same nature as the laws of a community." Were it not for this dim awareness, Jefferson "would not have indulged in the somewhat in-congruous phrase 'We hold these truths to be self-evident' but would have said: These truths are self-evident, namely, they possess a power to compel which is as irresistible as despotic power, they are not held by us, but we are held by them; They stand in no need of agreement." Jefferson's awareness of the fallacy could be no more than dim because he was caught in a period of transition. The new political developments of his time were "nowhere matched by an adequate development of new thought." In particular, "there was no avoiding the problem of the absolute . . . because it proved to be inherent in the traditional concept of law. If the essence of secular law was a command, then a divinity, not nature but 'nature's god', not reason but a divinely informed reason, was needed to bestow validity on it."[78]

Fortunately for the American republic, this problem was a theoretical one. This "bondage" to the "conceptual and intellectual framework of the European tradition" did not, Arendt argues, determine "the actual destinies of the American republic to the same extent as it compelled the minds of the theorists." For if it had, she speculates (somewhat naively), "the authority of this new body politic in actual fact might have crumbled under the onslaught of modernity—where the loss of religious sanction for the political realm is an accomplished fact—as it crumbled in all other revolutions. . . . what saved the American revolution from this fate was neither 'nature's god' nor self-evident truth, but the act of foundation itself." In short, Arendt believes that in practice, the "We hold," the performative part of Jefferson's "incongruous phrase," won out over the constative part, the reference to self-evident truths. This saved the American revolution because the "We hold" constitutes the only sort of power that is "real" and "legitimate," the sort of power that "rest[s] on reciprocity and mutuality" and comes into being only "when men join themselves together for the purpose of action" by binding "themselves through promises, covenants, and mutual pledges."[79]

The appeal to self-evidence stands in opposition to the "We hold." It expresses not a free coming together but an isolated acquiescence to compulsion and necessity. The appeal therefore coerces and disempowers. It violates the integrity of politics and denatures and disables its practice. Recall Arendt's insistence on the autonomy of the political realm and on the sui generis character of politics. She argued that politics should not be held to standards external to it, that it has two precepts of its own: forgiving and promising. These precepts are unique in that they are both performatives; indeed, it is that feature that makes these two practices, ordinarily thought of as the subject of ethics, profoundly political in an Arendtian schema. As performatives, they cannot be judged true or false, right or wrong. And they cannot make sense in isolation. Performative utterances necessarily take place in concert and require spectators for their success: they must be witnessed, judged, and remembered if they are to bring something into being that did not exist before. In my view, Arendt wants to celebrate the American Declaration of Independence as a purely performative speech act, but in order to do so she must disambiguate it. She dismisses its constative moments and holds up the Declaration as an example of a uniquely political act, an act available uniquely to human beings, an authoritative exemplification of human power and worldliness.

The performative "We hold," on Arendt's account, empowers an existing community inasmuch as it constitutes a free coming together and gives public expression of an agreement to abide by certain rules in the community's subsequent being together. The "We hold" is a promise and a declaration. It signals the existence of a singularly human capacity, that of world building:

> There is an element of the world-building capacity of man in the human faculty of making and keeping promises. . . . The grammar of action: that action is the only human faculty that demands a plurality of men; and the syntax of power: that power is the only human attribute which applies solely to the worldly in-between space by which men are mutually related, combine in the act of foundation by virtue of the making and the keeping of promises, which, in the realm of politics, may well be the highest human faculty.[80]

The source of power in this world-building act of foundation is the speech act itself, the declaration of the "We hold." And the act of foundation is the source of its own authority as well. In short, power and authority are interdependent on Arendt's account.[81] The authority of the world built by power derives from all that is implied by the fact that world is the product of power rather than strength or violence. (What is implied is that it is the product of free action by equals who act in concert, bound together by mutual promises and reciprocity for the sake of bringing something new into being.) Properly understood and performed, the act of foundation requires no appeal to a source of authority beyond itself: "[I]t was the authority which the act of foundation carried within itself, rather than the belief in an immortal Legislator, or the promises of reward and threats of punishment in a 'future state,' or even the doubtful self-evidence of the truths enumerated in the preamble to the Declaration of Independence, that assured stability for the new republic." Thus, Arendt squares Sièyes's circle by finding the source of authority in the act of foundation, thereby making appeals to an absolute, transcendent source of authority not merely illicit but redundant and unnecessary. Arendt's political performative does not require the blessing of a constative in order to work. Nor, Arendt claims, did the American Constitution: the preamble to the Declaration, she argues, "provide[s] the sole source of authority from which the Constitution, not as an act of constituting government but as the law of the land, derives its own legitimacy."[82]

Arendt thereby seems to have found for the new world the new thought it needed to enable it to conceive of a founding that secures law for a community without appealing to a law of laws and without lapsing into foundationalism, the thought that salvages political authority for an age unable or unwilling to support the authority of tradition and religion. One might say that her project is to save authority, to find a way to sustain it, because she realizes that without it there can be no politics. In a world devoid of authority, we are denied the opportunity to exercise our "human capacity for building, preserving, and caring for a world that can survive us and remain a place fit to live in for those who come after us."[83]

This reading of Arendt may initially appear implausible because of what Richard Flathman calls the essentialist character of her account of authority. Flathman notes that Arendt asserts "a necessary connection between *in* authority and a quite definite and complex constellation of values and beliefs about tradition and religion [meaning that of ancient Rome]." According to Flathman, it follows from Arendt's argument that once "this particular constellation of values and beliefs has disappeared, *in* authority has *thereby* disappeared as well." Furthermore, Flathman argues, given Arendt's insistence that power and authority are interdependent, it is curiously inconsistent that she both claims that authority has disappeared from the modern world and insists that power has not.[84] On my reading, however, the problem disappears, for Arendt is understood to be claiming that a certain kind of authority, the kind that sustained the Roman republic together with tradition and religion, has disappeared in modernity. This is not, as Arendt says, "'authority in general', but rather a very specific form which had been valid throughout the Western world over a long period of time." And it is this specific form of authority, "authority as we once knew it, which grew out of the Roman experience of foundation and was understood in the light of Greek political philosophy," that "has nowhere been reestablished."[85]

In *On Revolution*, Arendt gives an account of an alternative form of authority, the authority inherent in the performative Declaration of Independence and in the practice of constitution making that "preceded, accompanied, and followed" it "in all thirteen colonies." Both, she argues, "revealed all of a sudden to what an extent *an entirely new concept of power and authority*, an entirely novel idea of what was of prime importance in the political realm had already developed in the New World, even though the inhabitants of this world spoke and thought in the terms of the Old World."[86] Arendt understands that we cannot recover the lost form of authority that sustained Rome for so long; it is untenable in modernity. But neither can we exercise our world building capacities in a world without authority. If we love the world, if we are committed to world-building—to politics—we must find another form of authority, one that can be sustained in modernity. Only then will we experience the privilege of a kind of political action that is not just revolutionary.[87]

Revolutions are frequent in the modern age (and peculiar to it) because of the failure of traditional authority.[88] But most revolutions themselves fail for the same reason. They seek to ground their reconstitution of the political realm in the same sort of traditional authority whose very untenability made their own revolution possible. Arendt tries to get out of this vicious circle by offering an alternative conception of authority, one that inheres not in an untenable absolute, or in a law of laws, but in the power of reconstitution itself.[89]

Only the modern conception of authority is viable for modernity because it requires for its sustenance not a shared belief in particular deities or myths but a common subscription to the authoritative linguistic practice of promising. Consequently, it assumes a preexisting community, but not in the strong sense of "homogeneity of past and origin" which is the "decisive principle of the nation state."[90] This is a community in a weaker sense, bound together by common linguistic practices, not even necessarily by a single, common, inherited, first language. This is a community whose members understand and subscribe to performative practices. Such a community should be able to sustain this new kind of authority, in Arendt's view—assuming, that is, that it can overcome its nihilistic craving for a law of laws, for a source of authority that is transcendent or self-evident, assuming that it can see and be satisfied with the power and authority inherent in its own performatives.

Conversely, one might say not that Arendt seeks to salvage authority for the sake of politics but that she seeks to salvage politics for the sake of authority. To see Arendt's politics as a response to modern nihilism is to make sense of her claim that we need politics for the sake of the world. We cannot live without standards or some stability and yet our traditional sources of stability are no longer viable. Consequently, we are left to the devices of politics and action. Politics is more important than ever because it is the only alternative to violent domination, the only source in modernity of legitimate rules possessed of authority and capable of addressing "the elementary problem of human living-together."[91]

Arendt's description of the signing of the Mayflower Compact is enlightening in this context. The parties to the Compact

> obviously feared the so-called state of nature, the untrod wilderness, unlimited by any boundary, as well as the unlimited initiative of men bound by no law. This fear is not surprising; it is the justified fear of men who have decided to leave civilization behind them and strike out on their own. The really astounding fact in the whole story is that their obvious fear of one another was accompanied by the no less obvious confidence they had in their own power, granted and confirmed by no one and as yet unsupported by any means of violence, to combine themselves together into a "civil Body Politick" which, held together solely by the strength of mutual promises "in the Presence of God and one another," supposedly was powerful enough to "enact, constitute, and frame" all necessary laws and instruments of government.[92]

Like the parties to the Compact, the founders of the American republic built small "islands of security" in an "ocean of contingency" through joint action, promising, and constitution making, performatives that are not solipsistic because they presuppose a plurality of participants who subscribe to a shared authoritative practice of promising and not nihilistic because, by virtue of their power, they are the guarantors of their own authority. Arendt can do no better than this because of her conviction that the "realm of human affairs" is "relative by definition."[93] Political action has no anchor.

The Undecidability of the American Declaration of Independence

Arendt's claim that political action has no anchor rests on her too easy dismissal of the constative moments of the Declaration. She does not see that her cherished performative, "We hold," is itself *also* a constative utterance. She brackets the problem by suggesting that the "we" does not exist as such prior to the Declaration; on her account, after all, action does not postulate an actor, it occurs ex nihilo. But this creates problems for her other claim that the "we" stands as the guarantor of its own performance. The problem is addressed by Derrida in his own reading of Jefferson's draft of the American Declaration of Independence, a reading that, like Arendt's, focuses on the document's curious structural combination of constative and performative utterance. Derrida argues that

> The "we" of the declaration speaks "in the name of the people." But this people does not yet exist. They do *not* exist as an entity, it does *not* exist, *before* this declaration, not *as such*. If it gives birth to itself, as free and independent subject, as possible signer [of the Declaration], this can hold only in the act of the signature. The signature invents the signer. This signer can only authorize him- or herself to sign once he or she has come to the end, if one can say this, of his or her own signature, in a sort of fabulous retroactivity.[94]

On Derrida's account, the signers are stuck in Sièyes's vicious circle. They lack the authority to sign until they have already signed. The American founders' invocation of the name of the laws of nature and the name of God manifests this predicament. They appealed to a constative, according to Derrida, not, as Arendt would have it, because of a failure of nerve or because they underestimated the power of their own performative but because they did not overestimate its power. To guarantee that power and secure their innovation, they had to combine their performative with a constative utterance. They needed "another 'subjectivity' . . . to sign, in order to guarantee it, this production of signature," for "in this process . . . there are only countersignatures."

> It is still "in the name of" that the "good people" of America call *themselves* and declare *themselves* independent, at the instant in which they invent for themselves a signing identity. They sign in the name of the laws of nature and in the name of God. They *pose* or *posit* their institutional laws on the foundation of natural laws and by the same coup (the interpretive coup of force) in the name of God, creator of nature. He comes, in effect, to guarantee the rectitude of popular intentions, the unity and goodness of the people. *He founds natural laws and thus the whole game which tends to present performative utterances as constative utterances.*[95]

Founding, promising, or signing, cannot occur ex nihilo: "For this Declaration to have a meaning *and* an effect there must be a last instance. God is the name, the best one, for this last instance and this ultimate signature"; that is, "God" is the name Derrida gives to whatever is used to hold the place of the last instance, the place that is the inevitable *aporia* of founding (or signing or promising).[96] In short, Derrida, like Rousseau (and yet quite unlike Rousseau), sees that to break Sièyes's vicious circle, to posit the law of institutional laws, *"il faudrait des dieux."*[97]

The moral of Derrida's story is that no act of founding (or signing, or promising) is free of this aporia—this gap that needs to be anchored— and this is a structural feature of language. This gap that marks *all* forms of utterance is always filled (whether or not we acknowledge it) by a deus ex machina, if not by God himself then by nature, the subject, language, or tradition. Arendt sees that this aporia is a structural feature of all performatives (though not of all language). But she insists that the aporia, the gap that marks all performatives, can and should be held open. She understands that there is often a felt human need to fill this gap, but she does not see it as a systemic, conceptual, or linguistic need. Quite the contrary. The difference between her position and Derrida's on this point is made clear by their different assessments of the American Declaration's combined performative and constative structure.

Unlike Arendt, Derrida does not see the Declaration's structural combination of performative and constative utterance as incongruous. It is not a question "of an obscurity or of a difficulty of interpretation, of a problematic on the way to its (re)solution," because "this obscurity, this undecidability between, let's say, a performative and a constative structure, is *required* in order to produce the sought after effect." The insecure performative is not always and necessarily anchored by another utterance. The "We hold," on Derrida's account, is capable of anchoring itself not because of its powerful purity as a performative but because it is in fact both a constative and a performative. It is unclear whether "independence is stated or produced by this utterance." And its rhetorical force derives in large measure from this unclarity, from the fact that *one cannot decide* which sort of utterance it is, constative or performative.[98]

For Derrida, the combined constative and performative structure of the document and its "We hold" illustrates beautifully a structural feature of all language: that no signature, promise, performative—no act of foundation—possesses resources adequate to guarantee itself, that each and every one necessarily needs some external, systemically illegitimate guarantee to work. This need marks the Declaration of Independence just as it marks more quotidian utterances. "This happens every day" (indeed, "every signature finds itself thus affected"), Derrida says, "but it is fabulous."[99]

For Arendt, however, the Declaration's constative moments are marks of impurity, tainting what is really and ought to have been a purely performative act. She does not see that her cherished performative, "We hold," is also a constative utterance. And so there is no undecidability here for her. The other constative moments of the Declaration are unfortunate errors or lapses, marring but not obviating modernity's greatest moment, the moment when a new revolution splendidly completed its course in the founding of a republic whose authority rested exclusively in the power of the performative "We hold." The power of this utterance as a performative is sufficient to produce the sought after effect. Acts of founding are not aided but compromised by the unnecessary and illicit reliance on a constative.

As evidence for her claim that the Declaration and its performative *We hold* are the sole source of authority for the Constitution, Arendt notes that "the Constitution itself, in its preamble as well as in its amendments which form the Bill of Rights, is singularly silent on this question of ultimate authority."[100] But there are two ways to read this silence. The alternative sees this same silence as evidence that the constative structure of the Declaration *is* a guarantor of constitutional authority. Recall that Arendt identifies speech with power and characterizes violence as "mute."[101] Recall too that, in her view, constatives are violent, despotic, and disempowering: they are not the products of shared public agreement; they demand an isolated acquiescence to a truth. They are not held by us, we are held by them. In short, they silence us; hence Arendt's insistence that they are illicit in the realm of action, the realm of speech.[102] Consequently, the fact that the Constitution is silent on this question of ultimate authority is not overwhelming evidence that the authority of the republic inheres in the performative "We hold." That silence can be read equally well as evidence that the constative moments of the Declaration contribute importantly to the establishment of ultimate authority in the new republic. The silence can do no more than confirm the undecidability Arendt resists.

Arendt resists this undecidability because she seeks in the American Declaration and founding a moment of perfect legitimacy. Insofar as the authority of the founding derives from a constative, it is rooted not in power but in violence. This undecidability, then, delegitimates the republic and so, for the sake of her moment of pure legitimacy, Arendt must do away with it. What she does not see is that the American Declaration and founding are paradigmatic instances of politics (however impure) because of this undecidability, not in spite of it. Derrida's point, like Nietzsche's, is that in every system (every practice), whether linguistic, cultural, or political, there is a moment or place the system cannot account for. Every system is secured by placeholders that are irrevocably, structurally arbitrary and prelegitimate. They enable the system but are illegitimate from its vantage point.[103] The question is, what placeholder fills this place, the place of the last instance, in Arendt's account?

Arendt fills the place of the last instance with a fable, her fable of the American revolution and founding. From a Derridian perspective, it is appropriate that she turns to a fable to hold the place; for all placeholders, according to Derrida, including those that are constative in structure, are fables. When Derrida claims that the signer's authorizing himself to sign by signing is a "fabulous retroactivity," he signals to us that this retroactivity is enabled by a fable: "There was no signer, by right, before the text of the Declaration which itself remains the producer and guarantor of its own signature. By this fabulous event, by this fable which implies the structure of the trace and is only in truth possible thanks to the inadequation to itself of a present, a signature gives itself a name."[104] Arendt herself recognizes this "inadequation to itself of a present"; her historical fable is an acknowledgment of it and a response to it. Thus, her criticism of the American founders for their inability to conceive of a beginning that was not rooted in the past must be in the service of her fable, for she too proves to be unable to conceive of such a totally present event.

Arendt turns to the Declaration in the hope that it will provide her with the resources to fill the gap in her own theorization of a politics of founding. The historical event inspires the fable but it does not bind it. Arendt dismisses, among other things, the constative structure of the Declaration of Independence and insists that the Declaration's pure performative was a sufficient guarantor of the authority of the new republic—in order to fill the place with a fabulous faith, the faith that the American founding fathers did not need gods to found a legitimate republican politics and so neither do we. Like all her spectators' stories, Arendt's fable is meant to define and enable new horizons of possibility. It is meant to inspire us, just as classical examples of founding emboldened the American revolutionaries.[105] The fable must take the place of the constative in order for Arendt to theorize a viable politics for modernity, a politics born not of violence but of power, a nonfoundational politics that is legitimate, authoritative, stable, and durable.

Arendt claims that this fable is the product of her commitment to memory, to the recovery of the American revolutionary spirit; but it invents that spirit. It claims to be a dereification, a recovery of origins; but it erases the violence and ambiguity that marked the original act of founding. And the effect of Arendt's fable is the same as that of all legitimating fables: to prohibit further inquiry into the origins of the system and protect its center of illegitimacy from the scrutiny of prying eyes.

Arendt seems to recognize this. At the end of *Willing*, she acknowledges that she has come to an impasse. Her account of freedom, natality, and the will "seems to tell us no more than that we are *doomed* to be free by virtue of being born, no matter whether we like freedom or abhor its arbitrariness." The only way out of this impasse, Arendt argues, is through "an appeal to another mental faculty," that of judgment.[106] Judgment is the faculty used by the spectators who turn actions into stories. It is the faculty used by Arendt as a spectator of the American Revolution and founding. Her fabulist rendering of those events is meant to bridge the impasse of freedom, the abyss that afflicts all performative utterance, all declarations of independence, all acts of founding.

Intervention, Augmentation, and Resistibility: Arendt's Practice of Political Authority

In spite of their apparent irreconcilability, it may be possible to bridge— or at least to negotiate—the impasse between Arendt and Derrida. If instead of dismissing the constative moment of founding we treat it as an invitation for intervention, we could respect Arendt's prohibition against anchoring political institutions in an absolute while still acknowledging Derrida's insight that *all* acts of founding are necessarily secured by a constative. By this strategy of intervention, we do not deny the constative moment of founding, but neither do we succumb to its claim to irresistibility. We resist its irresistibility. Our intervention testifies to the resistibility of the constative anchor and it posts our opposition to the attempt to "put the law *above* man," to secure the law of laws from all (political) intervention.

This notion of resistibility is at the center of Arendt's re-covered conception of authority for modernity. Recall that for Arendt an absolute is illicit in politics because it is irresistible. God, self-evident truths, natural law, are all despotic because they are irresistible. Because they are irresistible, they do not persuade to agreement, they command acquiescence. Thus, it is in virtue of their irresistibility that they are antipolitical. Resistibility is the sine qua non of Arendt's politics (hence her confinement of the irresistible body to the private realm).

On Arendt's account, it is this feature of resistibility that distinguishes secular law from divine command, political authority from religious devotion. The American founders invoked God (and a whole series of constative anchors) because they (mistakenly) believed that the "essence of secular law was a command." Their political development, she argues, "was nowhere matched by an adequate development of new thought" and this is why "there was no avoiding the problem of the absolute". It was the New World's failure to distinguish secular law from divine command that left it unable to comprehend the fact that "power under the condition of human plurality can never amount to omnipotence, and laws residing in human power can never be absolute."[107]

Derrida recognizes this fact. His deconstruction of the American Declaration is in the service of this recognition. He exposes "the whole game which tends to present performative utterances as constative utterances." But he knows that this exposure cannot bring the game to an end. The game proceeds, and Derrida, by his very intervention, declares himself a player. In so doing, he joins Arendt in proclaiming his commitment to resistibility. Like her, he refuses to allow the law of laws to be put, unproblematically, *above* man, but he recognizes, more deeply than does Arendt, that the law will always resist his resistance.[108] His unwillingness to passively accept that is a commitment to politicization, resistibility, and intervention. And his strategy of intervention is not only consistent with Arendt's own account of the practice of political authority, as I read it; it is required by it.

Arendt's theorization of authority builds on the close connection in Roman thought and practice between the concept of authority and a practice of augmentation:

> The very concept of Roman authority suggests that the act of foundation inevitably develops its own stability and permanence, and authority in this context is nothing more or less than a kind of necessary "augmentation" by virtue of which all innovations and changes remained tied back to the foundation which, at the same time, they augment and increase. Thus the amendments to the Constitution augment and increase the original foundations of the American republic; . . . *the very authority of the American Constitution resides in its inherent capacity to be amended and augmented.* This notion of a coincidence of foundation and preservation by virtue of augmentation . . . was deeply rooted in the Roman spirit.[109]

Because republics do not rest on one world-building act of foundation but are manifestly committed to augmentation, to the continual preservation and amendment of their foundation, they are uniquely endowed with political vigor. Not so the American republic, however. In it, augmentation gave way to permanence; "there was no space reserved, no room left for the exercise of precisely those qualities which had been instrumental in building it." This was, Arendt argues, "no mere oversight"; the American founders, intent on "starting something permanent and enduring," succumbed to the charms of the irresistible absolute. As a result, the experience of free political action remained "the privilege of the generation of the founders." That privileging, Jefferson felt, was an injustice. No constitution was perfect and none should be treated with "sanctimonious reverence." Consequently, he greeted the news of Shay's rebellion with enthusiasm: "God forbid we should ever be twenty years without such a rebellion," he said, echoing Machiavelli's advice to princes to reinvigorate their rule with a repetition of the violence of their founding about every ten years.[110]

Arendt does not endorse this reliance on violence as a way to reinvigorate the republic. But she does admire Jefferson's later idea of a ward system, a system he came to see as "the only possible non-violent alternative to his earlier notions about the desirability of recurring revolutions." The ward system, Arendt says, could correct the fatal flaw of the Constitution (which "had given all power to the citizens, without giving them the opportunity of *being* republican and of *acting* as citizens") by subdividing counties into small republics in which every citizen would have an opportunity to participate in the activity of politics.[111]

Like Machiavelli, Arendt believes that this commitment to political action is uniquely republican. Republics generate and maintain power, as action in concert, better than any other form of regime. The source of their power is their internal difference and plurality. Republics are born of an act of power, a promise, made by diverse individuals who, in promising, do not give up their plurality and individuality. "The mutual contract where power is constituted by means of a promise, contains *in nuce* both the republican principle, according to which power resides in the people, . . . and the federal principle, . . . according to which constituted political bodies can combine and enter into lasting alliance without losing their identity." The republican recognition that difference and plurality are the sources of power is manifest in the republican commitment to an institutional separation of powers, a commitment born not of a fear of power but of devotion to it. The institutional separation of power, Arendt argues, generates new power. Just as in Machiavelli's view the Roman commitment to augmentation (as territorial expansion) was invigorated by the internal conflicts between the Senate and the people, so in Arendt's view republican augmentation (as amendment) is invigorated by institutional difference and agonistic action, by citizen conflict as well as cooperation.[112]

Like Machiavelli, Arendt believes that one of the points of politics is to found institutions that will last. And, like Machiavelli, she believes that republican forms of government are blessed with a longevity unmatched by other forms of political association.[113] Machiavelli believed that the durability of republics was due to the inner diversity that provided them with more resources than any other form of regime to adapt to changing circumstances. He saw the world of politics as a world in flux, a world much like Nietzsche's, in which survival entails expansion.[114] His commitment to republicanism was indebted largely to his commitment to find a form of political association capable of some durability or perpetuity in a world whose contingency would otherwise be unendurable (a world Nietzsche later referred to as his "Siberia").

Arendt, too, attributes the durability of republics to their power to expand, a power she admires. But the power of which she speaks does not involve conquest. And the expansion of which she speaks is not one of territorial acquisition; it is one of augmentation.[115] On her account a republic, properly constituted, empowers its citizens to a degree unparalleled by any other form of political association. It offers them opportunities for political activity other than revolution by committing itself institutionally to continual world-building. And this is clear not only from Arendt's accounts of action and participation but also from her account of authority. Indeed, her views are aptly summarized by Hanna Pitkin's description of Machiavelli's account, in which "republican authority must be exercised in a way that further politicizes the people rather than rendering them quiescent. Its function is precisely to keep a political movement or action that the people have initiated . . . from disintegrating into riot, apathy, or privatization."[116]

This republican commitment to political action is important to Arendt for two distinct but related reasons. The first is connected to her motif of self-realization. In her view, human beings denied the opportunity to exercise their world-building capacities live an impoverished life, a life that is somehow less than human, a life without freedom, without happiness.[117] The second reason is connected to Arendt's re-covered conception of authority for modernity. Where other theorists of authority, such as Rousseau, believe that the problem of authority is how to put the law *above* man, that is, how to make the law of laws irresistible, Arendt believes the problem is how to prevent the law of laws from becoming irresistible: she rejects the command model of authority as inappropriate for the human condition of living together in a secular and political world. A practice of authority centered on an irresistible law of laws is inappropriate for the postfoundational age for which Arendt theorizes a politics and it is also deeply antipolitical. It prohibits the practices of augmentation and amendment she valorizes and it encourages a withdrawal from active politics; it deactivates politics.

Recall Arendt's claim that the American founders correctly perceived that the authority of any body politic derives from its beginning but mistakenly believed that a beginning was "something which must have occurred in a distant past." The "great good fortune" of the American republic was that this mistaken belief lost out. The success of the revolution "was decided the very moment when the Constitution began to be worshipped"; for that constitution worship, Arendt argues, evidenced the fact that the republic was built on a beginning that was very present: "If their attitude towards Revolution and Constitution can be called religious at all, then the word 'religion' must be understood in its original Roman sense, and their piety would then consist in *religare*, in binding themselves back to a beginning." This constitution worship has always been "ambiguous," its object "at least as much the constituting act as it was the written document itself." Consequently, Arendt can say both that the "American remembrance of the event" of constitution is what keeps the authority of the republic "safe and intact" and that the "very authority of the American Constitution resides in its inherent capacity to be amended and augmented."[118] For Arendt, this commitment to augmentation maintains a republic and its revolutionary spirit by, in a curious sense, keeping its beginning always present.

Derrida identifies this same structure of maintenance. He calls it "*survivance*," by which he too means a kind of preservation through augmentation. Here, as with Arendt, survival is not produced by the maintenance of a present into a future in the way a fixed monument seeks to preserve the presence of what is past. For Derrida, maintenance is an augmentation that takes place by way of translation, by way of a translation that is called for and "heard in" the original text. Just as on Arendt's account the Constitution calls out to be amended, so Derrida's text calls out to be translated: it is not present, yet. This is not translation in the ordinary sense: just as Arendt's performative founding could never be content merely to transmit a sense of obligation or produce obedient subjects, neither can Derrida's act of translation be "content merely to transport a content into another language, nor just to communicate or to transmit something," merely to produce comprehension. Translation augments, necessarily. It does not merely copy, or reproduce; it is a new linguistic event, it produces "new textual bodies." It does not simply preserve an original in a practice of mere repetition, it dislodges the constative yearnings of the original and finds there the point of departure for a new way of life; hence Derrida's claim that this is not *survivance* "in the sense of posterity . . . but of 'more living' "; in the sense of *"plus de vie* and *plus que vie."* This "augmentation," says Derrida, is "what survival is." And this augmentation is arguably like Arendt's practice of authority, which responds to the text or document that seeks to preserve and refer to the past moment of founding by augmenting it with another event, with another speech act, or, as in this case, by an act of translation.[119]

   This structure of maintenance is also explored by Machiavelli, who sees the importance of maintaining the act of foundation, understands that human institutions need frequent revitalization, and seeks that revitalization in the "return to beginnings," a kind of invitation to augmentation. As Pitkin points out, this return to beginnings may be read as a way of frightening the population back into obedience, but there is also another way to think about it. "Perhaps," she suggests, "one should construe the forgetfulness that gradually corrupts a composite body as reification: a coming to take for granted as 'given' and inevitable what in fact is the product of human action." This reification distances citizens from their political institutions. From this perspective, Pitkin argues, the return to origins does not signal the recurrence of violence but a return "to the spirit of origins, the human capacity to originate." If we assume here that "in the beginning lies not chaos but human capacity," then we can see that Machiavelli's return to beginnings is, as are Nietzsche's genealogies and Derrida's deconstructions, a dereification and a political intervention.[120]

   Arendt, like Machiavelli, sees that a beginning too firmly rooted in the past is in danger of becoming reified and foundational. Our commitment to augmentation and amendment may derive from our reverence for a beginning that is in the past; but our practices of augmentation and amendment make that beginning our own, not merely our legacy but our own construction and performative. The commitment to augmentation protects that which was glorious because it was a performative from being sanctified and turned into a law of laws, an absolute whose irresistibility would ultimately and necessarily destroy the uniquely political character of the republic.[121] On this reading of Arendt, augmentation is both a necessary condition of politics and constitutive of one form of the activity itself. What Leo Strauss says of Machiavelli applies equally to Arendt: "Foundation is, as it were, continuous foundation."[122]

Since on Arendt's account the practice of authority consists largely in this commitment to resistibility, the practice of authority turns out to be, paradoxically enough, a practice of deauthorization. On this account then, deauthorizing projects like Derrida's and Machiavelli's, and the adoption of a posture of intervention, become *part* of a practice of authority and not simply an unauthorized assault on the institutions of authority from some outside. This inclusion is the genius of Arendt's account.

It is noteworthy that, for both Derrida and Arendt, the moment of intervention is the moment of politics. But for Derrida politics *begins* with the entry of the irresistible absolute; it is the impossible superimposition of constative on performative utterance that occasions the Derridian intervention, an intervention that is political. For Arendt, however, politics *ends* with the entry of the *antipolitical* (because irresistible) absolute. Arendt's intervention consists in her insistence that acts of founding can and should resist the urge to anchor themselves in an absolute. But Arendt's account of authority as a practice of augmentation and amendment does not, in my view, commit her to this insistence. It commits her only to the insistence that we treat the absolute as an invitation for intervention, that we declare ourselves resistant to it, that we refuse its claim to irresistibility by deauthorizing it. This, in effect, is what Arendt herself tries to do in her own interventionist critique of the constative structure of the American Declaration of Independence. Inspired, perhaps, by Nietzsche's counsel to seek "a past from which we may spring rather than that from which we seem to have derived,"[123] she calls on us to do the same.

Making Space for Arendt's *Virtù* Theory of Politics

In Arendt's politics, institutions and individuals are always incomplete, forever calling out for augmentation and amendment. Like Nietzsche's self as a work of art, like translation on Derrida's account, Arendt's politics is never a fait accompli. Her rendering of authority as a practice of augmentation evidences her commitment to the perpetuity of political contest and to the view that in politics, in authorship, and in institutions it is not possible to get it right. These commitments are the hallmarks of any *virtù* theory of politics.

Virtù theories of politics reject, problematize, or resist any attempt to ground political authority unproblematically in a law of laws that is immune to contestation or amendment. Arendt perceives, as does Kant, that the characteristic feature of a law of laws is its inherent irresistibility. This is its attraction for Kant: its compulsion, irresistibility, and certainty. For Arendt, however, the irresistibility of the law marks the closure of political space and the beginning of despotism. Thus, the reverence on which her politics builds is very different from the Kantian variety: for her, the object of reverence is an act of constitution that offers itself as an invitation to augmentation and amendment. Arendtian reverence activates.

Arendt's politics takes seriously Nietzsche's claim that "the will to a system is a lack of integrity," a claim that rests on the supposition that the contingent world is partly resistant to (never simply completed and enabled by) attempts to order it. Those whose project is systematization can achieve their goal, Nietzsche charges, only if they lie and conceal the resistances that evidence the inadequacy and the impositional character of their system. For Arendt, these spaces of worldly and contingent resistance to systematization are the spaces of politics. For her, we might say, "the will to a system is a lack of politics." This formulation is consistent with her concerns about the displacement of politics in an age of modern bureaucracy, administrative politics and normalization, an age of system. The mark of true politics, for Arendt, is resistibility and a perpetual openness to the possibility of re-founding. Like Nietzsche, she is attracted to *virtù* as an alternative because it "rouses enmity toward order." Too much order closes down the spaces of contestability, the spaces of politics. Arendt's account of politics, law, and institutions is, like Nietzsche's, devoted to the preservation of the contest. Like Nietzsche, she admires the agon and seeks to protect it from closure, from domination by any one idea, truth, essence, individual, or institution.

Arendt's politics is devoted to the generation and preservation of the spaces of politics and the spaces of power. But when she talks about the spaces of power, she means more than the agon, the site of the contest, and she means more than the agora, in which public discussion takes place, although she means these too. But she also means that the spaces of the in-between must be maintained by political and civic institutions as well as by such political and civic virtues as respect and friendship. And she means that the spaces within persons, the spaces that mark their multiple resistances to the domination of autonomy and the imposition of subjectivity, must not be closed. This is why the inner multiplicity of the self and the plurality of the republic are conditions of action and politics. Both evidence space and belie, indeed resist, systematization. Finally, Arendt can also be taken to be referring to the aporia of promising and of all performative utterance; these too are spaces she would like to hold open—free from constative intrusion. These are all the spaces of Arendt's politics. The insistence that they be closed expresses a resentful need for a too stable or too ordered order. The art of keeping them open is, for Arendt, part of the task of politics. Attempts to overcome the spaces of plurality or multiplicity, she warns, will result in "the abolition of the public realm itself" and the "arbitrary domination of all others," or in "the exchange of the real world for an imaginary one where these others would simply not exist." The only way to prevent such an exchange, and to preserve space for the other, is by protecting the spaces of politics. And this, on Arendt's account, is the task of power: power "keeps the public realm, the potential space of appearances between acting and speaking men, in existence." And Arendt herself tries to do this, not only in her account of republican institutions but also through her account of the self.[124]

On Arendt's account, the inner plurality of the self is the source of its vigor. Were the self completely and exhaustively constituted in the mode of subjectivity, it would have no spur to action, no excess to animate or dislodge it, no fissures that might mark its openness to risk and its need for augmentation. Tormented by inner conflicts in the private realm, the self is released from its cycles of ordinariness by the rupture that is action. The self as subject is disrupted and the rupture creates the space for the emergence of the actor and his heroic identity. The episode is an event, from the standpoint of predictable and cyclical nature, "a miracle."[125]

The rupture creates a foundling, an actor momentarily without a past, without a birthright, without causal antecedents.[126] This is of paramount importance to Arendt's account because the attribution to the self of a deep identity or nature, ontologically grounded or given, allows the meaning of its performative utterance to be derived not from the performance but from the identity of the performer, not from the doing but from the being behind the doing. The being behind the doing of the act of foundation would, in turn, become the absolute, the external justification and source of authority of that act of foundation. The justification of any particular political form of life would be foundational and the disruptive unruliness of Arendtian action would be tamed.

But is it not the case that this unruliness has already been tamed—by Arendt herself? Her notoriously uncompromising public-private distinction protects the sui generis character of her politics by prohibiting the politicization of issues of social justice. According to Arendt, these sorts of occupations belong not to politics but to the traditional realm of the household as Aristotle theorized it. Issues concerning race, gender, ethnicity, religion are also barred from politics. These are private realm traits, on Arendt's account, natural, essential, and imitable characteristics of all human beings as such, not at all the stuff of virtuosic action. No wonder, then, that her readers are often puzzled as to what those citizens "talk about together in that endless palaver of the *agora*."[127] Voluptuously described, Arendt's politics turns out to seem rather arid; but it is not totally devoid of content. Her citizens might discuss constitutional issues—of founding and interpretation—they might focus on the rule of law and debate the terms of their mutual association, they will probably declare war and peace, and they may even address environmental issues so that they might prevent or at least delay the destruction of the very earth beneath their feet and preserve the most palpable condition of worldliness we have.

Nonetheless, Arendt's vision of politics remains rather constricted. Throughout my reconstruction of her political thought I have emphasized the rupture of Arendtian action, its politicizing component, its commitment to resistibility, its animus to responsible subjectivity, its enmity toward too much order, its perpetual augmentation of institutional settlements and individual identities. But in so doing I have seriously underplayed the rather vast and highly ordered space that provides the background condition of Arendtian action, the private realm, a realm in which the exhilaration of action is the real *vetitum*. Once reminded of the rather deep and stable settlements of the private realm, the alleged exhilarations of action's disruptions start to ring false. It is hard to make out the much vaunted ocean of contingency from here. The disruptions of action seem to leave so much in place: god, capital, technology, gender, race, class, ethnicity—none of these is touched by Arendt's politics. Or is it?

Arendt insists that her public-private distinction is nonnegotiable, but its politicization and attenuation are called for by her own account of politics and action. Indeed, any reading of Arendt that takes seriously the agonistic, virtuosic, and performative impulses of her politics must, for the sake of that politics, resist the a priori determination of a public-private distinction that is beyond contestation and amendment. I incorporate elements of this resistance into my reading of Arendt because her confinement of action to certain permissible sites and objects conflicts with her own theorization of action. Action is, after all, boundless, excessive, uncontrollable, unpredictable, and self-surprising. If action surprises its actors, why should it not also surprise Arendt, its author? If action is boundless and excessive, why should it respect a public-private distinction that seeks, like a law of laws, to regulate and contain it without ever allowing itself to be engaged or contested by it?

Arendt's own theorization of politics, as well as her own commitment to interpretation as a practice of augmentation, mandates a radicalization of her account of action. But there is one thing forever in the way of this radicalization, and that is Arendt's own nonnegotiable distinction between the public and private realms. Indeed, as it turns out, there is more than one thing in the way: Arendt secures her public-private distinction with a multitiered edifice. The distinction spawns numerous binaries, each one a new layer of protective coating on the last, each one meant to secure that much more firmly the distinction that resists the ontologizing function Arendt assigns to it: performative versus constative, "We hold" versus "self-evident truth," self versus body, male versus female, resistible versus irresistible, courageous versus risk-aversive, multiple versus univocal, speech versus silence, active versus passive, open versus closed, power versus violence, necessity versus freedom, action versus behavior, extraordinary versus ordinary, inimitable versus imitable, disruption versus repetition, light versus dark—in short, public versus private.

Why so many? In the very drawing of the distinction, where the drawing is an extraordinary act in Arendt's sense (it has the power to create new relations and realities), Arendt is caught in a cycle of anxious repetition. Binary distinctions and adjectival pairs are heaped, one on another, in a heroic effort to resist the erosion of a distinction that is tenuous enough to need all of this. Tenuous, indeed: there are, in Arendt's account, numerous instances of the permeation of these distinctions. Arendt is quite straightforward about the fact that the public realm is all too easily colonized by the private; it is to this problem that she responds in *The Human Condition* and in *On Revolution* when she considers the consequences for politics of the rise of the social and the urgency of poverty, respectively. Her candor tempts us to think that these distinctions are, above all else, drawn to protect the public from the private realm's imperialism. But the converse is also true. It is equally important to Arendt to protect the private realm's reliability, univocality, and ordinariness from the disruptions of action and politics.[128] Arendt domesticates not only behavior but also action itself: she gives action a place to call home and she tells it to stay there, where it belongs. But, of course, it refuses.

Here is the real risk of action—in this refusal. The self-surprising quality of action is not limited to the fact that action does not always turn out as we would have intended it to; or even to the fact that we, as actors, are never quite sure "who" it is we have turned out to be. Action is self-surprising in another sense as well, in the sense that it happens to us; we do not decide to perform, then enter the public realm and submit our performance to the contingency that characterizes that realm. Often political action comes to us, it involves us in ways that are not deliberate, willful, or intended, in ways that cannot be fully captured or captivated by agent-centered accounts. Action produces its actors; episodically, temporarily, we are its performative production. On Arendt's account, the American revolution happened to the American revolutionaries: "But the movement which led to the revolution was not revolutionary except by inadvertence." And, sometimes, particularly in her account of willing, action happens to the private self, initially in the *private* realm.

Arendt treats willing as an antecedent of action, but it is a funny kind of antecedent because it actually defers action. Caught in a reflexive, internal, and potentially eternal dynamic of willing and nilling, a dynamic that it is incapable of arresting, the will awaits redemption. And when that redemption comes, it comes in the form of action itself. Action liberates the self from the will's paralyzing "disquiet and worry" by disrupting its compulsive repetitions. Action comes in, as it were, to the private realm; it happens to the as yet unready and not quite willing (because still also nilling) subject in the private realm. Like a *"coup d'etat,"* action "interrupts the conflict between *velle* and *nolle*" and redeems the will. "In other words," Arendt adds, "the Will is redeemed by ceasing to will and starting to act and *the cessation cannot originate in an act of the will-not-to-will* because this would be but another volition."[129]

Examples of public-private realm cross-fertilizations abound; they are as manifold as the distinctions that are supposed to account for their impossibility, their perversion, their monstrosity. What is to prevent us, then, from attenuating the public-private distinction? What would be the punishment for unmasking the private realm's natural or constative identities of race, class, gender, and ethnicity, for example, as really the sedimented products of the actions, behaviors, and institutional structures and norms of individuals, societies, and political cultures? What is at stake?

At stake, for Arendt, is the loss of action itself, the loss of a realm in which the actionable is vouchsafed. This is a real cause of concern, especially given the astonishing and disturbing success of the "innumerable and various rules" of the social in producing normal, well-behaved subjects. But to vouchsafe it Arendt empties the public realm of almost all content. Things possessed of content are constatives, after all, sites and forces of closure, in Arendt's theorization, irresistible obstacles to performativity. Her effective formalization of action, her attempts to safeguard action with her nonnegotiable public-private distinction, may contribute more to the loss or occlusion of action than any rise of the social, than any closure of (would-be) constation.

But neither the self-defeating character of the distinction between public and private nor its permeability, inexactness, and ambiguity are reasons to give it up. Instead, they suggest the possibility of attenuation. What if we took Arendt's own irresistibly lodged distinction to be a line drawn in the sand, an illicit constative, a constituting mark or text, calling out to be contested, augmented, and amended? And what if we began by dispensing with the geographic and proprietary metaphors of public and private? What if we treated Arendt's notion of the public realm not as a specific place, like the agon, but as a metaphor for a variety of spaces, both topographic and conceptual, that might occasion action?[130] We might be left with a notion of action as an event, a "miracle," a disruption of the ordinary sequence of things, a site of resistance of the irresistible, a challenge to the normalizing rules that seek to constitute, govern, and control various behaviors. And we might then be in a position to identify and proliferate sites of political action in a much broader array of constations, ranging from the self-evident truths of God, nature, technology, capital, labor, and work to those of identity, of gender, race, and ethnicity.[131] We might then be in a position to *act*—in the private realm.

Arendt would no doubt be concerned that these amendments of her account politicize too much, that, as Nancy Fraser puts it on her behalf, "when everything is political, the sense and specificity of the political recedes."[132] For Fraser, Arendt's theorization of politics highlights a paradox: if politics is everywhere then it is nowhere. But not everything *is* political on this amended account; it is simply the case that nothing is ontologically protected from politicization, that nothing is necessarily or naturally or ontologically *not* political. The distinction between public and private is seen as the performative product of political struggle, hard won and always temporary. Indeed, the paradox is reversible: the impulse to secure, foundationally, the division between the political and the nonpolitical is articulated as a concern for the preservation of the political but it is itself an antipolitical impulse. Arendt knew this; this was the basis of her critique of the constative, foundational ground of the Declaration of Independence. This is what motivated her to apply performativity to the self-evidence of the Declaration. This is what led her to denaturalize and deessentialize the Declarations's anchors of nature and God. The same impulse can motivate the application of performativity to Arendt's public-private distinction, as well as to the essentializing attributes, attitudes, roles, and identities of Arendt's private realm.

If it can be said that the founders succumbed to the charms of the irresistible absolute because they were tempted by permanence, might it not also be said that Arendt succumbs to the charms of nature and essentialism because she is tempted by order, if not by "nature's god" and the self-evident equalities it secures then by "nature" itself and the daily predictabilities and routines (as well as the sex, race, and class differences) it stabilizes? If the constations of the Declaration mask what are really performative actions, might that not also be true for the constations of the private realm? Might it not be the case that Arendt *mis*takes performative effects in the private realm—the constitution of selves into embodied, raced, classed, and gendered subjects—for constative natural facts? Is there not in Arendt's own deauthorizing reading of the Declaration license to interrogate her essentialism and to proliferate the sites of her politics by applying her theorization of the extraordinary to the realm of the ordinary?

The dispersal of the agon is also authorized by another, somewhat different moment in Arendt's theorization of politics. Arendt understood that there were times in which the exigencies of a situation forced politics to go underground. She looks to the underground politics of occupied France and valorizes its proliferation of sites of resistance, its network of subversive political action.[133] "Occupation" might not be a bad term for what Arendt describes as the "rise of the social" and the displacement of politics by routinized, bureaucratic, and administrative regimes. In the absence of institutional sites, politics might well go underground, looking to locate itself in the rifts and fractures of identities, both personal and institutional, and doing so performatively and creatively, with the hope of establishing new relations and realities.

At issue here is the location and construal of political space. Perhaps unduly influenced by her own reading of ancient Greek political thought, Arendt sometimes seems to assume that political space has to be an empty site, situated in a stable space, an agon or an agora, rather than an unstable fissure in an otherwise highly ordered and settled practice or identity. As a result, Arendtian action runs the risk of starting from nowhere and encountering or engaging nothing at all.[134] And her characterizations of action as disruption, resistance, augmentation, and amendment seem to lose their force. What would a politics that was free of constation look like? What would action resist and disrupt if it were never challenged by a law of laws, if its mise-en-scène was not constituted by absolutes? How would performative foundings—of republics and identities—stabilize themselves without their epic moments of undecidability, without relying on the miscegenation of constation and performativity? Arendt does not answer these questions directly. But the problematic assumptions that engender them are belied by her own politicizations, amendments, augmentations, and interventions, in particular by her own interventionist reading of the American Declaration and founding in which she too resists the irresistible and contests the incontestable.

This reading of Arendt licenses the application of her own strategy of intervention to the would-be closures of the would-be private realm. Instead of containing the private realm lest it sully the pristine innocence of action, action's generative power can be used to proliferate the sites and subjects of politics, to include resistance to system, the aggravation of fissure, and the disruption of process in the private realm. It might call attention to the extraordinary measures that reproduce ordinary life, daily. It might find spaces of performativity and resistance in the rifts and fissures of private realm identities and institutions.

The possibility of a politics of performativity situated in the self-evidences of the private realm is explored by Judith Butler, who focuses in particular on the construction and constitution of sex and gender. Butler unmasks the private realm's constations—effectively described by Arendt as the mindless, tiresome, and oppressive repetition of the univocal cycles of nature—as performatives that daily reproduce sex and gender identities. These performances, Butler argues, are the enforced products of a regulative practice of binary gender constitution centered on and by a "heterosexual contract." But these acts are "internally discontinuous," the identities they produce are not "seamless." (They are Derridian iterations—imperfect repetitions—that make permanence impossible while fostering its illusion.) The "multiplicity and discontinuity of the referent [the self] mocks and rebels against the univocity of the sign [sex/gender]." There are possibilities of "gender transformation" in these spaces of mockery and rebellion, "in the arbitrary relation between such acts, in the possibility of a different sort of repeating."[135] A subversive repetition might performatively produce alternative sex and gender identities that would proliferate and that would, in their proliferation (and strategic deployment), contest and resist the reified binaries that now regulate and seek to constitute the identities of sex and gender exhaustively.

The strategy is to unmask identities that aspire to constation, to deauthorize and redescribe them as performative productions by identifying spaces that escape or resist administration, regulation, and expression. These are spaces of politics, potentially spaces of performative freedom. Here action is possible in the private realm because the social and its mechanisms of normalization consistently fail to achieve the perfect closures Arendt attributes to them too readily, without resistance. This failure of the social to realize its ambitions means that it is possible to subvert the concretized, petrified, reified, and naturalized identities and foundations that paralyze and displace politics and to broaden the realm of the actionable, to resist the sedimentation of performative acts into constative truths and to stand by the conviction that in politics and in identity it is not possible to get it right. This impossibility structures the needs and repressions of Arendt's public *and* private realms. And it provides good reasons to resist the sedimentations of private realm identities as well as the foundationalisms of founding documents.

My radicalization of Arendt's account of political action and my democratization and proliferation of its sites, situations, and effects ought not to be taken as a rejection of the basic insights that ground her distinction between public and private realms. Pitkin sees in that distinction (as Arendt constructs it) a refusal to theorize politics as a practice or venue of the representation of interests and of shared material needs and concerns, and she rightly criticizes Arendt for her failure to accord these important issues the attention they deserve.[136] But Pitkin fails to appreciate the promise in Arendt's vision. There is promise in Arendt's unwillingness to allow political action to be a site of representation of "what" we are, of our reified private realm identities. In Arendt's view, a politics of representation projects a commonality of identity and interests that is imagined, impositional, and ill-fitting; and it obstructs an important alternative: a politics of performativity that instead of reproducing and representing "what" we are generates "who" we are by episodically producing new identities, identities whose "newness" becomes "the beginning of a new story, started—though unwittingly—by acting men [and] to be enacted further, to be *augmented* and spun out by their posterity."[137] The distinction between "who" and "what" we are need not map neatly onto a public-private distinction, however; it may be less binary and more ambiguous than Arendt supposes. But her connection of political action to the performative production of identities rather than to their constative representation opens up possibilities of political proliferation, reclaiming the practice of politics from representative, state-centered, and state-centering institutions and treating that reclamation not as an impertinence but as part of a practice of political authority that calls for the perpetual augmentation and amendment of the constitution and practice of politics.

CHAPTER FIVE

Rawls and the
Remainders of Politics

Embedded in the principles of justice there is an ideal of the person that provides an Archimedean point for judging the basic structure of society.

—John Rawls

He found the Archimedean point, but he used it against himself; it seems that he was permitted to find it only under this condition.

—Franz Kafka

After Arendt's frustrating refusal to include social and economic issues in her account of politics, Rawls's liberal theory of justice might come as something of a relief. His constitutional democracy is sensitive to the predicaments of "permanent minorities," attentive to the temptations and subversive effects of individual and class interests, devoted to narrowing the range of socioeconomic inequalities, supportive of tolerance in the political order, and downright magnanimous to conscientious objectors. What could possibly be wrong with an ideal like this?

Rawls's ideal of institutional justice is meant to provide a critical lever or standard by which to measure the real institutional arrangements of contemporary democratic societies and political cultures. Most do not fare well by this standard. But the ideal is not temporary. In the course of its development in *A Theory of Justice*, Rawls becomes more and more beholden to his ideal, more and more invested in securing the conditions of its approximation, maintenance, and automaticity (but not those of its self-overcoming). At the same time, possibly as a result of this process, the Rawlsian scheme develops certain pathologies of its own, most of which Rawls fails to confront or explains away. My reading of Rawls traces this pattern of increasing investment, the consequent engendering of pathologies, and the denial or dismissal of them as incidental, inessential infelicities that do not affect the viability or rationality of the scheme.

These infelicities, unacknowledged or depoliticized, are the remainders of politics. But Rawlsian citizens are not cognitively and politically empowered to recognize them as such. In Part III of *A Theory of Justice*, Rawls invites us to spend some time in justice as fairness and we meet several interesting characters there: the criminal and the law-abiding public faced with its need to punish him, the indolent laborer and the citizens who willingly soften his economic hardship, the fanciful fellow who counts blades of grass in a park and the rational community that is puzzled by him, the irresponsible rogue who does not reason deliberatively about his good and the responsible life planners who disapprove of him. In the end—a bleak moment on the horizon of Rawls's imagination—the citizens even confront the specter of a horde of criminals rising up against (or within) them, but, Rawls assures them, the rationality of the scheme is nonetheless secure.

Each encounter is a didactic opportunity, a chance for Rawls to teach us how to decide the tragically undecidable dilemmas of politics. But Rawls does not think these dilemmas are undecidable. For each one there is a right answer, without remainder. Each solution is rational and justifiable, unmarked by power, violence, or tragedy. Rawls imagines a political culture whose fundamental conflicts (between liberty and equality) are "settled,"[1] a civic culture that engenders no resistances to itself, a practice of punishment that sparks no remorse, a potentially radical redistributive taxation scheme that provokes no resentments; he offers us a virtue theory of politics untouched by the disruptions of *virtù*, a political economy untroubled by politics. If we have trouble envisioning this ideal, it is because our intuitions are contradictory and in need of rational systematization or because our perspective is skewed, corrupted by the unjust institutions in which we live. From the right vantage point, however, and in the right setting, we can reason to the right resolutions. This is the task Rawls assigns to politics and to political theory: to isolate the right vantage point, to establish the right setting, to facilitate the identification of these right resolutions, to dissolve the remainders of politics rather than engage them.

Rawls believes that a politics without remainders is possible because he assumes that a set of institutions can be so well—and so thinly— conceived and so well-ordered that it fits, without excess, the selves it presupposes and the subjects it engenders. He assumes that his well-ordered institutions will produce well-ordered subjects who are comfortable in (and not also resistant to) their subscription to practices of self-containment and self-concealment, practices reminiscent of those on which Kant relies. Politics, in the guise of juridical administration and enforcement, stabilizes the relation of fittedness that Rawlsian rationality is supposed to guarantee.

But resistances, personified by the unruly characters we encounter in Part III, keep surfacing in this well-ordered regime. Rawls disciplines offenders and reasons with eccentrics. In each case, he confidently reassures (but also warns) us that the responsibility for the dissonance is not institutional but personal, not political but psychological. But Rawls cannot finally depoliticize these characters and the dissonances they personify. Each signals a rift where Rawls seeks closure. Each represents the continual need to reinscribe subjectivity on the self. Each testifies to the lack of fit between the self and the Rawlsian juridical order.

Rawls's strategy of depoliticization does not dissolve the remainders of politics. Instead, they return; they seem to be forever popping up in his text, in his thoughts. Why? Could it be that they are somehow engendered by the demands of the scheme itself? Could it be that instead of being marginal curiosities these figures are actually necessary components of a scheme that is constantly defining itself against some other? Could it be that Rawlsian rationality is not sufficient to itself, that justice as fairness is forced to draw on otherness as a resource to secure itself even as it insists that one of its greatest merits is its refusal to treat others merely as means and not also as ends in themselves?

Reconciliation or Politicization?

Rawls's project has an enduring appeal because it animates and engages a desire for just settlements while tapping into the sense of disempowerment that shapes most of those living in this age of the megastate.[2] It is hard to resist the pull of Rawls's image of a just union of social unions in which all citizens—nurtured by the primary good of self-respect and the material goods that are its precondition—are full members. Indeed, this ideal draws some of its energy from insights that are also central to *virtù* theories of politics. But Rawls betrays those insights in his eagerness to protect the founding and maintenance of justice as fairness from the disruptions of politics.

For example, Rawls notes (with Max Weber) that the modern state exercises "a final and coercive authority over a certain territory" and population. It "affect[s] permanently men's prospects in life."[3] One response to this circumstance might be to politicize the relationship between citizens and the state, to call on citizens—in the name of a radical democratization—to decenter the state as the privileged site of political action by creating, in Nancy Fraser's phrase, "multiple publics" and by recognizing those multiple publics that already exist, even in the face of the state's long-standing denial of them.[4] But this is not a response Rawls considers. In the name of a more democratic politics, he recenters the state that other democratic activists are actively involved in decentering.[5]

Reconciliation, not politicization, is Rawls's goal in *A Theory of Justice*. Aided by the imaginary of the contract illustrated by the original position, Rawls identifies the conditions under which self-respecting citizens might be reconciled to the arbitrariness of state power and to the state's monopoly on the legitimated means of violence. By theorizing a state-centered arrangement that free and equal rational beings could consent to if they were ever given the opportunity to do so, Rawls distracts attention from the fact that the opportunity never actually arises. Satisfied that justice as fairness approximates a voluntary scheme, Rawls wagers that citizens will not *experience* the state as a coercive institution.[6] As a result, Rawlsian citizens are allowed, indeed subtly encouraged, to become relatively passive consumers of the state's goods and services, impervious to the possibility that their survival as a democracy might require them to engage and resist—not simply reconcile themselves to— the state's status as the privileged and legitimate bearer of political power and coercion.[7]

Rawls sees all the advantages of reconciliation—the state distributes the goods, services, and constitutional guarantees that secure justice and stability—but he is inattentive to its drawbacks. He seeks a reconciliation without remainders. But that means that when the scheme does find itself face to face with some of its own remainders (as it does, most dramatically, when it confronts and punishes criminals, the citizens whose experience of the state as a coercive power is perhaps the least subtle or ambiguous), it is surprised, it responds quite violently, and it judges itself to be thoroughly justified in doing so. Disempowered by their reconciliation to the state and its powers, desensitized to the remainders of politics, Rawlsian citizens find it difficult to articulate or politicize this violence. But they are no less subject to it, no less parties to it.

Rawls's closure of political space continues apace as he moves farther to secure the reconciliation he seeks: no set of arrangements should "encourage propensities that it is bound to repress and disappoint." Any regime that fails to elicit "the pattern of special psychologies" that "either supports its arrangements or can be reasonably accommodated by them" is unjust and unstable.[8] Rawlsian justice and stability require that the gaps between institutional promise, individual expectations, and delivery be closed. Rawls means to criticize the hypocritical tendency of regimes to preach one set of principles while practicing another. But the effect of his provision goes beyond that worthy intent.

The propensity of institutions to generate expectations that they then disappoint is a feature of political life, a feature that should be engaged, not suppressed. The generation of expectations is a process that resists the kind of control Rawls seeks. But, more important, the gaps between promise and delivery, between expectation and experience, are spaces of politics in a democratic regime. They are undoubtedly, as Rawls fears, a site of resentment, but they are also a site of idealism, of critical reflection and action. The promulgation of an ideal that closes these spaces has a depoliticizing effect that resonates throughout Rawls's regime and makes it harder, not easier, for Rawlsian citizens to be true to (to rise to the challenge of) the spirit of the democratic scheme Rawls envisions.

Rawls's next founding insight (an insight that *virtù* theories of politics also draw on) is especially endangered by the closure of political space. Committed to pluralism, Rawls's liberal democracy insists that no single comprehensive vision of the good life may dominate the political space.[9] But Rawls sees no *positive* connection between politics and pluralism. He makes no provision for the politicizations necessary to maintain plurality in an age of social homogenization. Rawls imagines a private realm in which different forms of life coexist as lifestyles; there is no contest among them. None feels threatened by the existence of the other. None maintains itself at the cost of the other's existence.[10] But in political life spaces of plurality and difference are often closed by the sedimentation or naturalization of a dominant culture's form of life: its own particular vision of gender identities becomes a standard by which all men and women are measured. Its family structures become a norm of health, safety, and normality. Its attitudes toward work and leisure become moralized. Its approved directions of sexuality are touted as natural, not contingent, and deviations from them are treated accordingly, as curiosities, evils, or illnesses. Without the resources of politicization, those (like Rawls's grass counter) who deviate from these norms find that their rights are protected in Rawls's regime but that they themselves are (at best) disrespected. Rawls does not address this inequity. Unrelated to the basic structure, it is not the subject of justice. But what if it is a *product* of Rawls's effective depoliticization of difference? What if genuine pluralism is a *casualty* of the public-private distinction that Rawlsian justice postulates as the *condition* of pluralism's possibility?

Rawls does not engage these questions, but when he turns his attention to his next founding insight his argument takes on a new, politicizing energy. The practice of desert, Rawls argues, is incoherent, aporetic, unstable. It rewards differences (in talents and abilities) that are "arbitrary from a moral point of view."[11] The bases of desert are not themselves deserved ("all the way down"[12]). Rawls's politicization of the practice, his deessentialization of its foundations, leads the parties in the original position to reject antecedent moral worth as a basis of distribution and to commit themselves to a potentially radical redistributive taxation scheme. This is Rawls's difference principle and it "expresses a conception of reciprocity" in which "men agree to share one another's fate, . . . to avail themselves of the accidents of natural and social circumstance only when doing so is for the common benefit."[13]

The difference principle and the rejection of desert on which it is based have a powerful appeal. But so does the practice of desert. The mesmerizing pull of desert is not finally overcome by Rawls's critique; it returns to haunt justice as fairness when Rawls reaches for antecedent moral worth (or unworthiness) to account for the presence of criminality in a just regime and to justify its punishment. In so doing, he relies on desert to serve its traditional function: it explains the inexplicable, it makes sense of evil and justifies our dealing harshly with it. Problematically, the reappearance of desert also endangers the difference principle; but Rawls, because he does not acknowledge desert's return, makes no provisions for its engagement.[14] Another space of politics is closed precisely at the point at which justice as fairness most needs the resources of politicization.

The Politics of Originating Positions

We might think of *A Theory of Justice* as making two major claims, each distinctly problematic. The first is the claim that the "first task in the theory of justice is to define the initial situation so that the principles that result express the *correct* conception of justice from a philosophical point of view."[15] (*Is* that the first task in theorizing justice?) The second is that Rawls's own construction of the original position, the two principles chosen there, and the kind of union of social unions realized by their adoption give satisfactory expression to the philosophically correct conception of justice. (*Do* they?) I focus first on the formal construction of the original position as the starting point of a theory of justice, and then on the features of the society, justice as fairness, that Rawls hopes or speculates will be produced by the adoption of the two principles he favors.

Rawls's reliance on the original position to provide the founding force for justice as fairness testifies to his preference for reconciliation over politicization.[16] Some readers of Rawls have suggested that the original position has depoliticizing effects (or undesirable political effects). But no one has concentrated on the drift of the position, on its movement within Rawls's text from a contractual situation, to a perspectival position (a speculative beginning?), to a self-ordering mantra.[17] The original position's drift does not mar the theory; it is one of the keys to the theory's success. Indeed, the theory needs—it presupposes—the continued success of all three dimensions of the original position long after the founding of justice as fairness. As contract, the original position renews a sense of shared social purpose; as perspective, it implies an individual commitment to justice and reconciliation; as mantra, it consolidates the self into the stable subject Rawls takes as his starting point.

In its best known capacity, the original position represents a contractual situation in which Rawls's two principles of justice are chosen and agreed to.[18] The process is purely procedural: "there is no independent criterion for the right result; instead there is a correct or fair procedure such that the outcome is likewise correct or fair."[19] The fairness of the procedure is secured by several constraints, most famously by the veil of ignorance, which restricts the parties' knowledge of the details of their empirical identities and situations ("those contingencies which set men at odds and allow them to be guided by their prejudice"[20]). The veil greatly simplifies the process of coming to agreement, but simplicity is only part of the point.[21] It also ensures that the parties' choice is moral, not self-serving. From behind the veil, they are unable to choose principles of justice that will advance their own particular interests or reward their own particular talents.[22] The veil of ignorance allows Rawls "to define the original position so that we get the desired solution," a solution "that nullifies the accidents of natural endowment and the contingencies of social circumstance as counters in the quest for political and economic advantage."[23]

But the veil of ignorance also subverts Rawls's description of the original position as a meeting place, a choice situation, a site of negotiation and agreement. Rawls claims that "the principles of justice are the result of a fair agreement or bargain," but agreements or bargains postulate a plurality and difference that are absent in the original position. Rawls concedes the point when he says that "we can view the choice situation in the original position from the standpoint of one person selected at random. If anyone after due reflection prefers a conception of justice to another, then they all do, and a unanimous agreement can be reached." Since the original position isolates a rational choice, "the differences among the parties are unknown to them," the "deliberations of one person are typical of all," and "each is convinced by the same arguments." Thus, although Rawls suggests that we "imagine that the parties are required to communicate with each other through a referee," he knows that "such a referee is actually superfluous"; the "parties have no basis for bargaining in the usual sense."[24]

Since the parties meet in the original position simply as beings possessed of the capacity to reason, the original position is guaranteed to produce, not a mere agreement, but unanimity. "Once knowledge is excluded, the requirement of unanimity is not out of place and the fact that it can be satisfied is of great importance. It enables us to say of the preferred conception of justice that it represents a genuine reconciliation of interests."[25] The absence of interests from the original position, however, makes it difficult to say in what sense they can be said to have been reconciled. At best, Rawls offers a process that seeks to reconcile the parties to the fact that some of their interests will not be served by justice.

Two moments in the account, thus far, signal the original position's first drift from contract to perspective: the twin requirements of correctness and unanimity. As Michael Sandel points out, "'any agreements reached' in the original position are fair, not because the procedure sanctifies just any outcome, but because the situation guarantees a particular outcome[26]—in Rawls's words, a "correct" outcome. At the same time as the original position moves from a pure procedure to a guarantor of correct outcomes, the parties' plurality slides to unanimity, and the language of agreement and choice gives way to that of acceptance and acknowledgment. "Ideally," Rawls says, the "acknowledgment [of the two principles] is the only choice consistent with the full description of the original position. The argument aims eventually to be strictly deductive."[27]

The ideal, then, is to close the space of politics and interpretation at the moment of founding, to install in the regime a self-identical base, a transparent moment in which the self and Rawls's two principles meet in perfect, mirrored, harmony.[28] Rawls's ideal is to render his fair "choice" situation safe, calculable, and deductive, to shelter it from the risk and the politics of (mis)interpretation just as Austin (sometimes) sought, with the resources of context, to protect performatives from the risk of misfire.

At this point, the dimension of agreement fades from the position and in its place we find a perspectivism, a positioning from which the truths of justice can be more clearly discerned, acknowledged, but not chosen. As agreement slides into acquiescence, silence settles on the parties, a silence Arendt would take to be characteristic of submission to a truth, to reason, or to a necessity dictated by an overdetermined context.[29]

Sandel notes the incompatibility of choice and acknowledgment as well as the disjunction in Rawls' references to agreement and unanimity in an original position that is occupied by a single party. But Sandel resolves these problems, noting that it makes sense to say that the (single party) original position produces an agreement if we think of each party as agreeing "to a proposition" rather than with others "with respect to a proposition." Agreement in this sense "does not require more than a single person." Neither, however, does it "involve an exercise of will." It is an act of cognition. On Sandel's account, the parties in the original position do not choose principles, they "grasp something [that is] already there." Here there is no "decision that *decides* anything except whether I have got it right." Rawls's language of choice is a decoy; acknowledgment is the deep truth of the original position.[30]

The fact that Rawls' allegedly voluntarist original position can be read as a site of cognitive acknowledgment is of major interest to Sandel since, for him, the moment of cognitive acknowledgment is the true moment of politics. But, although Sandel is right to note the drift of Rawls's language from choice to cognition, he moves too quickly to supplant choice and identify cognitive acknowledgment as the real "truth" of Rawls's original position. Perhaps the real truth of the position is not choice *or* acknowledgment but the position's drift from one to the other. Perhaps the truth of the original position is its structural undecidability, its reliance on the overlapping and incompatible languages of (performative) choice and (constative) acknowledgment, of power and knowledge, or, in more Rawlsian terms, of contract and perspective. On this reading, the second dimension of the original position supplements the first; it does not replace or supplant it.[31]

The original position's second, perspectival dimension reassures the parties in the face of the disruptive, performative power of the first. Rawls's wariness of politics means that the founding of justice as fairness has to be quickly converted into an act of maintenance, the choice of principles domesticated into an acknowledgment of them, the radicality of desert's politicization stabilized by the reassurance of the familiar.[32] From the start, the parties are told that the point of the Rawlsian procedure is not to create new and startling possibilities or to subvert established modes of thinking but "to clarify and order our thoughts," to "fix" ideas we already have about what is fair and just. "There are questions which we feel sure must be answered in a certain way." The original position is a "natural guide to [this] intuition."³³ It operates as a much needed heuristic device designed to isolate morally relevant considerations, to simplify, clarify, order (and also consolidate) what Rawls takes to be a stable body of moral and prudential beliefs.

Rawlsian justice needs clarity, fixity, and stability to function smoothly, and so it seeks out the predictability of administration, protecting it from the disruptions of politics whenever possible; hence the insistence that the choice of the principles in the original position is final.³⁴ Finality, one of the constraints of the fair choice situation, is meant to prevent the parties from choosing provisional principles of justice for now with the intention of revising them at some later date. Thus, once the practice of desert has been rejected, it must not resurface. Once out of the original position, the principles of justice are settled. They frame the process of constitutional construction,³⁵ and the resulting constitutional principles, together with the two principles of justice, regulate the legislative process. Nothing settled in the first three stages of the founding is contestable in the last stage, which is purely administrative, occupied solely with the "application of rules to particular cases by judges and administrators, and the following of rules by citizens generally."³⁶

The progressive closure of contest in this regime does not mean that the citizens may never again enter the original position.³⁷ On the contrary, they may do so at any time. But their reentry is part of a continuing process of *depoliticization;* its function is not to open up alternative possibilities or to investigate any unexpected effects of their initial agreement but to consolidate existing practices.³⁸ The effect is to displace political action with introspection. If the original position is rightly conceived, each repetition of its operation will produce the selfsame outcome.³⁹ As Rawls puts it, if the original position is to "be interpreted so that one can at any time adopt its perspective, [i]t must make no difference when one takes up this viewpoint, or who does so." No matter who enters the original position, no matter when, "*the same principles are always chosen.*" Thus, the possibility of its perfect repetition is a condition of the original position's success as a perspective.⁴⁰ But Rawls's celebration of the position's repeatability exceeds its perspectival needs and suggests that the position has drifted again, this time from critical, distancing, filtering perspective to a mantra-like ritual that orders the self into the form of rational subjectivity the original position (in its other two dimensions) actually presupposes.

If the result is always the same, why repeat the experiment? One possible answer postulates both the original position's contractual and perspectival dimensions. Over the life of a regime or a person, new dilemmas arise, new data emerge, new institutions come into being, and a renewed commitment to confront them together is called for or a fresh perspective on them is needed. But this answer works only if we ignore the claim that the role of the veil of ignorance is to ensure "not only that the information available is relevant, but that it is *at all times the same.*"[41] The perfect and unchanging repeatability of the position indicates that its operation is prized for something other than its outcome. If the operation is repeated perpetually, perhaps that is because the Rawlsian subject is never a fait accompli. Perhaps it signals the regime's perpetual need to reinscribe unruly subjects into the order. Perhaps Rawls counts on the original position to issue not only in an intersubjective agreement among selves but also (repeatedly) in an intrasubjective ordering of the self according to the dictates of Rawlsian rationality and justice.

The reliance on the original position to produce the self it presupposes means that the position is never really original; it is always already being repeated, and this is a condition of its capacity to *originate* Rawls's virtue model of politics. But, more important, the myth of originality surrounding the position has effects that resonate throughout the political life of the regime: the reliance on the original position establishes a hierarchical divide between an original, pure, prepolitical, noncontingent, introspective position and all other subject positions and positionings that constitute and condition human lives and possibilities. (The *point* of the original position is to "correct for" the latter.) The original position is *the* position, not *a* position, and the result of its enthronement as a single, sovereign perspective is a paradoxical combination of an enormous politicizing and subversive potential (illustrated by Rawls's deessentialization of desert) with a practice of repetition that betrays that potential and serves the regime's needs of maintenance and consolidation with powerfully depoliticizing effects.[42]

One effect of the original position's sovereignty over other positionings is Kantian: from the perspective of a speculative beginning, politics is seen as a sign of failure, a Fall; it is unoriginal. Structured by an ideal that displaces politics with administration, justice as fairness's first and pervasive impulse is to depoliticize, medicalize, punish, disavow, or suppress—to administer—the remainders that signal the ideal's impossibility. When Rawlsian citizens experience dissonance (in themselves or in others), the default is to return to the original position and confirm that, from its perspective, the outlaw impulse, desire, or activity in question is indeed irrational or unjust. In effect, the original position's myth of origins encourages citizens to respond to dissonance with introspection, a practice that supports the regime's broader efforts to privatize, naturalize, or dissolve dissonant remainders rather than politicize them. The point is powerfully illustrated by Rawls's account of punishment and criminality.

The Practice of Punishment

In *The Genealogy of Morals*, Nietzsche envisions a society so powerful that it does not need to punish: "A society might attain such a *consciousness of power* that it could allow itself the noblest luxury possible to it—letting those who harm it go *unpunished*. 'What are my parasites to me?' it might say. 'May they live and prosper: I am strong enough for that!' " Nietzsche's imagined society does without punishment not because its laws are "right" or because its citizens become increasingly obedient but because it overcomes justice (the insistence on right) with mercy, a kind of magnanimity that is "beyond the law."[43] The scenario is not merely naive. That it initially strikes the reader that way is one of the most telling points of the reflection. The image of a society so powerful that it does not *need* to punish is meant not to make us yearn unrealistically for the realization of the ideal, but to invite us to reflect critically on why and how societies punish, to think about punishment (its gravity, its sites, and its frequency) as a measure of societal need rather than individual deviance, as a signal of social weakness rather than administrative resolve.

In *A Theory of Justice*, Rawls also envisions a society that does not need to punish.[44] But if Rawls' ideal society does without punishment, that is not because it is powerful enough to afford magnanimity but because its institutionalization of justice makes magnanimity unnecessary: criminality does not surface in a well-ordered regime. Rawls wagers that citizens governed by relatively just institutions will acquire a "corresponding sense of justice."[45] Well-ordered institutions engender well-ordered selves, and this secures the regime's stability.[46] Gradually, the citizens' felt need to reenter the original position disappears. The disruptions of dissonance and resistance, both inter- and intrasubjective, diminish.

Hence Rawls's wager that his scheme will pass the formal tests of stability and congruence. The "strains of commitment" will not be too burdensome in justice as fairness, and the institutional order will be congruent with the members' conceptions of the good.[47] But the wager is premised on the assumption that the institutions of justice as fairness fit and express the (core) self without remainder. As Rawls puts it, the original position, by bracketing the contingent attributes and worldly features that set people at odds, and the difference principle, by refusing to distribute scarce resources as moral rewards for contingently distributed natural talents, give "expression [to] our nature as free and equal rational beings."[48] *This* expressivism is what underlies Rawls's belief that justice as fairness does not ask too much of its subjects.

But Rawls's expressivist ground is insecure. His identification of a human (moral) nature with a free and equal rationality soon gives way to the admission that some beings are free and equally rational but others are oddly irrational, even immoral, even when raised in a just regime. His identification of the core of the self with freedom and reason is soon tempered by the admission that there are some selves whose core constitution is anything but rational. Rawls tries to turn these figures to his advantage by making an example of them. He stabilizes his expressivist assumptions by contrasting his free and equal rational beings with a now spectral other, the "bad character."[49] Unfortunately, his expressivism leaves him unprepared for the character on whom he relies. From Rawls's perspective, the bad character is so bewilderingly deviant that Rawls is forced back into a discourse he disavowed: the discourse of antecedent moral worth.

The purpose of the criminal law, according to Rawls,

> is to uphold basic natural duties, those which forbid us to injure other persons in their life and limb, or to deprive them of their liberty and property, and punishments are to serve this end. They are not simply a scheme of taxes and burdens designed to put a price on certain forms of conduct and in this way to guide men's conduct for mutual advantage. It would be far better if the acts proscribed by penal statutes were never done. Thus a propensity to commit such acts is *a mark of bad character*, and in a just society legal punishments will only fall upon those who display these faults.[50]

Rawls permits punishment, as a practice, to work as an incentive scheme, but he insists that individual punishments must be justified deontologically, not consequentially. The consequentialist justification of individual punishments leads too easily to a willingness to punish the innocent in order "to promote effectively the interest of society."[51] That would undermine the priority of right as well as punishment's incentive structure, which depends on the public belief that only the guilty are punished.

Justice as fairness boasts that it punishes persons only for acts they commit, but it is actually the brand of character from which these actions emanate that it outlaws. Actions are *guided* by punishment's incentives, but characters are *criminalized* by punishment's retribution. In Rawls's regime character is a thoroughly juridical concern, even if it is not actually punished in the absence of actions that speak it.

And yet, this concern with character seems to be very much at odds with Rawls's other commitments regarding the self, particularly with his rejection of antecedent moral worth as a basis of distributive justice and, related, with his treatment of the self as the bearer of attributes and talents that belong to it only contingently. Rawls does not say that the person with a bad character *deserves* his punishment, but he is markedly less charitable toward this person than he is toward other citizens of justice as fairness. The citizen who is incapable of holding a job because he is indolent is not, on Rawls's account, responsible for his situation. The fact that he has this attribute and not others is "arbitrary from a moral point of view." This is why Rawlsian citizens agree to "share" his "fate" and treat the distribution of talents and abilities as "common assets." They do not, however, take the same view of the criminal possessed of bad character. They do not offer to share the burden of the criminal's fate. They do not view *his* moral failings as a common liability. The account would be more consistent if punishment was allowed to work simply as an incentive scheme; but it is not, for two reasons.[52]

First, one of the most important features of Rawlsian justice is that it approximates a voluntary scheme and, therefore, need not (indeed must not) rely (at least not overtly) on coercion as an incentive for subscription. Second, there is a big difference between the fact that some people command higher wages and social rewards than others and the fact that some people heed their sense of justice while others do not. The difference between the indolent laborer and the criminal, on Rawls's account, is that the former is moved by certain attributes that are only contingently his whereas the criminal is unmoved by his sense of justice even though that sense is deeply and rationally his, whether he affirms it or not. Indeed, by failing to affirm his sense of justice, by committing himself to a conception of the good that is incongruent with principles of right, the criminal denies his own moral personality.

This part of Rawls's argument is "connected with the Kantian interpretation" according to which "the desire to act justly and the desire to express our nature as free moral persons turn out to specify what is practically speaking the same desire." The desire is satisfied when we affirm the sense of justice. By affirming the sense of justice, we "realize our nature." By denying it, we do not: "What we cannot do is express our nature by following a plan that views the sense of justice as but one desire to be weighed against others. For this sentiment reveals what the person is." Contingent talents and attributes do not reveal what the person is. They tell us nothing about whether a person is of good or bad character. Only the sense of justice reveals that.[53]

To some, however, the sense of justice is not so self-revealing. Rawls appeals to these people explicitly, giving them three reasons for compliance, but presumably these people are unmoved by his appeals: the desire to act justly and the desire to express their nature as free moral persons are not overriding desires to them. They do not care about the psychological costs of deception or about the loss of spontaneity and naturalness that, Rawls warns, are bound to result from the need to disguise their free riding in a system whose conception of justice is public. Perhaps there are compensating pleasures to be had in beating the system, even when the system is just. Or perhaps they prefer the disguise that enables their free riding to the one they would have to assume in order to fit themselves into the community of justice as fairness. Thus, they apparently are unmoved by Rawls's final appeal as well, the promise of sharing in the good of belonging to this cooperative scheme. Rawls may be correct when he says that, "to appreciate something as ours, we must have a certain allegiance to it." Yet these people might respond that, "to have a certain allegiance to something, we must first appreciate it as ours." The device of the original position is supposed to solve this problem of chronology and identification, but Rawls admits that some people will just fail to identify with the regime. For people such as these, there is nothing internal—no sense of loyalty, no identification, not even rational self-interest—to prevent or discourage them from devoting themselves to conceptions of the good that are not congruent with the principles of justice. For people such as these, the three reasons for compliance simply do not persuade; perhaps these are people that will not be reasoned with.[54]

This limitation on reason and reasoning is what forces Rawls to confront the problem of punishment. But it is not to those who are to be punished that he addresses himself. He justifies punishment to those who mete it out, to those who adhere to and identify with the scheme, to those whose rationality is modeled by the original position. The only concern here is whether citizens can punish others and exact retribution without dirtying their hands, without being haunted by remainders. *Is* it just for those "who do affirm their sense of justice" to require others who do not "to comply with just institutions?"[55]

Rawls answers yes, without remainder; it is just to enforce compliance in justice as fairness. Since the question is posed behind the veil of ignorance, punishment is justified without explicit recourse to responsibility or desert; Rawls relies solely on rationality. The parties, having agreed to the principles see that "it is rational to authorize the measures needed to maintain just institutions." As for those who find, after the veil of ignorance is lifted, that "being disposed to act justly is not a good for them," well, they "cannot deny these contentions." Rawls concedes that it "is, of course, true that in their case just arrangements do not fully answer to their nature, and therefore, other things equal, they will be less happy than they would be if they could affirm their sense of justice. But here one can only say: *their nature is their misfortune.*"[56]

Confronted by those unfortunate enough to experience a rift between themselves and the regime, Rawls comes as close as he ever does to admitting that justice as fairness is built on an ineliminable moment of arbitrariness: some will feel at home, completed and realized by the constructions of justice as fairness, and others will not. To those who do not, to those who fail to affirm their sense of justice, their nature is their misfortune is all that Rawls can say. When, however, the problem is not the inability of a citizen to affirm his sense of justice but that citizen's inability to command a high income in the marketplace, Rawls instructs us to say something very different: his nature is *our* misfortune. If this is not an inconsistency it is only because, on Rawls's account, talents and attributes are randomly and inequitably distributed among persons, whereas the sense of justice is assumed to be equally available to everyone. The problem is that some cannot *affirm* their sense of justice.

We might think that the distribution of this inability to affirm is, like the distribution of talents and attributes, arbitrary from a moral point of view, but again there is a difference. Justice as fairness is not required to respond to the first arbitrariness because it *does* respond, rationally, to the second by ordering its institutions in accordance with the two principles of justice. In so doing, it has done all that can reasonably be expected of it. It has set up a just basic structure according to principles that those not disposed to act justly would themselves affirm from the standpoint of the original position.[57] It has eliminated thereby all the environmental factors, all the injustices both arbitrary and systemic, that in other regimes motivate persons to criminal behavior.

Does this not account for Rawls's insistence that the object of punishment in justice as fairness is bad character? In justice as fairness, what else could it be? There is no perpetual underclass here; homelessness is not a systemic problem. There is genuine equality of opportunity, as well as a public commitment to the equal consideration of others and reciprocity in the course of economic advance and development. In the absence of systemic injustice, there is nothing that can account for criminal behavior; criminality must be a symptom of sheer perversity, orneriness, a tic of some kind, a defective character. Criminality, in short, must be an assault on the system from some outside, from some mysterious and terrifying state of nature: it must be sociopathic.[58]

The key to Rawls's account of punishment, and one probable reason for its brevity, is that the system is simply not responsible for the production of criminality.[59] Criminality is extrasystemic. What this means, however, is that the notion of antecedent moral worth (or, in this case, unworthiness) whose viability Rawls denied in his account of distributive justice is now assumed in order to account for and justify institutions of punishment and their regulation of compliance.[60] By contrast with distributive justice, which responds only to institutionally generated demands and expectations, retributive justice is there precisely to respond to extrainstitutionally generated demands, expectations, and resistances.[61] By blaming the latter on bad character, justice as fairness effectively assumes responsibility only for the production of good characters, of those fortunate enough to find themselves well fitted to the constructions of justice as fairness. Like many parents in denial, justice as fairness will confess only to having raised its good children. It is mystified by the others. Who can tell where they came from? ("They must have made a mistake at the hospital.") Rawls is driven to this chimera because of his own insistence that justice as fairness not "encourage propensities that it is bound to disappoint."[62] If justice as fairness is to pass this test, it must deny responsibility for the criminal propensities present in the regime because those propensities are the very ones this regime is out to disappoint.

The same logic governs Rawls's discussion of envy, an "inexcusable" and irrational attitude in a regime so rationally ordered. Once again, the primary concern is to delineate the responsibility for the disruption. Does it emanate from the self or from the regime and its institutions? Is it a feature of political life or is it a private or natural (dys)function? Does the range of permissible inequalities and the terms of their permissibility give rise to this potentially destabilizing passion or is it generated, inexplicably, from an outside source? Rawls argues that envy is excusable and *therefore* politically significant only when it is the product of injustice; only then is it "not irrational" because only then is it occasioned by "circumstances where it would be unreasonable to expect someone to feel differently."[63]

As a just society, justice as fairness "eliminates the conditions that give rise to disruptive attitudes" like envy by treating self-respect as a primary good, by limiting the range of inequalities, and by requiring that inequalities be justified to the least well off. In this well-ordered society, then, the rational individual "is not subject to envy," and that means that when envy does surface in Rawls's regime it is as a disruptive attitude, irrational, inexcusable, inexplicable, and, most important, extrasystemic.[64]

Rawls wagers that, as the rational capacities of subjects in justice as fairness are heightened by living in a well-ordered regime, injustice and envy will diminish and maybe even disappear. He assumes that "men's propensity to injustice is not a permanent aspect of community life; it is greater or less depending in large part on social institutions, and in particular on whether these are just or unjust." And so he concludes that "a well-ordered society tends to eliminate or at least to control men's inclinations to injustice."[65] The claim that certain levels of inequality or other forms of injustice are bound to give rise to greater and more virulent forms of envy and other disruptive feelings is plausible. Less plausible are the rest of the assumptions in the Rawlsian package: that a set of institutions can assert such strict intentionalist control over the expectations to which it gives rise; that institutions and aspirations can be ordered in a way that fits and expresses the self without remainder; that resistances will not be aggravated but rather alleviated by the demands and aspirations of a rational regime; and, therefore, that subjects in this regime do not need the resources of politicization because the conditions for successful reconciliation can and have been met. These are the assumptions that lead Rawls to treat sources of disorder, forces of unsettlement (and politicization?), as *outside agitators.* Envy and criminality disrupt a system that claims not to engender them, a system that insists that the outside agitators need only be removed—punished, banished, or suppressed—and order will be restored.

One result of this approach is Rawls's refusal to recognize the phenomenon of criminality as a valid test of the arrangements he advocates. The fact that some (or even many) persons exist for whom the right and the good are not congruent does not have the standing to call into question the justice of justice as fairness.[66]

> It can even happen that there are many who do not find a sense of justice fits their *good;* but if so, the forces making for stability are weaker. Under such conditions *penal devices will play a much larger role* in the social system. The greater the lack of congruence, the greater the likelihood, other things equal, of instability with its attendant evils. *Yet none of this nullifies the collective rationality of the principles of justice;* it is still to the advantage of each that everyone else should honor them.[67]

Here the argument shifts as the tests of stability and congruence give way to rationality, but this is a rationality that need not move anyone. Even if many people find themselves ill fitted to the scheme, it would still be the case that it is to the advantage of each that everyone else should honor it. Even if the propensity to injustice and the will to envy are never diminished and are perhaps even aggravated, even if punishment plays a heavy-handed role in maintaining stability, the rationality of the scheme is not in question. What *would* have the power to nullify the collective rationality of the scheme? How frequent and how grave would punishments have to be before the rationality of the scheme would be problematized, or even affected, by phenomenal outcomes? Rawls says that it would have to be frequent and violent enough to make the scheme practically untenable. But that could just as well mean that as long as punishment works, as long as it keeps the lid on those whose nature is their misfortune or succeeds in putting them away, then *their* nature will not become *our* misfortune.[68]

This is not the scenario Rawls envisions. His confidence in his expressivist wager is so great that he speculates that "in a well-ordered society sanctions are not severe and may never need to be imposed."[69] His confidence is Kantian. Kant, too, thought that "*the more closely the legislation and government were made to harmonize with this idea* [that a constitution ought to allow 'the greatest possible human freedom in accordance with laws which ensure that the freedom of each can coexist with the freedom of all the others'], *the rarer punishments would become,* and it is thus quite rational to maintain (as Plato does) that none would be necessary at all in a perfect state."[70] In the Rawlsian (and Kantian) ideal, the state punishes rarely not because it is magnanimous or powerful (in Nietzsche's senses) but because its citizens are law abiding; its subjects are, for the most part, well ordered. But the ideal has an ambiguous effect on punishment. Because Rawlsian punishment is so thoroughly justified by the bad character, because it is so well deserved, those who punish are not sullied, not even touched, by their actions. By justifying punishment so well, Rawls removes or relaxes all doubts and reservations, all ambivalences, all remnants of power and arbitrariness. He makes life neat and easy after the founding . . . for those whose nature is their good fortune. He does not explain, however, why we should idealize a practice of punishment in which the citizens who punish have no hesitations about the use of power, no ambivalence about inflicting punishment, no remorse about depriving others of their liberty or exacting time from a human life.

Rawls seeks closure for punishment, but it is elusive. His return to antecedent moral worth to justify punishment and define criminality is ill at ease with his admission that some (and possibly many) citizens are simply unlucky to be ill fitted to the regime's needs. Rawls knows that they do not deserve their ill fittedness; it is their contingent misfortune. And yet it is at precisely this moment that desert reappears in the account. Why? Is it because this is the moment at which Rawls is most anxious to disavow any relation between his well ordered subjects and the other? Were it not for this disavowal, there might be room to consider the possibility that the expressivist wager actually plays a role in the production of *bad* characters, as well as good ones. There might be room to think about the bad character as a remainder of Rawls's politics. Is this the possibility that Rawls is anxious to rule out: that he himself turns the unfortunate misfit into the bad character who deserves what he gets in order to protect and stabilize the just order that the Rawlsian wager has enabled up to this point?[71] Or is the role of the expressivist wager in the production of the deserving criminal more subtle than that? Does the citizens' public faith in the success of the wager simply leave them so unprepared for the appearance of misfits and criminals that they react (as does Rawls himself) with a shock, surprise, and condemnation that serve both to justify the suppression of the other and to consolidate the citizens themselves into a "we," a we that can punish without remorse or remainder?[72]

If the demonization of the other into an antecedently bad character is one of the effects of the institutionalization of Rawls's wager, that is a powerful reason to reject the project. From a *virtù* perspective, the task of a theory of justice is not to justify punishment so well that it is moved beyond the reach of politicization but to insist that, although justification is always a part of the practice of punishment, it is never seamless, never complete.[73] The problem with Rawlsian punishment is its aspiration to univocality. Rawls imagines a practice in which there is no moral anguish, no unruly excess, no joy in another's suffering, no troublesome doubts, only a sense of justice. But justifications of punishment are not so well ordered. They always draw on a range of conflicting assumptions and beliefs (vengeance, rehabilitation, self-preservation, or, as in Rawls's own case, desert and the need for stability), and this marks punishment as a tragic situation, in Bernard Williams's sense: it is never simply the right thing to do.[74] It is not something that we ever get right. Punishment draws on a palimpsest of justifications because no single set of assumptions or beliefs is capable of putting our doubts to rest. And this is appropriate. Because of its pervasive, violent effects on human and political life, punishment is one of the most important sites of politicization in any set of arrangements. Its rifts should not be sealed. These are spaces of politics, power, and resistance, and they should be preserved, even aggravated, for the sake of the remainders of politics.

Rawls's ideal, however, is to leave no space for these sorts of questions, alternatives, and remainders to come up. By treating punishment as an expression of right, not power, he seeks to reconcile citizens to a practice that might otherwise disturb them. The reconciliation empowers citizens to maintain and protect their sets of arrangements. But it disempowers those (bad characters as well as others) who might seek to politicize the practice of punishment. Moreover, Rawls's apparently thoroughgoing rejection of desert as a principle of distribution leaves the citizens unprepared to engage it on its return as the ground of retributive justice. These depoliticizng effects are problematic because they are justified, after all, by a wager. If the wager turns out to be wrong, if the regime fails to take, if some or even many citizens find that their nature is their misfortune, the result is not more politicization and resistance, by Rawls's own admission, it is more punishment. The frequency of punishment in itself signals nothing more than the fortuitous presence in the regime of a large number of bad characters. It does not testify to any failure of the regime or its aspirations. And the citizens, dispossessed of the cognitive and political resources to analyze, trace, or engage this sequence of events, are disempowered to resist or politicize them within the frame of justice as fairness.

Drawing on the *virtù* perspective, I read Rawls through the lens of a counterwager generated by the Nietzschean claim that the self, an original multiplicity, has no univocal core and is therefore not only enabled by its construction into a subject but always resistant to it as well. Up to this point, I have granted Rawls his assumption that the space of punishment is intersubjective, but the *virtù* counterwager invites further reflection on this front: is there not an *intrasubjective* dimension to punishment too?[75] The spectral power of the bad character is diminished somewhat and the force of the *virtù* counterwager enhanced if we think of the criminal and the bad character (much as the overman of Nietzsche's imagining) as personifications of those aspects of the self that are resistant to the formation of responsible subjectivity. From this perspective, resistance is located not only in distinct individuated subjects possessed of (or by) bad character; it is experienced (to a greater or lesser extent) by all subjects and so the criminality Rawls punishes retributively is, contra Rawls, an integral part of the subject. Likewise, the inexcusable envy that rises up unaccountably in some, on Rawls's account, might be taken to represent a range of disruptive attitudes and impulses that are rationalized into silence by the would-be well-ordered subjects of this well-ordered regime.[76]

If dissonance and resistance mark all subjects to some extent, then the parties deliberating in the original position are underinformed on some important points. They know that they may turn out to be black or white, middle or lower class, highly talented or unremarkable. But they are not told that they may turn out to be one of those unlucky louts whose nature is his misfortune, a bad character who is committed to a conception of the good that is incongruent with the principles of right and unable to affirm his sense of justice. They do not consider the principles of justice from the perspective of the outlaw even though each of them is likely to experience outlaw impulses and even though some of them are likely to find that they are themselves outlaws in this regime. They do not know that there is an ineliminable element of arbitrariness at the very foundation of this regime and that its effects and reverberations will be felt by most of them daily. The parties assume that they will be well and easily fitted to the Rawlsian order and that expectation will often be disappointed. Moreover, if and when that expectation is disappointed, the citizens are discouraged from politicizing their disappointment. The potentially political space, the space between expectations and experience, is closed in justice as fairness, disappointment is privatized, and introspection—not political action or organization—is counseled.

The *virtù* theorist counters Rawls's wager with a wager of her own: she speculates that a set of arrangements that chastens its aspirations to closure is less likely than justice as fairness to convert resistances into criminality, otherness into bad character. The renunciation of closure invites the articulation of resistances instead of branding them as antecedent irrationalities for which the system is not responsible and to which it need not respond responsibly. By relaxing the demand that subjects "fit" identities—by renouncing expressivism—it diminishes the propensity to self-loathing, vengeance, and violence fostered by regimes that profess themselves free of any part in subjectivity failures. The counterwager does not insist on its own truth in opposition to Rawls's; it calls attention to the effect of the Rawlsian wager in the day-to-day life of the scheme. The question, then, is not which wager is right but what effect each has on the society that is founded on its ground. Which one is more sensitive to the remainders of politics? Which one produces remainders less insistently? Likewise, the question raised by the need to punish is not whether punishment can be justified but what effect its being justified has on the way that punishment is practiced in Rawls's regime.[77]

The *virtù* counterwager is just a wager, too, but if it fails, the result will be more politics than one might anticipate, not more punishment. Or, better, since any increase in punishments is assumed to be politically significant, the increased frequency of punishment is, contra Rawls, taken as a signal that something political is amiss and increases in punishment are, therefore, resisted, not depoliticized; they are seen as a reflection of a societal need that bears examination, not as an independent measure of the number of bad characters resident in the regime.[78] Moreover, those engaged in this political contest of resistance will be empowered in part by the unruliness of punishment's justifications.[79] Thus, if a *virtù* theory can do better than Rawls's it is not because it escapes the problems Rawls faces but because it recognizes the impossibility of such an escape and engages that impossibility politically, institutionally, and discursively.

A regime that is more rather than less politicized is surely not everyone's ideal.[80] Pace Arendt, the more political or politicized life is not necessarily the more rewarding or self-realizing. But what if, in our anxiety to displace politics, we find that the depoliticization of arrangements and institutions that are stabilized (at least partly) by power tends (as it does in Rawls) to produce more punishment? The choice may be between the uncertainty and contingency that more politics brings and the cultural as well as personal confidence and self-assurance that are all too often maintained by punishing or otherwise suppressing the external and internal other. Given that choice, there are good liberal as well as radically democratic reasons to prefer the former.

Irresponsible Rogues and Idiosyncratic Misfits

The bad character is just the most obvious of several silenced others in Rawls's regime, and punishment the most graphic of several depoliticized, silencing practices.[81] In Part III of *A Theory of Justice*, as Rawls defends the viability and stability of the scheme while imagining the enrichments its full realization might bring, other moments of dissonance arise and other more subtle strategies of consolidation are brought to bear on them. Rawls asks whether citizens will find that justice as fairness is a good place to live, and he concludes that it is indeed a fulfilling arrangement for those whose nature is their good fortune. As for others who break no law but whose experience of the regime is more dissonant and less satisfying, Rawls finds that they have no ground for complaint: they may not be in a position to share in the best goods the regime has to offer, but their rights are respected and they themselves are tolerated.

Like Kant, for whom the juridical establishment of a veneer of morality contributes to the development of morality in the species, Rawls believes that the construction of a veneer of rationality tends to enhance individual rationality.[82] But what is it like to live among these citizens, with their greatly heightened rational capacities, with their confidence in their own ways of life and in the regime that makes it all possible? What is it like to be a citizen who violates no right but deviates only from the best the good has to offer? What is it like to be an underachiever in this society? What is it like to be odd—not evil, not intolerant, not criminal—just odd, the least well off, not economically, but socially? Are Rawlsian citizens people with whom one could be happy living if one was not quite like them, if one was not quite as taken by the force of the right as they are, or if one was not quite so reasonable?

At their best, Rawlsian citizens live responsible and well-planned lives. "Responsible to [them]selves as one person over time," each develops a rational plan of life that has "a certain unity, a dominant theme." The subject who does not treat himself as an "enduring individual" but "rejects equally the claims of his future self and the interests of others is not only irresponsible with respect to them but in regard to his own person as well." The principle of responsibility, Rawls explains, resembles a principle of right: "The claims of the self at different times are to be so adjusted that the self at each time can affirm the plan that has been and is being followed. The person at one time, so to speak, must not be able to complain about actions of the person at another time."[83] For responsible Rawlsian subjects, a life plan that can be affirmed is one that steers them clear of risk, remorse, and disappointment. By contrast with Nietz-sche's vision of responsibility as part of a process of self-overcoming in which an affirmation of the present moment in eternal recurrence tests for lingering moments of ressentiment, Rawlsian responsibility is part of a process of self-unification that seeks not to overcome but to avoid ressentiment and remorse, to sidestep or suppress rather than confront or engage the tragic elements of the human condition.[84]

Deliberative rationality supports the practice of responsibility Rawls describes. Ostensibly a voluntary activity, rational deliberation is a mat-ter not of right but of the good, a private matter. Subjects are more likely to be happy if they do deliberate but they are not required to do so, merely encouraged.[85] Deliberative rationality operates as a kind of ra-tional stoicism, instructing subjects to "adjust their conceptions of the good to their situation," to have a "coherent set of preferences between the options open to [them]."[86] They do not resent the fact that more options are not available to them. The subject "does what seems best at the time and if his beliefs later prove to be mistaken with untoward results, it is through no fault of his own."[87] Remorse, in this situation, is as irrational as envy was earlier.[88] Indeed, this is one of the great merits of rational deliberation: it ensures the subject against remorse, regret, or resentment, or at least against the rational variants of these emotions.

This insurance is supposed to empower subjects, in part by freeing them from a sense of blame for contingent misfortune. But their em-powerment derives from an initial *disempowerment*, from the subject's rational limitation of herself, of her imagination and aspirations to a realistic plan of life.[89] Moreover, a case can surely be made for the claim that those who are rationally ensured against contingent misfortune are that much more, not less, vulnerable to it when it does strike.[90] As Nietzsche and Machiavelli point out, the self that turns itself into a castle or fortress succeeds only in creating a dangerous illusion of strength. Pitted against castles and fortresses, *fortuna* almost always has the advan-tage. Real power inheres in mobility and adaptability to worldly con-tingency, in a willingness to meet it on its own terms.

In a similar vein, the "fortressing" of the subject, its construction into a rational, risk-averse, remorse-avoiding creature, renders it less, not more, capable of democratic citizenship. The level of control on which these rational subjects will insist is ill at ease with the vicissitudes of democratic politics and action. These subjects are less likely to join together as democratic citizens than they are to be joined together as a population to be managed by the state. For example, it is hard to imagine those among this society's least advantaged *demanding* the justification due them whenever inequalities are increased. Will those justifications simply flow out of the top economic ranks and trickle down? What is their force as justification if they are merely supplied by those in power and not demanded by those who must be satisfied by them?[91] Surely it will not be difficult to satisfy these people who learn daily to expect no more than they are likely to get?[92] It seems that, just as the original position reconciles subjects to state power and violence, deliberative rationality (still backed by the perpetual return to the original position) reconciles subjects to their socioeconomic conditions and, in so doing, undercuts the potential for politicization that democratic citizenship presupposes.

In *The Gay Science*, Nietzsche captures the impossibility of reconciliation without self-overcoming in a single brief phrase: "By doing we forgo."[93] Rawls, by contrast, envisions a doing without any tragic forgoing. He idealizes a relatively remainderless existence in which subjects experience their misfortunes without blame, the empowerment of reconciliation without its attendant disempowerments, the thrill of an enhanced control over their lives without the loss of a sense of abandon in living. Is it irrational for the Rawlsian subject to resent planning her life as a career? Is nothing forgone in this unification of a life? What about promiscuity, spontaneity, experimentation, the will to live in the present?

The promiscuous or spontaneous subject is not as supported by the regime as are Rawls's rational deliberators. Deliberative rationality is a voluntary activity but one held in high—and public—esteem. Although rational deliberation is an option, not a requirement, there is nonetheless some moral pressure to conform with its requirements, pressure from Rawls in *A Theory of Justice* and pressure from one's fellow citizens in the context of justice as fairness. Rawls does not discuss the nondeliberating character in any detail, except to say that she is free to abstain from deliberation, but he does have something to say about the subject who does not deliberate well. The poor deliberator probably suffers from "various shortcomings of knowledge, thought, and judgment," all of which Rawls characterizes as defects. The knowledge that guides subjects, Rawls argues, "is necessarily incomplete, their powers of reasoning, memory, and attention are always limited and their judgment is likely to be distorted by anxiety, bias and a preoccupation with their own affairs." According to Rawls, "some of these *defects* spring from moral faults, from selfishness and negligence." Amid all this talk of defects and moral failure, what happens to the sense of blamelessness that is supposed to follow from a rational deliberation that consists merely in doing one's best?[94] Amid all this talk of moral failure, deliberative rationality as a simply *voluntary* activity begins to recede. Perhaps justice as fairness cannot allow deliberative rationality to be so strictly voluntary because it performs a function too necessary to the scheme: it produces and maintains the stable subject of Rawlsian distributions and justification.

Rawls provides a more complete portrait of the nondeliberating subject's lot when he introduces a "fanciful case"—"someone whose only pleasure is to count blades of grass in various geometrically shaped areas such as park squares and well-trimmed lawns. He is otherwise intelligent and actually possesses unusual skills, since he manages to survive by solving difficult mathematical problems for a fee." Rawls says that "we would be surprised that such a person should exist," and we certainly would be if we lived in justice as fairness.[95] Citizens of the regime are expected to be capable of and interested in better and more meaningful conceptions of the good than this. Something (antecedent) must be wrong with this fellow. Or at least that is the first thought Rawlsian citizens will have when they see him. That is why the behavior of this character who is not like them necessarily poses a question to them. They *cannot* just pass him by. There is no ground for juridical interference—he is self-supportive and he is bothering no one—but justice as fairness does sanction some nonjuridical interventions.

First, Rawlsian citizens consider whether counting blades of grass is really part of this person's conception of the good. Since this is a society in which justification plays an important mediating role, they may begin by asking the grass counter to give an account of himself. Rawls envisions a benign, even nurturant exchange, but the effects of justification exceed his intentions. As soon as the citizens stop to ask the grass counter to justify his activity, they begin to sound a bit more like the police than like mere passers-by. They have stopped in order to decide what to do about this person, as if he were at their disposal. They have stopped in order to interrogate him.

"Faced with his case we would try out other hypotheses. Perhaps he is peculiarly neurotic." Now the "we" is like a case worker. Faced with idiosyncrasy, Rawlsian citizens see neurosis as a tempting explanation. It explains so much and leaves the promises of justice as fairness intact, just like their attribution of criminality to bad character did. Rawls says nothing about what the citizens should do if the grass counter is neurotic, but it seems likely that they would, at the very least, urge him to seek psychiatric counseling. If it turns out that he is not neurotic, "if we allow that his *nature* is to enjoy this activity and not any other," intervention is still justified. It cannot be ruled out unless and until the citizens ascertain "that there is no feasible way to alter his condition."[96] In short, their efforts to alter his condition are worthy. They need only respect the bounds of feasibility, by which Rawls presumably means that they should not violate the priority of right.

In the end, the "definition of the good forces us to admit that the good for this man is indeed counting blades of grass." But the fact that the admission is *forced* suggests that, although justice as fairness is supposed to support each individual's self-esteem, it does not do much for the grass counter's. His fellow citizens may not violate his rights in their dealings with him, but they do not treat him with the same respect they accord to others whose conceptions of the good are less opaque to them. They may treat him with liberal respect, but he is not accorded teleological respect, the juridically unenforceable basis of the valued primary good of self-respect.[97] Is there anyone in this "fanciful case" who shows a "willingness to see the situation of others from their point of view?" Do those who interrogate the grass counter act as if they are "prepared to give reasons for [*their*] actions?" And are these people likely "to do small favors and courtesies" for the likes of the grass counter? All three of these practices are features of Rawls's practice of mutual respect, but all are absent from the citizens' engagement with the grass counter. Indeed, there is reason to think that the citizens will warn their children to stay away from that man in the park because, even though he seems harmless enough, they do not want to take any chances. ("Better safe than sorry" *is* the phrase by which responsible, rational deliberators live.) If, as Rawls says, the "self-respect" of the parties "and their confidence in the value of their own system of ends cannot withstand the indifference much less the contempt of others," then the grass counter is not improved by the citizens' interventions, he is undermined by them.[98]

The grass counter will be surprised and disappointed to find that his behavior commands intervention at all. On the basis of his own reflections in the original position, he expects to be left alone in justice as fairness. Why would anyone bother (about) him? He expects a civic and civil indifference of his fellow citizens, but that is not what he gets. His fellow citizens are constituted by the very psychological profile to which justice as fairness aspires to give rise. They are as self-confident and self-possessed as Rawls hopes they will be. But their self-confidence has a flip side: backed up by the right, these people are as likely to be arrogant as they are to be self-confident, perhaps even smug. Sure that they know best, they assume that the burden is on those who are different to prove otherwise, or to resist, with sheer stubbornness but never with violence, the citizens' efforts to help, treat, or cure them. In a society such as this, composed of people such as these, there tends to be a fair amount of pressure on everyone to develop and pursue conceptions of the good that will win the approbation of their neighbors.

Rawls introduces the grass counter to illustrate justice as fairness's neutrality among individual conceptions of the good, but the example has a countervailing force to it. It also illustrates the practical tendency of a depoliticizing juridical neutrality to enhance the normalizing power of majority social judgments and cultural norms. Or better, in this case, it illustrates the practical nonneutrality of a juridical structure intended to give rise to precisely the sorts of citizens to whom it seems that the maintenance of their own form of life requires that they interrogate the other, examine him, account for him, and make him justify himself . . . to them. There is little room here, for example, for the Nietzschean "spirit who plays naively—that is, not deliberately but from overflowing power and abundance," a spirit who plays with blades of grass but also with things that are "called holy, good, untouchable, divine." Nietzsche's free spirit has an ideal but it is his own: he "should not wish to persuade anybody" to it, he would not want to justify it, because he would not "concede the right to it to anyone" and he demands the same courtesy in return. "This is what I am; this is what I want:—you can go to hell!" he screams in protest.[99] How would the well-meaning citizens, police officers, and caseworkers of justice as fairness respond to the grass counter who spoke to them this way?

To highlight the normalizing components of this imagined situation is not to call for callous indifference to others in place of Rawls's interventionism. It is to say that the problem is more complicated than that and that Rawls does not seem to be sensitive enough to the political dimensions of his intervention or to their complicating effects. For example, the gap between the grass counter's expectation (of indifference) and experience (of intervention) is a site of politics, but Rawls never addresses it. The interrogation itself is a political intervention, an exercise of power for the purposes of identity formation, maintenance, and closure, but Rawls does not treat it that way.[100] The citizens seek to make the grass counter more like them, but Rawls sees no imposition here, only nurturance and aid. The citizens' practices of consolidation and closure are depoliticized and their eagerness to bring the grass counter—the underachiever, the oddball, the eccentric—into the fold is left unexamined.

Once examined, however, their eagerness raises the possibility that it is not arrogance but a sense of instability that drives Rawlsian citizens to seek out and normalize difference wherever feasible.[101] Does the grass counter speak to or personify those parts of the self that resist Rawlsian orderings? Does his presence in the park, therefore, make it more difficult (or that much more necessary) for the citizens to insist that ill-fittedness as well as bad character are antecedent to the scheme? Do the citizens try to convert the other because the fact that he strikes a dissonant chord in the self shakes their expressivist faith and opens the door to the disturbing Nietzschean claim that otherness is actually produced by the forms of moral and responsible subjectivity they value? As Nietzsche puts it,

> those moralists who command man first of all and above all to gain control of himself thus afflict him with a peculiar disease; namely, a constant irritability in the face of all natural stirrings and inclinations—as it were, a kind of itching. Whatever may henceforth push, pull, attract or impel such an irritable person from inside or outside, it will always seem to him as if his self-control were endangered.[102]

With his self-control always at stake, always in doubt, the responsible subject is anxious to distance himself from whatever pushes, pulls, attracts, or impels him from inside or outside. He cannot silence his disruptive internal impulses as long as what he sees as their external manifestations persist. Is this why Rawlsian citizens are unable simply to pass by the grass counter? Justice as fairness is supposed to be neutral with regard to individual conceptions of the good, but the sheer irresponsibility (in the Rawlsian sense) of grass counting pushes, pulls, attracts, impels the citizens. They respond to it as they do to their own impulses to irresponsibility, with demands for justification, treatment, rationalization, all meant to bring the relief of closure.

But the Rawlsian subject's self-control is not only endangered by the other, it is also enabled and secured by it. The well-orderedness of the citizens draws some of its energy from their definition of themselves in opposition to dissonant characters; their identification as citizens is nourished by their efforts to help, interrogate, or cure the other; hence their *need* to decide what to do about him. The other's presence in the regime destabilizes Rawlsian self-orderings but it also secures the practice of justification that consolidates those self-orderings. In short, Rawlsian justification has a performative dimension: it produces and consolidates the justifying subject it presupposes. Does that mean that the citizens relate to the other more as a means (to the consolidation of the just order and its population) than as an end in himself?

Rawls intends the opposite. If dissonant characters and impulses keep surfacing in his text, he would say, it is because he is committed to a traditional philosophical assumption that others must be given reasons for compliance, that his position must be justified to those who are resistant to it. Philosophy does not preach only to the converted and it does not simply exclude those who do not agree; it offers rational arguments and hopes to persuade others, to justify itself to them. This practice of philosophical justification is not uncontroversial: Stanley Cavell dissociates himself from one aspect of it—"I am not as keen as others seem to be to let the worth of moral theory depend on its being able to (re)convince a convinced scoundrel"—but he does not criticize it directly.[103] It is worth criticizing, however. One effect of Rawlsian justification is its management of confrontations with the other to the satisfaction of the "we" that dominates discourse and argument, the "we" whose nature as free and equal beings is assumed and expressed (but also produced) by the two principles. If Rawlsian justification means to reassure the "we" that its political order is indeed just, is that because the "we" senses, perhaps, the dissonance of the remainders of politics and, indeed, experiences them as resistances? And might those experiences not be the consequences rather than the occasions of a practice of justification that (at the founding, in reflective equilibrium, in the difference principle) strives to eliminate or dissolve the remainders of politics rather than engage them?

Liberal and Other Alternatives

Like Kant, Rawls sees the enterprise of political association as "typically marked by a conflict as well as an identity of interests." And like Kant's citizens, Rawls's citizens believe that "social co-operation makes possible a better life than any would have if each were to try to live solely by his own efforts." But Rawls's citizens have none of Kant's ambivalence about sociability. Kant's postulate of unsocial sociability is modified by Rawls to form the circumstances of justice. The unsocial urge noted by Kant and heightened by Nietzsche becomes in Rawls a "conflict of interests" that arises out of the fact that "men are not indifferent as to how the greater benefits produced by their collaboration are distributed." The transformation of intrasubjective dissonances into the more manageable conflict of interest facilitates Rawls's claim that he seeks simply "to reduce disagreements and to bring divergent convictions more in line."[104] The perspective of *virtù* calls attention to these dissonances, to their resistance to alignment, to their daily effects and reverberations in a regime that assumes their absence, and to the potentially undemocratic effects of their being remaindered. Informed by Arendt's theorization of authority as a practice of augmentation that is committed not to entrenchment or settlement but to the utopian possibility of a perpetual Nietzschean self-overcoming, this perspective highlights the closures of contest that form the base of the Rawlsian project and it politicizes them. The contrast between *virtù* and virtue theories of politics helps to raise tacit assumptions to the level of critique. But in the case of Arendt and Rawls, the contrast may also be somewhat misleading since Rawls's closure of political space for the sake of justice is perfectly compatible with Arendt's position.

Like Rawls, Arendt also depoliticizes justice. In her private realm, the realm of economic distributions, there are no spaces of politics. Efficiency, elite and authoritative decision-making, and bureaucratic administration are the sovereign mechanisms of Arendtian justice, too. These are the elements in Arendt's account that a *virtù* theory has to overcome. In a sense, then, Rawls's theory of justice is thoroughly Arendtian. Indeed, his displacement of politics with administration fulfills (it does not offend) Arendt's fantasy of the household; Rawls even describes the parties in the original position as heads of households. But, he also fulfills Arendt's nightmare of the household, which is precisely that household concerns, once prominent on a political agenda, leave no space for the appearance of the extraordinarily disruptive *political* action Arendt celebrates. Rawls is too devoted to the administrative success of justice to take the risk of Arendtian politics.

In their different ways, both Arendt and Rawls are insensitive to a tragic dimension of their respective theorizations of a modern democratic politics: economic justice, as they each theorize it, requires a predictability, an administrative control that is uneasy amid the tumult of democratic political action. Given the choice between justice and politics, Rawls opts for the former in the belief that the disruptions of politics (as opposed to the smooth managements of administration) are symptoms of *injustice* and that, therefore, they will not be missed once absent. Arendt opts for the latter in the (benighted) belief that it addresses an ontological need that justice leaves untouched. But must the choices be confined to these two irreconcilable options? Might the dilemma not be a product of

Arendtian and Rawlsian insistences? A *virtù* theory of politics argues—in opposition to both Arendt and Rawls—that increases in justice will come with the proliferation, not the diminution, of political sites, with a politicizing rather than conciliatory response to the state's monopoly on the administration of justice.

In choosing justice over politics, Rawls does not have the last word on the liberal side, however. There are some liberal theorists who reject the choice Arendt and Rawls take as given and confront the ineliminability of politics in a way that Rawls never does, even while rejecting Arendt's claim that the elimination of politics would constitute a deep ontological disappointment. Most famous, perhaps, is Isaiah Berlin's refusal to privilege politics as the centerpiece of human activity while at the same time acknowledging that the source of that refusal—his commitment to value pluralism—makes politics an ineliminable feature of human life.[105]

Influenced by Berlin but writing from a more consequentialist perspective, Richard Flathman envisions a more politicized liberalism in which the state's role in establishing and maintaining rights settlements is not merely accepted and celebrated, it is challenged and the challenge is treated as *part of* a practice of rights that might enhance rather than diminish justice (property rights are among those whose contestability is heightened). On Flathman's account, the practice of rights is no longer owned and operated by the state. Rights are moderated by a practice of "civil encroachment" much as authority is moderated by civil disobedience. The invocation of a right does not necessarily settle matters; on the contrary, it might well have unsettling effects, just as the invocation of authority in a political culture hospitable to civil disobedience does not necessarily settle matters; it may well provoke resistances with unsettling effects. These unsettling effects are not simply unwanted remainders that Flathman tolerates. They are part of a valued institutional process that amends and augments the structure of rights and authority, contesting, resisting the state's monopolistic relation to both. Thus, the best effect of civil disobedience (and correspondingly of civil encroachment) is that "argumentation about the merits of the law or command not only continue after its adoption or promulgation but take on added forcefulness and drama. It is more difficult for those who support the adopted law or command to say, 'Well that's settled, let's go on to other things'. It is even more difficult for them to say, 'We won that one, let's go out and win another'." Flathman refuses the choice between justice and politics that Arendt and Rawls assume for the sake of a liberalism in which politics, while not celebrated as the privileged path to self-realization, always has a role to play in the lives of citizens who must live with the state.[106]

These alternatives are welcome rifts within liberalism. From their perspectives, Rawls problematically disempowers citizens by reconciling them without remainder to the juridical authority of the state;[107] and (what Berlin might call the monism of) Rawlsian rationalism is not a benign and agreeable means to institutionalize a private realm pluralism but a betrayal of a deeper (more disagreeable?) pluralism that mires these liberals in a politics they never quite celebrate, though neither do they condemn it tout court. These more politicized, less statist liberals call for more room than Rawls allows for political contest and unsettlement. They refuse to reduce politics to technique; they contest the hegemony of juridical administration by resorting to practices of politics that are more agonistic, more difficult, more sustained, sometimes engaging to their participants but not necessarily so. The charms of political action (or its lack thereof) are not its justification, however. (Re)founding, augmentation, and resistance are all part of political life, part of the same package of practices that brings founding, administration, authority, and sedimentation to political communities. The absence of (re)founding, augmentation, and resistance from political life indicates that spaces of politics are being closed. For some liberals, that closure does not secure the individuality and pluralism they value, it endangers them, and so their liberal commitments lead them to resist the statist closure of political space, to contest its effective marginalization of (re)founding, action, augmentation, and resistance.

The *virtù* theorist rejects the view that politics is solely an instrument of settlement, but she is not necessarily hostile, therefore, to the very idea of institutional arrangements. On the contrary, she favors those sets of arrangements that resist the temptation to ontologize the conditions of their existence. In a world not ordered to fit our institutional demands, populated by selves who are also not so obliging, highly politicized institutions that shift and proliferate the sites of politics are the best way to diminish the violence and the resentment that invariably haunt political arrangements.

There might be room in this *virtù* alternative for something like Rawls's difference principle because, whatever else it is, the difference principle is an institutional recognition of and response to the fact that socioeconomic inequalities are contingent, arbitrary, not morally justified, not expressive of a natural hierarchy or of some ideal order of things. From a *virtù* perspective, therefore, the aspiration of the difference principle is admirable: it admits the contingency of socioeconomic arrangements and inequalities, it releases subjects from a sense of personal responsibility for their place in the hierarchy, and it seeks to limit the range of inequalities so that no class will become thoroughly alienated and disaffected by bearing the brunt of economic violence in a regime. It sensitizes us to some of the remainders of politics.

The adoption of a difference principle for a *virtù* theory of politics, however (in the simple form of a public commitment to limit the range of economic and political inequalities—in distributions and opportunities), could proceed only by rejecting the rationalist packing in which Rawls wraps his difference principle. That packing works against the grain of the very thing the principle is designed to achieve (as, indeed, does the centrality of justification to its practice): as soon as subjects are released from responsibility for the inequalities that mark their lives and demarcate them from others, they are told that their (somewhat diminished) inequalities are justified. In short, the effect of the difference principle is twofold, and Rawls values both parts of the effect: the principle diminishes the range of inequality, but it also seeks to diminish the felt effects of the inequalities that remain by justifying them.[108] It grounds Rawls's claim that any envy, resentment, or recalcitrance felt by citizens in the context of a relatively just arrangement is irrational. In a relatively just society, it is their own responsibility to reconcile themselves to their situation. Like antecedent moral worth in Rawls's practice of punishment, responsibility returns to haunt the practice of distribution: subjects who in other respects have been told that they are not personally responsible for their contingent and arbitrary (from a moral point of view) situations are now told, nonetheless, that they are personally responsible for their failure to be satisfied with their lot in life. The effect, as Wolin points out in another context, is the "depoliticalization of the poor."[109]

Rawls cherishes the difference principle for its diminution of inequality but, most of all, he values its ability effectively to provide this sort of justification, a justification that acknowledges no remainders and licenses their suppression when they do surface (they are antecedent, irrational, inexcusable, criminal), thus settling the matter once and for all. In opposition to Rawls, the *virtù* theorist wagers that the very conditions of alienation and disaffection the difference principle is supposed to alleviate will be aggravated by its will to closure, that the remainders it seeks to dissolve will be engendered by it.

Rawls's dogged quest for a remainderless justification and reconciliation betray, they do not secure, the best impulses of his project—its commitment to inclusion, to reduce inequalities, increase political participation, alleviate alienation and resentment, level the socioeconomic playing field, and generally contribute to the empowerment of persons. Throughout *A Theory of Justice*, the citizens' responses to the other in themselves and in other persons testify not to a sensitivity to or respect for others but to an impatience, anger, hostility, and incomprehension that silences or coerces those whose dissonance destabilizes the Rawlsian order. The citizens' need to deny their part in the production of the other makes magnanimity impossible, and it either renders problematic their belief that the institutions that engender these outcomes are just or it signals a conflict that Rawls never acknowledges or engages, a conflict between (Rawlsian) justice and the ethical treatment of others.

CHAPTER SIX

Sandel and the Proliferation
of Political Subjects

It is precisely the insatiable identity principle that perpetuates antagonism by
suppressing contradiction. What tolerates nothing that is not like itself thwarts the
reconcilement for which it mistakes itself.
—Theodor Adorno

Friends are not concerned with what can be made of one another, but only with
the enjoyment of one another; and the condition of enjoyment is a ready
acceptance of what is and the absence of any desire to change or improve.
—Michael Oakeshott

It might seem obvious that if Rawls's liberal theory of justice as fairness is
a virtue theory of politics then surely so is Sandel's communitarian
account. But my interest in Sandel's account goes beyond the impulse to
label it. His is a provocative treatment of the role that politics might play
in the development, preservation, and consolidation of agency and identity in deeply situated subjects. Until now the merits of Sandel's *Liberalism and the Limits of Justice* have been assessed largely in terms of its
contribution to the liberal-communitarian debate, that is, in terms of its
success or failure in scoring philosophical and political points against
contemporary liberal thought. As a result, some of the book's best
insights have gone largely unremarked. From a *virtù* perspective, these
insights are rendered more visible; and so are the commonalities that
mark the apparently adversarial accounts of Rawls and Sandel.

Both Rawls and Sandel end up committed to virtue theories of politics,
but along the way Sandel raises some distinctive and important questions
about subjectivity. I raise these questions for reexamination by focusing
on three provocative insights developed by Sandel. First, he argues that
Rawls wrongly privileges a single particular conception of the self as

moral subject. Readers of Sandel, both communitarian and liberal, have since assumed that Sandel's point is simply that the communitarian conception of the self is preferable to the liberal conception on philosophical or epistemological and ethico-political grounds. And this is indeed where Sandel ends up by the end of the book. But he begins more subtly than that: against Rawls he argues that there is no single morally relevant description of subjectivity, that morally relevant descriptions of subjectivity are plural, and, indeed, that they ought to be proliferated. Rawls's antecedently individuated self is only one of three options Sandel mentions. The other two, Sandel argues, the intersubjective and the intrasubjective conceptions, may be more relevant than the Rawlsian variant in alternative moral settings. But Sandel himself prefers a single alternative moral setting, a communitarian setting, in which the intersubjective conception is ultimately privileged as the single morally relevant account of subjectivity. Sandel recasts Rawls's original position in order to generate the intersubjective conception, claiming not only that it is the necessary ground of a communitarian politics but also that it is the necessary ground of Rawls's difference principle, a principle of distribution Sandel himself endorses on communitarian grounds.

By implication, Sandel also argues that the Rawlsian subject is problematically univocal in its constitution, and that this univocality is secured by the distance from which the Rawlsian self relates to its (multiple) ends. Sandel's communitarian self is, by contrast, multiply and deeply constituted, subject to a variety of different—even conflicting—allegiances and identifications. But Sandel replicates the Rawlsian move: he domesticates his intrasubjective conception of the self by way of a practice of self-interpretation that is strikingly similar to Rawlsian practices of self-ordering of which Sandel is highly critical. As it turns out, the communitarian self is multiply constituted, but its multiplicity can be ordered and bounded, even univocally, in the recast original position; this self is not so radically multiple that it resists or exceeds, or somehow escapes the self's efforts to order itself (under the right conditions) into a coherent and unified agency.

Finally, Sandel criticizes Rawls for his failure to see the importance of encumbrance as a feature of the constituted self's subjectivity. Sandel comes much closer than Rawls to appreciating the elements of subjection involved in the constitution and production of subjectivity. But he theorizes an encumbrance that does not *subject*, one that is not weighty or difficult to bear, one that does not preclude or resist the self's ability to get a grip on itself and order itself coherently. In the end, Sandel's self has

good reason to celebrate its encumbrance: it is encumbered by communities that are only supportive and meaning-generative, communities
that locate and situate their members in a particularity of place and time
that is safe and reassuring. By tracing encumbrance to these sorts of
communities, to communities worthy of valorization and gratitude,
Sandel invests his discourse of encumbrance with a thoroughly positive
rhetorical flavor. To be encumbered is to be only enabled, not imposed
on; Sandel's subjects are constituted, situated, but not produced; encumbrance is a source of meaning and self-understanding but never a
source of mystification and self-alienation, except when community is
subverted by something outside itself. As a result, Sandel's community-
constituted self is in the end no more significantly encumbered than is
Rawls's liberal self. And power is acknowledged to be no more significant
in the production and maintenance of the communitarian subject than it
was in that of its liberal other.

Nonetheless, Sandel's initial impulses are instructive. His insights
regarding the multiplicity and potential proliferation of morally relevant
descriptions of subjectivity, the multiple constitution of the self as subject, and the quality of that constitution as at least partly one of encumbrance are all vitally relevant to a *virtù* theory of politics. And they
are important correctives to Rawls's liberal assumptions. But Sandel
retreats from each of these insights because he is out to win a war on two
fronts: he seeks not only to redress the abstractness of the Rawlsian
liberal self by theorizing a conception of the self as constituted subject
but also to fend off the specter of the "radically situated subject." Readers
of Sandel have paid scant attention to his brave battles on the second
front, probably because they themselves have little interest in defending
the radically situated subject.[1] On this exclusion, there is a deep and
abiding agreement among liberal and communitarian thinkers. From the
perspective of a *virtù* theorist, however, Sandel's construction of radical
situatedness as a specter and his anxious efforts to fend it off are worth
attending to because that specter is what drives Sandel back into the arms
of Rawls and firmly into the camp of a virtue theory of politics.

Two Kinds of Dispossession

The twin specters of radical unsituatedness (in the form of the liberal
self) and radical situatedness are represented by Sandel as two kinds of
dispossession, each typically symptomatic of departures from the moder-

ate situatedness communitarianism offers. These two kinds of dispossession animate Sandel's need to secure his middle option, a community-
constituted self that is protected from the dangers posed by these two
liminal cases.

Sandel's aim in *Liberalism and the Limits of Justice* is to build on an insight
he credits to liberalism: "Liberalism teaches respect for the distance of
self and ends, and when this distance is lost, we are submerged in a
circumstance that ceases to be ours." The self must establish and maintain some distance between itself and its ends or it will fall victim to
radical situatedness, to a complete and overwhelming submergence in
circumstances beyond its control. "But," Sandel adds, "by seeking to
secure this distance too completely, liberalism undermines its own insight." In its well-intentioned effort to empower the subject, liberalism
establishes too much distance between the self and its ends (through
antecedent individuation) and leaves the liberal self as disempowered as
its radically situated other.[2]

What liberalism has failed to appreciate is that there are not one but
two kinds of dispossession and, likewise, two "dimensions of agency"
capable of "repairing the drift toward dispossession." The first kind of
dispossession recalls Kant's account of reason's originary withdrawal of
the world from us: it "involves the distancing of the end from the self
whose end it once was. It becomes increasingly unclear in what sense this
is my end rather than yours, somebody else's, or no one's at all." As in
Kant, it is necessary to bridge the distance in order to heal the sense of
rupture and dislocation. But in Sandel's first scenario of dispossession,
the gap is bridged not by reason but by the will. The "faculty of agency
in its voluntarist sense" enters to relate the self "to its ends as a willing
subject to the objects of choice." The will enables the subject to "transcend the space" that distances it from its objects without effectively
closing that space. Complete closure would produce radical situatedness,
a leap from frying pan to fire.[3]

The second kind of dispossession describes the predicament of Kant's
first man *prior to* reason's disruptive concealment of the world from him.
Here the subject is radically situated, dispossessed because it is "possessed *by*" its desires or ends, "disempowered because undifferentiated
from its ends." This radically situated subject is, like Kant's first man at
the earliest stage, not yet conscious of himself as an end and therefore not
aware of himself as having ends. As Sandel puts it, "I am disempowered
in the sense of lacking any clear grip on who, in particular, I am. Too
much is essential to my identity. Where the ends are given prior to the

self they constitute, the bounds of the subject are open, its identity infinitely accommodating and ultimately fluid. Unable to distinguish what is mine from what is me, I am in constant danger of drowning in a sea of circumstance." This kind of "dispossession is repaired by agency in its cognitive sense, in which the self is related to its ends as a knowing subject to the objects of understanding."[4]

The dispossessed self and subject imagined in each of these scenarios is indeed imagined, however—an ideal type, a caricature of certain features and drifts that mark all selves and subjects to some extent. Each poses or posits a limit to agency, each marks the end point of a spectrum. As Flathman argues (albeit not with reference to Sandel), "the distinction between 'situated' versus 'unsituated' has no application to human action." Situatedness is a feature of all action "at least in the sense that all actions are the actions that they are by virtue of the public language and shared norms of some community or other."[5] And Sandel knows this: his deployments of these liminal, situated and unsituated, characters can be read as an illustration of the range as well as the bounds of the spectrum of situatedness. But his communitarian alternative is designed to emphasize the bounds over the range, to protect selves from their tendency to drift or be driven too far in either direction.[6]

One important consequence of this tendency, if it is left unchecked, is the loss of desert as a coherent practice and a defensible principle of distribution. The real cause of the downfall of desert, Sandel argues, is Rawls's radically unsituated self, not the much touted infinite regress to which the practice seems vulnerable. The real ground of Rawls's rejection of desert is, not that the bases of desert cannot themselves be deserved all the way down, but that they cannot be possessed by the antecedently individuated self "in the undistanced, constitutive sense necessary [on Rawls's account] to provide a desert base."[7]

The notion of desert requires "a *basis* of desert ultimately prior to desert," a being, as it were, behind the deserving, a moment of possession that anchors the practice. Possession, in turn, implies a "subject of possession that is not *itself* possessed (for this would deny its agency), a subject 'doing the possessing', so to speak," a being, as it were, behind the possessing. The relation between possession and desert is analogous, but the analogy is imperfect because desert's need for a "basis of desert which is not itself deserved" can be filled by "some subject of possession which is not itself possessed."[8] Desert is vulnerable to infinite regress only if we shy away from anchoring its place of the last instance with a creature more robust than that postulated by liberal theory.

Sandel does not shy away; he argues that desert's gap can be closed and the dispossession healed by stopping the drift toward the first kind of dispossession, by constituting a self capable of coherent possession. Nor does he worry about whether this closure is arbitrary. Real arbitrariness plagues only the deontological self that lacks any meaningful relation to its attributes. The communitarian constituted subject is plagued not by arbitrariness but by contingency. This problem, if it is a problem, is deferred: "There may be a certain ultimate contingency in my having wound up the person I am—only theology can say for sure."[9] On one reading, this deference implies that the problem is a problem only for those communities devoted to theological investigations and to the certainties in which they issue. On another, it implies that deference to theology on issues such as these is appropriate for all communities.

Sandel's deference to theology leaves him with the apparently more modest (but not unrelated) task of securing the possibility of coherent possession required by his account of agency. To that end he rejects Rawls's "sharp distinction between the subject taken as the pure subject of possession, and the aims and attributes it possesses." This distinction leaves the self "bare of any substantive feature or characteristic that could serve as a desert base." The pure subject of possession cannot deserve anything because it cannot possess anything. The Rawlsian self is disempowered by the very strategy that was meant to empower it; it is left dispossessed in a way that voluntarist agency, Rawls's only offering, cannot heal.[10]

In his quest for a more empowering notion of possession and agency, Sandel distinguishes three senses of possession, two of which are dangerously close to the pathologies of *dispossession* with which we began. "Depending on the sense of possession intended," Sandel says, "I may be described as the owner, the guardian, or the repository of the endowments I bear." The first and last options hold the same places on the spectrum marked by radical unsituatedness and radical situatedness, respectively. The middle option is the one Sandel finds most attractive. Guardianship fits best with "various communitarian notions of property" and it also provides Rawls's difference principle with the subject of possession it needs.[11]

The Communitarian Subject of Possession

Robert Nozick's critique of Rawls's difference principle provides the occasion for Sandel's rehabilitation of it for communitarian ends. According to Nozick, the difference principle's treatment of "natural talents as a common asset" does "not take seriously the distinction between persons."[12] It is no better than the utilitarian bête noire Rawls criticizes: it leaves some to the mercy of others, violating the Kantian principle of respect for persons that prohibits the use of persons merely as means.

Sandel argues that Rawls has two avenues of defense available. He might claim that the difference principle does not violate mutual respect "because not *persons* but only 'their' *attributes* are being used as means to others' well-being." But this defence so thoroughly distinguishes the self from its "contingently-given and wholly inessential attributes" that it leaves the self "radically disembodied" and incoherent. Moreover, as Nozick objects (with Sandel's approval), there is in any case no comfort for those "thick with particular traits" in being told that the "purified men within us are not regarded as means."[13]

The second avenue of defense, although no more likely to be embraced by Rawls than the first, is the one Sandel himself favors. Rawls could "deny that the difference principle uses me as a means to others' ends, not by claiming that my *assets* rather than *person* are being used, but instead by questioning the sense in which those who share in 'my' assets are properly described as 'others.'" The problem of just distribution is one of those moral settings in which "the relevant description of the self may embrace more than a single empirically-individuated human being." If Rawls would only recognize this, if he would only allow for the proliferation of morally relevant descriptions of subjectivity, then he could tie "the notion of common assets to the possibility of a common subject of possession." He could then ground his difference principle in an intersubjective conception of the self.[14]

The intersubjective conception also resolves another problem plaguing the difference principle. As Sandel rightly points out, Rawls's claim that talents and attributes are arbitrarily distributed "argues only against the proposition that the individual owns them or has a privileged claim to their benefits, not in favor of the proposition that some particular society owns them or has a privileged claim with respect to them." The claim succeeds only in deprivileging individual claims; it is not in and of itself sufficient to privilege "general social ends" over "individual ones." Rawls needs to justify the difference principle's privileging of general social ends *independently*, and the only way to do that, Sandel argues, is by resorting to "some conception of a wider subject of possession." In short, the problem is that Rawls's approach leaves the question of belonging unsettled: to whom do these talents and attributes belong? The intersubjective conception and the notion of guardianship that goes with it can give an answer. Rawls's difference principle cannot because the question is never put before it.[15]

Finally, and perhaps most important of all to Sandel, the move to ground the notion of common assets in the intersubjective conception actually empowers the person whose talents and attributes are to be put to general social ends. Even "if I cannot be the owner I can at least be the guardian of the assets located 'here', and what is more, a guardian for a community of which I count myself a member."[16] Guardianship may not look like the best option from the standpoint of ownership, but the indefensibility of the ownership thesis is already presupposed by the difference principle. And, from Sandel's perspective, in which the spectral repository thesis looms as the only other alternative, guardianship looks very good indeed.

From a *virtù* perspective, however, Sandel's deployments of the intersubjective conception and the guardianship thesis are deeply problematic. He relies on the intersubjective conception to stop the infinite regress of desert and fill the aporia that makes desert so vulnerable to charges like those made by Rawls. Rawls's great insight regarding the arbitrariness of the social practice of desert is thereby erased. And the importance of power in Sandel's settlement of the issue of belonging (and in the maintenance and consolidation of this settlement) is neglected or silenced, as we see below. Sandel does all this because the possibility of a legitimate or legitimated belonging is very important to him. Like Rawls, he knows that the aporias of social practices have the power to subvert the closures to which communitarians (and liberals, in their way) aspire. Talents and attributes *must belong to someone*, to some subject of possession; there must be some title if the claims of community are to be articulated, consolidated, and adjudicated.

Having identified the gap in Rawls's difference principle, Sandel opts for a more sophisticated instrument of closure: the community-constituted subject located in a wider subjectivity, the communitarian subject of possession. I argued in Chapter 5 that the difference principle (or something like it), divested of its rationalist aspiration, could be pressed into service on behalf of a politics that rejects or resists the will to closure, a politics devoted to recognizing and responding institutionally to the arbitrariness that marks each individual's success or failure in accommodating and approximating the demands and values that constitute her political, social, and economic culture. Sandel takes a different view: the problem with the difference principle is not that it seeks too much closure but that it achieves far too little. It has gaps that must be plugged. Its grounding in an argument about the ineliminably arbitrary character of the practice of desert is not only mistaken but dangerous: it is a sore reminder of the inability of human practices to attain the closure to which Sandel aspires. It broadcasts Nietzsche's disturbing and potentially disruptive claim that "the will to a system is a lack of integrity." But there is a solution with integrity, Sandel claims, if we are only willing to embrace it: the communitarian subject of possession can settle the question of belonging.

Sandel is right that Rawls's argument from arbitrariness does not *settle* the question of belonging, but Sandel's own arguments are also animated and powered by unarticulated assumptions and undefended stopping points. The question of belonging is settled by Sandel, but it is settled arbitrarily. What force brings his proliferation of morally relevant descriptions of subjectivity to a halt at the magic number three? Once the proliferation has begun, what rationale stops it here rather than there? Why is it less arbitrary for Sandel to stop here, at the number three, than it was for Rawls to stop there, at the number one?

Sandel never addresses these questions directly; instead, he marshals the criteria of appropriateness and indebtedness to mark the boundaries he wants to secure. Both are left untheorized but both are important in the fabulist narrative of community Sandel has to tell: the communitarian subject knows that "since others made me, and in various ways continue to make me, the person I am, it seems appropriate to regard them, in so far as I can identify them, as participants in 'my' achievements and common beneficiaries of the rewards they bring." I am indebted to them for my being my self. People like me, participants in common endeavors, regard themselves "less as individuated subjects with certain things in common, and more as members of a wider (but still determinate) subjectivity, less as 'others' and more as participants in a common identity."[17]

The parenthetical proviso in this passage protects Sandel from the charge that the wider subjectivity is so wide as to be indeterminate. Sandel includes it because he wants to secure the difference between his communitarian subject and the radically situated subject: his subject is situated but not submerged, part of a subjectivity that is wider than a single individual but not so wide as to make it impossible to sort out the bounds of its identity, determinately.[18] But the need for a boundary does not settle the issue of where a boundary line should be drawn, of whether its site is arbitrary, natural, right, essentially contestable, or fluid. And none of these considerations settles the question of how the border should be treated: should it be patrolled by border guards or left vulnerable and undefended? Is its installment a temporary and rough approximation or a great and permanent victory for geographic correctness?[19]

From a *virtù* perspective, it is clear that the borders of Sandel's communitarian subject of possession are firmly drawn and subtly defended. Some but not all "others" are acknowledged as participants in my identity. It is *appropriate* to regard some as participants in "my" achievements and to leave other others out (or, indeed, to disavow them). The proliferation of morally relevant descriptions of subjectivity ends with an intersubjective conception in which the range of intersubjectivity is bounded by the inclusion only of those who identify with a particular community and who are identified by a particular community as its own. What criterion of identification governs the all-important standard of appropriateness here? What governs Sandel's refusal to consider whether subjects are indebted for their constitutedness to a wider array of others, to their enemies, their antagonists, to those they take pride in *not* being? Might I not, *together* with Sandel and in the spirit of his objections to Rawls, question the sense in which those who are figured in my consciousness as extrasubjective, outside or even enemies of "my" identity and community, "are properly described as others?" After all, figures who frighten and repel us play a part in our constitution as a "we," a "we" that is what it is (partly) insofar as it is not "them." Blackness plays a part in the constitution of whiteness, masculinity in femininity, master in slave, terrorist in state, and overman in herd. Perhaps the logic of indebtedness extends across the line of opposition that marks each of these pairs. At least (as Sandel said to Rawls), Sandel must provide an *independent* argument to account for why it does not.

In *The Alchemy of Race and Rights*, Patricia Williams reports the story of two Stanford students, one black, one white, who argued about whether Beethoven was black. The argument spawned some racist actions, and in the end the white student, who had initially protested that it was ridiculous to think that Beethoven was anything but white, yielded after being confronted with proof that Beethoven was indeed of mulatto ancestry. The white student found that Beethoven's music sounded different to him subsequently.[20] This is one of many examples on which Williams relies in her superb illustrations of the depth of identity investments in America and the range of juridical and institutional protections that work to protect identity investments, particularly the investment that whites have in not being black. In effect, Williams argues that in America logics of indebtedness are firmly lodged on one (sometimes shifting) side of an identity-other opposition. In this way, logics of indebtedness generally tend to reinforce oppositional structures. And this is what Sandel's logic of indebtedness does, by bounding the self in quite determinate ways and by insistently distinguishing friend from enemy (although not along racial or racist lines): the debt stops here.

But this is not the only logic of indebtedness. Indebtedness is a potentially powerful instrument of subversion as well. Nietzsche uses notions of debt and indebtedness to subvert or dislodge such entrenched oppositions as we-them, friend-enemy, identity-other. As Nietzsche indicates in "Homer's Contest," the self's talents, attributes, and identities are generated as much by contest and agonistic engagement with others as they are by the nurturant support provided by those who are, or imagine themselves to be, like oneself. Hence Nietzsche's acknowledgment of a debt to his enemies; he is grateful to them for providing him with a spur to life. Indeed, his gesture to his enemies goes *beyond indebtedness* all the way to a magnanimity that exceeds the capacities of Sandel's intersubjective conception and, in *The Genealogy of Morals*, to honor.[21] As Nietzsche sees it, his greatest talents are generated by engagement with adversaries and by his effort to disrupt, destabilize, and get some distance from the beliefs and presuppositions that constitute his community. Would Sandel's community want to claim *these* talents—of disruption, destabilization, and distance—for itself? In cases like this, communities tend to rely on the logic of indebtedness to issue not claims of appropriate appropriation but rather demands that the critic be silent for the community's sake. The demand for silence or restraint is, of course, a different kind of appropriation; it too invokes a wider subject of possession, and it too is empowered by a debt claim, a claim that in this case calls on the individual to acknowledge the extent to which he owes his talents and attributes to the community, precisely by renouncing them or refraining from their use.

Sandel's insight against Rawls is that the bounds of the self are more porous than Rawls allows, but Sandel will not let the bounds of the self become too porous. There is little largesse in Sandel's "enlarged self-understanding."[22] It is constituted only by friends and not by enemies. The only argument Sandel offers in defense of his particular boundaries of subjectivity is the one implied by his claim that one's talents and attributes, even one's identity, are nurtured and enabled by one's community. The bounds of subjectivity are drawn by debt and enforced by gratitude. But the self's identity, talents, and attributes are at least as likely to be the products of its *resistances* to community constitution as they are to be the products of hothouse care. Western figurings of the haunted artist, the rebel thinker, the born-again Christian, and the transvestite all exemplify and inculcate the point. It is at least insufficient to say that one owes one's community a debt for forming one's character when one is conscious of one's character and talents having been formed by deliberate acts of rebellion and less deliberate resistances to the terms of identity set by one's home communities.

Occasions for Politics

Sandel's deployment of a logic of indebtedness is puzzling because the invocation of debt already implies noncompliance and this implication seems to be at odds with his assumptions regarding the depth of the self's community constitutedness and self-identification. It implies moments where the happiness and easiness that permeate his account of the identification of self with community are strained and tensed to the point of unhappiness and uneasiness.

This is the first of two moments of dissonance I focus on in Sandel's account. It is implied by Sandel's description of community as a claim maker, as an entity empowered to make *legitimate* claims (and to legitimate some claims and not others).[23] The fact that this community has a practice of claim making implies that it is vulnerable to identification failures and to resistance or noncompliance. Sandel's introduction of claiming invites the following politicizing questions, although he does not pose them: what happens when individuals resist these claims? what happens when the community's claim that the self is only the guardian of its talents and attributes, and not their owner, is rejected by particular selves? Sandel tries to circumnavigate these questions and the dissonance they generate by describing the self as a thoroughly community-constituted subject, possessed of and indeed animated by the enlarged self-understanding that is presupposed and required by the intersubjective conception. As a subject/member of a community, I am likely, Sandel says, to experience the enlistment of "my" assets or life prospects into community service less as a violation of mutual respect "and more as a way of contributing to the purposes of a community I regard as my own." I do not feel imposed on because the enlistment is justified not by "the abstract [Rawlsian] assurance that unknown others will gain more than I will lose, but [by] the rather more compelling notion that by my efforts I contribute to the realization of a way of life in which I take pride and with which my identity is bound."[24]

Because it is justified so compellingly, Sandel supposes that the enlistment does not compel; it is not a conscription, it is an enlistment.[25] And it is, like the encumbrance that justifies it, a happy one. I do not resent the enlistment and I do not regard it as an imposition because the happiness that structures the situation does so exhaustively. Sandel moves quickly from epistemological claims about the situatedness and constitutedness of selves in and by communities to normative claims about indebtedness, obligation, and allegiances, and on to projections of happy self-identifications and even self-realization.[26] In the face of these projections, it is at first difficult to imagine or identify the *source* of the dissonance that gives rise to community practices of claim making and to which the community, as claim maker, responds. But Sandel provides an important clue.

Although he tends to talk about the constituted self as a member of a single, univocal community, constituted by a single, unified identity, Sandel does occasionally suggest a more plausible and more politically fecund alternative which provides the setting for the second moment of dissonance in his account. As it turns out, Sandel's subjects identify with a plurality of communities to which they are variously related: "Each of us moves in an indefinite number of communities, some more inclusive than others, each making different claims on our allegiance." In the context of claim making, it might be more apt to put the point in a less subject-centered and voluntarist way: each of us is moved by several communities, each of which defines allegiance and betrayal in ways that are not necessarily compatible with each other or capable of being reconciled without remainder. Either way, however, Sandel's subjects are partly constituted by some communities, partly by others, constituted more deeply and enduringly by some than others. The subject has "various attachments" that make "respective claims" on it, and not all of them can be satisfied partly because the subject's abilities are limited but also because these various claims conflict with each other.[27] Here, in this pluralism of constitution, is the second moment of dissonance, the recipe for conflict Sandel needs to account for the presence of politics and contest in communitarian surroundings, and for that of claim making as well.

In this moral setting of multiple and conflicting constitutive claims, Sandel's intrasubjective conception is the most morally relevant conception of the self. The intrasubjective conception highlights the (cognitive and moral) predicament of the moderately situated self, a self constituted partly by several different communities and not fully or exhaustively by any one. This self is in conflict, pulled in different directions simultaneously. As Sandel conceives of it, the problem is not notably different from the one that troubled possession: the terms and subject of possession had to be clearly delineated and the question of belonging settled in order to safeguard distributive practices; likewise, from the vantage point of the intrasubjective conception, some normative or genetic account of belonging needs to be supplied so that the subject might clarify and come to know the terms and facts of her membership in various communities. This safeguards practices of obligation and allegiance. To which community does this subject really belong? On whose behalf is she the guardian of the talents and attributes she has at her disposal?[28]

Practices of obligation and allegiance are not the only things that depend on answers to these questions. Sandel believes that agency itself is endangered by this intrasubjective conflict unless the self can sort out its situation and the terms of its situatedness. He never considers the possibility, celebrated by Nietzsche and Arendt, that intrasubjective multiplicity and conflict (recall the many souls of Zarathustra and the remnant of inner resistance that marks Arendtian action) might be spurs to action, sites of agency, important sources of empowerment and power that may be disabled by some coherent subjectivities. Sandel assumes that agency demands particular patterns of coherence and that it postulates particular patterns of ordering for selves and others. For the sake of agency, intrasubjective fissures must be healed.

But the communitarian subject, too often a victim of cognitive dissonance (especially in liberal surroundings), is so plurally and deeply constituted that she cannot heal herself without help. Sandel sees that the constituted self is constituted along so many dimensions of subjectivity that she *cannot* know herself. But this does not lead him to follow Nietzsche in critically reevaluating the project of self-knowledge. Nor does it lead him to follow Arendt in her insistence that introspection as a practice has no part in politics and action. Instead, Sandel rushes to refurbish practices of self-knowledge and introspection and to celebrate them, without reservation, as part of a practice of politics as friendship. He turns the self-transparency that was Rawls's premise and assumption into a goal: it is a fragile achievement that can be won and maintained under certain conditions.

Politics as Friendship

The problem for Sandel's constituted subject is to achieve agency, and the only way that she can do that is by sorting out her relation to her constituting communities. Self-knowledge and self-interpretation are the roads to agency and away from radical situatedness. Because of the depth of its constitutedness, the "challenge to the agent" is "to sort out the limits or the boundaries of the self, to distinguish the subject from its situation and so to forge its identity." This subject is not radically situated because it can exercise and achieve agency by seeking self-understanding. On this account, "the predicament of the self would seem to approach the dispossession described on the *cognitive* account, in which the greater threat to agency is not the distance of the self from its purposes and ends but rather the surfeit of seemingly indispensable aims which only sober self-examination can hope to sort out."[29]

But the agent engaged in this introspection is not alone. In Sandel's communitarian regime self-reflection is an activity taken up by "persons encumbered in part by a history they share with others." Consequently, for the constituted self, knowing oneself is "a less strictly private thing" than it is for the deontological self who necessarily deliberates on its own. "Where seeking my good is bound up with exploring my identity and interpreting my life history, the knowledge I seek is less transparent to me and less opaque to others." Self-reflection becomes deliberation with a friend, a process of "offering and assessing by turns competing descriptions of the person I am, and of the alternatives I face as they bear on my identity." The process is one of discovery and "I may say in retrospect that my friend knew me better than I knew myself."[30] Communitarian friendship reoccupies the site of Rawls's original position: it is a site of politics as deliberation under certain ideal circumstances, ideal because they presuppose and secure the isolation, acknowledgment, and affirmation (but really the production and maintenance) of a morally relevant description of the self.

Here, politics as friendship is empowering, enabling, clarifying. The retrospective glance is grateful, the friendship unambiguous, the processes of exploration and interpretation unthreatening. The agent that stands at the end of the process is discovered, not produced; the friend who helps to identify that agent does so by virtue of an enhanced vision into the soul of the other, not as an expression of his own investment in the production and maintenance of certain kinds or patterns of friendly identities. Here, the friend turns out to be right or, more accurately, to have been right all along. The would-be agent had to come to see that, with the help of his friend.

On this account, the respect that is an integral part of Kantian friendship drops out, and with it goes the secrecy that provides the paradoxical ground for a practice of friendship that Kant values precisely as a privileged site of communication. Relief and the (narcissistic) pleasure of a reflected self-knowledge take the place of the anxiety of discovery that sits at the heart of Kant's account of friendship. Anxiety turns to relief because the communitarian subject yearns more for the closure of a community identity than for the closure of the autonomy so valued by the Kantian subject, and because the world that houses Sandel's communitarian subjects is a safer place than that envisioned by Kant. Kantian friendship ends up as a paradoxical combination of secrecy and communication because Kant rightly sees that the qualities that make for friendship with others, with the other, are the very same ones that make for betrayal. There is no way to have one without the presence of the possibility of the other. Enmity cannot be held outside the bounds of friendship. Sandel, by contrast, disambiguates friendship (as well as community and politics) so that he might rely in safety on its power to diminish the self's opacity.[31]

Sandel's description of the role of friendship in the production and maintenance of agency/identity implies that there can be friendship before agency or, perhaps better, that friendship and agency are dynamically and mutually produced. Either way, there is a problem: how does one identify friends, or distinguish friends from enemies, before one's own identification of oneself as, let us say, a member of one community rather than another? Consider the dilemma facing the subject who is multiply constituted by communities in conflict: what if one is a woman, raised as an orthodox Jew with the concomitant expectation that she will fulfill traditional gender roles and identities while at the same time socialized in a society that espouses gender equality and renegotiates traditional gender roles daily? Which community's members are her friends? Which ones know her better than she knows herself? How could she know if she chose wrongly? Perhaps it is apt to recall in this context the familiar parental refrain when the child begins to assert her identity in opposition to that of her home community: she has "fallen in (as if to a deep well) with the wrong crowd." She has "not been herself" since she met them. "We hardly recognize her, she is so changed." They are "not really her friends." She does not know who her true friends are. Hers is a cognitive failure, not a subversive choice or a moment of clarity or simple resistance. For the sake of her community identity, she is refused even the dignity of being charged with sheer perversity or willfulness. And the community that claims her is disabled from *engaging* the dispositions and dissonances she personifies.[32]

The possibility of falling in with the wrong crowd or of choosing the wrong friends with whom to deliberate about ends and identity problematics raises two problems: first, it implies that choice may be more central to Sandel's cognitive politics than he might otherwise allow; second, if this is the case, it suggests that meaningful choosing might be *postulated* by the practice of friendship, in which case it turns out that agency and even identity (and the distance from ends that makes them possible) are presupposed rather than produced by Sandel's practice of friendship. The closure to which the friendship engagement aspires (as a performative production) turns out to be already harbored within it (as a constative truth), waiting to be discovered. Sandel might respond that, in his communitarian society, one does not choose one's friends, one comes to acknowledge them; perhaps friends are more like family, loved ones who cannot be chosen because one is born to them. This response presupposes the intersubjective conception, but not its intrasubjective other. It minimizes the dilemma of friendship posed by the subject's multiple, even mongrel, and ambivalent constitution. And it ignores the fact that in the case of the intrasubjective conception there is no clear and unproblematic answer to the question, who are my real friends?

Sandel's retreat from the premise of proliferation, his unspoken resumption and privileging of the intersubjective perspective alone, compels politics as friendship to renege on its promises of openness and deliver only on its promise of closure. In *Liberalism and the Limits of Justice*, friendship is packaged as a practice of self-interpretation that offers deeply situated subjects a lever, an opportunity for distancing, reflection, and perspective. Politics as friendship opens up possibilities, it proliferates political subjects, it creates new and potentially important politicizing spaces between subjects and the ends that constitute them, spaces of reflection and critique. These are the spaces that enable agency, on Sandel's account: the communitarian subject, "awash with possible purposes and ends" that threaten "always to engulf it," must "turn its lights inward upon itself" and "inquire into its constituent nature" if it is to be an agent rather than a victim of circumstance.[33] But, as it turns out, Sandel valorizes these new spaces of light, of proliferation, distance, openness, and agency, because they are the necessary conditions of a closure he values above all else, the closure of affirmation, of affirmed identity. Here the object of value and the site of agency is not the fissure but the sealant. Affirmation is the intended product of friendship, the product of a cognitive politics that offers its subjects the deep and sealing fulfillment of closure, the fulfillment that comes from knowing and acknowledging the ends that are constitutively, and now seamlessly, theirs.

The ultimate aim of friendship in Sandel's community politics is to affirm and reinforce identification with community. Sandel tends to neglect this part of the scenario, or to underplay it, but the structure of reinforcement is quite clear if we think about the scenario of friendship and friendly exchange from the vantage point of the occasions of Sandel's politics as friendship. What occasions friendly exchange and self-examination in Sandel's introspective politics as friendship? Why do friends enter into the picture at all? The encounter is occasioned, not by the self's frustrating inability to satisfy all the legitimate but conflicting claims made on it by plural communities, but by some felt rift in identity, a mysterious unease, misidentification, confusion, or opacity in self-knowledge—perhaps, even, a felt resistance. This is when friendship enters. The friend enters to correct (what he insists is) a cognitive failure. At this juncture, when dissonance might become withdrawal or resistance, when the aggravation of fissures might lead to the proliferation of political subjects and subjectivities, friends enter to heal the self, to secure its identity, *and* theirs, to *identify* the subject and supplement it, to provide it with the sealant of a closure that it cannot attain by itself. Sandel relies on languages of openness, distance, and proliferation to sell his product of community closure.[34]

The character of Sandel's practice of friendship as a practice of reinforcement and perpetual reintegration is most visible from the (often dissonant, even discordant) perspective of the intrasubjective conception, a conception Sandel entertains very briefly before allowing it to recede and then disappear from his account. The disappearance allows Sandel to advertise politics as friendship as a source of completion and supplementation that only enables. Sandel does not abandon the intrasubjective conception altogether, however; he cannot afford to. His theory needs, indeed presupposes, the intrasubjective conception to account for politics at all. Only by presupposing the intrasubjective conception can he sustain his claims that the subject starts out "awash with *possible* purposes and ends" and that its identity is "the product rather than the premise of its agency."[35] Moreover, without the dissonance that the intrasubjective conception personifies (as it were), without the pluralism presupposed by Sandel, and without its attendant conflicts, self-reflection is not likely to be a felt need; there would be no adequate, reliable, and meaningful occasion for the deliberation and shared introspection Sandel values. If the self was not multiply and inexhaustively and fractiously constituted, if it was singly, exhaustively, and univocally constituted, it would lapse all too easily from community constitutedness into the radical situatedness Sandel is anxious to fend off. As he knows, radically situated subjects have no call to deliberate about themselves and their ends. Radically situated subjects have no occasions for politics.

But Sandel has to rid himself of the problematic aspects of the intra-subjective conception if it is going to occasion the sort of consolidating politics he seeks without also undermining it. To that end, he implicitly assumes that the multiple ends and identity formations of the intrasubjective conception are susceptible to harmonization and ordering in the right setting, given the right hothouse politics. The mongrel has a pure-bred within it. Without this implicit assumption, Sandel's own intrasubjective conception would be deeply resistant to his own regime's inter-subjective goals.

Morally Deep Questions

Sandel's identification of politics as friendship with the task of harmonization brings him uncomfortably close to Rawlsian practices of self-reflection in opposition to which he delineates his own position. The communitarian subject is a "self-interpreting being," a "person with character" who "knows that he is implicated in various ways even as he reflects and feels the moral weight of what he knows." As evidence that his own conception is morally more substantial than Rawls's, Sandel points out that when the Rawlsian self reflects deliberatively it asks, "What ends shall I choose?" whereas the communitarian subject asks, "Who am I?" The latter question is in Sandel's estimation the more worthy and weighty "paradigmatic moral question." The moral impoverishment of the deontological self is manifest in its narrower "scope for self-reflection." It is "limited" to deliberation about its good in a way that "means no more than attending to wants and desires given directly to [its] awareness." Its agency consists in no more than an "exercise in 'efficient administration'."[36] Sandel presents the deontological self as a shallow chooser, an administrator, in opposition to the deeply deliberative (and professorial?) communitarian subject. But the opposition is tenuous.

First of all, on Rawls's account, the question "What ends shall I choose?" may or may not be a moral question. The paradigmatic moral question for Rawls is "How should we set up institutions that are well-ordered and just?"[37] This question is directed toward the moral end of framing the range of permissible pursuits, moral and otherwise, for members of a shared society. Moreover, given my reading of Rawls, this question is ultimately not terribly different from Sandel's "Who am I?" for the principles chosen in the original position are chosen because they reflect our answer to that question: "We are free and equal beings."

If we follow Sandel to the level of practical, daily life in justice as fairness, the difference he valorizes turns out once again to be tenuous. Although Sandel's self asks the supposedly deeper "Who am I?" whereas Rawls's asks the morally less worthy "What ends shall I choose?", the task for *both* is to efficiently administer an array of given and relatively unproblematic possibilities. Rawls's self chooses its conception of the good in light of its desires and the projects it is capable of realizing given its circumstances and legitimate expectations. Sandel's subject comes to understand who it is by surveying its plural attachments and distinguishing those that are more deeply constitutive of its identity from those that are less so. The plurality of desire and preference that characterizes the Rawlsian self becomes in the communitarian subject a plurality of constitution. The practice of choosing ends becomes a practice of identifying ends, of coming to know which ends are really constitutive of the self as subject. And the practice of ranking preferences becomes a practice of distinguishing deeper from more shallow attachments.

In short, both Rawls and Sandel take a pluralist view of the self's multiplicity. Selves and subjects start out multiply constituted but are amenable to the (self-)organization, administration, or identification each of these theorists advocates. There is no excess that exceeds the ordering that enables the self for certain patterns of life, no resistance engendered by that patterning.

Both the Rawlsian practice of choice and the communitarian practice of cognition take as their point of departure the plurally constituted self, the intrasubjective conception, constituted on the one account by multiple preferences, on the other by competing identities and allegiances. And both assume that these multiplicities need to be hierarchically ordered if the self is to be stabilized (by way of practices of interrogation, introspection, and identification) into coherent agency. But this point of departure destabilizes the opposition between knowing and choosing on which Sandel's critique of Rawls turns. As with the communitarian practice of friendship, knowing oneself cannot be finally distinguished or separated from choosing oneself if one takes seriously (as Sandel initially does, as an initiating move) the (tragic?) perspective of the intrasubjective conception. To know oneself *is* to choose oneself when one is multiply constituted as well as powerfully formed by and implicated in complicated identity and community dynamics. And perhaps Sandel knows this: perhaps this is another reason for his ceasing to take the perspective of the intrasubjective conception seriously. Only by dropping it entirely is he able to secure the distinction between knowing and choosing that is so crucial to his case against Rawls. Knowing is safely and distinctly different from choosing only from the rather more radically situated perspective of the intersubjective conception.

Typically, Sandel moves back and forth between the intersubjective and intrasubjective conceptions. When moved by his need to distinguish his own position from that of the radically situated subject, Sandel proliferates political subjects and perspectives to include that of the intrasubjective conception. But when the perspective of the intrasubjective conception leaves him open to the charge of efficient administration, Sandel moves back to the intersubjective perspective. In the absence of its intrasubjective population, however, the intersubjective conception looks uncomfortably like its radically situated other. Thus, Sandel is driven back into the arms of Rawls by his desire to fend off the specter of radical situatedness (by way of the intrasubjective conception whose plural constitution may protect it from *radical* situatedness but also engenders its need for Rawlsian efficient administration). He then drops the intrasubjective conception (for whom knowing necessarily involves Rawlsian choosing) in order to protect his cognitive politics from looking like Rawls's voluntarist politics.

This back-and-forth movement does not secure Sandel's all-important distinction between knowing and choosing; it advertises the distinction's instability. To stabilize the distinction, and to secure it, Sandel introduces a notion of authenticity. The multiplicity of the subject's constitution is illusory. Beneath it lies a real unity, an authentic (constative) self that holds the whole operation together, that eschews the performativity of self-fashioning in favor of the reassurance of constative self-discovery. Constation relieves the aporetic anxiety of performativity, just as friends relieve the anxiety of the dissonant self regarding its place (or lack thereof) in a community. Unity is the telos of the communitarian subject; the multiplicity so well illustrated by the intrasubjective perspective is merely a due to be paid on the road to closure. The pull of competing identities and allegiances does no more than provide the necessary mise-en-scène for the reward of identity, just as the spooky castle on a hilltop sets the scene for the challenges and resolutions that are the stuff of gothic romance.

The question posed by and to the communitarian subject is not "Who am I?" but rather "Who *am* I, really?"[38] The "really" speaks volumes. As it turns out, there is a right answer to the question—really. Constation comes in to hold the place, to supplement the *aporia* of identity in a plural society and in a plural self. The intrasubjective perspective turns out to be temporary, perhaps morally relevant in certain circumstances but not a moral ideal. This is probably best illustrated by Sandel's own very temporary consideration and subsequent abandonment of the intrasubjective conception in favor of his own intersubjective ideal.[39]

But the intrasubjective conception cannot be so easily abandoned by Sandel. The larger argument of his book is addressed to it throughout; indeed, the book is occasioned by the perspective of the dislocated and conflicted individual. How is the intrasubjective individual to answer the morally deep identity question? Is she supposed simply to pick one of her multiply constituting identities, in Isaiah Berlin's word to "plump" for it? How would she know the truth of one from the falsity of multiple others? Why is she supposed to assume the truth of a oneness in contradistinction to the falsity of an otherness of multiplicity? What if the truth of her competing, multiple identities is that all of them are incomplete, and fractious, each one actually dependent on the others for stability even while it protests that it alone is independent from and antagonistic to them? What if no single one of this subject's competing identities is self-sufficient and complete enough to stand on its own even if chosen to do so sincerely and knowledgeably? What if her multiplicity is not only a site of conflict but also a site of supplementation, of mutual, reciprocal support? What if intrasubjective conflict is the truth of her identity, and the rifts in her subjectivity the sites of her agency, not obstacles to it? Perhaps there is no identity so perfect, so seamless, so well-fitted to her that she could wear it, be it, perform and live it without resentment, without sadness, without yearning, without guilt, hatred, and even violence.

I pose these questions to highlight the supplementary work done in Sandel's scheme by a powerful set of speculative and contestable assumptions about the self and its relationship to itself and others in the mode of subjectivity.[40] Is there no political community capable of building on the premise of the perpetual inadequacy of identities to the task we assign them? Is it not possible to envision a set of arrangements that valorizes positive possibilities in the experience of dissonance in subjectivity, rather than valorize exclusively the good fortune of harmony and self-realization?

Sandel's response to this imagined dissonant subject is to represent her within his intrasubjective conception in which the subject is multiply constituted by several univocal and self-sustaining identities. This strategy allows him to treat the problem of dissonance as if it were merely a pluralist's dilemma. Identity itself is left untouched, healthy and univocal, even in the face of an intrasubjective dissonance. And this strategy leaves Sandel with a solution: the multiply constituted subject is advised to deny her multiplicity or to overcome it by coming to know (or picking) one (healthy and univocal, complete, and self-sufficient) identity as really hers and assimilating the others to that core identity, while rejecting those that resist assimilation. If the subject has trouble identifying her core identity, that is because she has turned to the wrong friends, fallen in with a bad crowd, spoken in the wrong language, or mistaken someone else's community for her own. This strategy treats her felt multivocality as at best epiphenomenal, at worst, her personal failure or perhaps her community's cognitive or political failure.

Consider, by contrast, Zarathustra's answer to Sandel's identity question: "I am who I must be; I call myself Zarathustra." Zarathustra refuses to answer the question in a single voice, with a single soul. His response unites the determinism or nonnegotiability of a constation with a celebration of performativity. His response is ambiguous, situated between terms and between categories, uncertain, tense, yet confident and self-aware. It turns down the volume on the "really" raised previously by the communitarian listener. "I am who I must be," a subject constituted by languages, conventions, practices, and powers; "I call myself Zarathustra," an agent capable of maneuvering creatively, innovatively, performatively, through the givenness of human life. It is not a response of bifurcation but rather of negotiation, continual, multiple, complex, and ongoing.

The ease with which Sandel slides from plural constitution to the naturalized constation of a unified identity illustrates the failure of even his intrasubjective conception to capture the dissonance, the multiplicity and excess, that forever haunts the formation of subjectivity and prevents it from achieving the closure to which it aspires. Sandel assumes that any lack of closure in the identity of the subject comes from a multiplicity that is exterior, from an environmental, plural constitutedness that, if sorted out in the right setting, in a better environment, can be uncovered to disclose an underlying and authentic and enabling unity. It is from this perspective that he criticizes Rawls for establishing "the priority of plurality over unity," claiming that, although "the principle of unity has an important place in justice as fairness, . . . it is not essential to our nature in the same way" plurality is. According to Sandel, Rawls locates conflict and the circumstances of justice in the nature of human subjectivity, whereas unity and commonality are treated as the "happy accident[s] of their circumstances." Sandel prefers to opt for a principle of unity that is "essential to our nature" and for an account wherein *conflict* is an "[un]happy accident," one that befalls communities from some outside, some extracommunity source.[41]

It is precisely against exteriorizing strategies and assumptions like these that Nietzsche invokes *virtù* and its antipathy to system and closure. No identity, no formation of subjectivity, can complete the self or constitute it univocally, expressively, or even plurally without engendering resistance to itself. *Virtù* is one of the perspectives from which the fissures in the would-be system of subjectivity can be identified and even aggravated. For Nietzsche, the virtue theorist's will to coherence is a will to closure, a will to efficient administration, a will that is antivital, a will that wills not.

The same is true of Arendt, who takes *virtù* to politics by way of her identification of action with virtuosity. On her account, the performative action whereby political communities constitute and reconstitute themselves episodically occurs in the very spaces that defy or resist the closure of administration, morality, behavior, nature, subjectivity, and identity. Were identity to cohere in the way valorized by Sandel, it would mean the end of politics, and the end of agency, because it would mean that political action would be unable to do the very thing Arendt counts on it to do: to disrupt the ordinary, to disappoint the will to efficient administration, to dislodge naturalized coherences, to give birth to the world anew. For Arendt, agency and action take place in the fissures that frustrate system, in the incoherences that so madden communitarians. As we saw in Chapter 4, Arendt rejects the view that political communities ought to constitute themselves on the basis of a shared and stable identity because identity-based foundings and maintenances, just like those based in the constation of god, truth, or natural law, threaten to close the spaces of politics, to homogenize or repress the plurality and multiplicity that political action postulates.[42]

A *virtù* theory of politics is devoted to preserving these sites of power, to resisting the urge to close them off with the supplementation of friendship, community, and identity. It locates spaces of politics in the nonidentity, the heterogeneity of political communities, and also in the resistances of the self to the normalizing constructions of subjectivity. It treats the self's agonistic ill-fittedness as a source of the generation of power, a signal that there are sites from which to generate alternative performativities and proliferate political subjects. For the sake of politics, it prefers these practices of generation and proliferation to those that affirm existing identities in a communitarian politics of reintegration.

From a *virtù* perspective, Sandel's initial premise of proliferation is promising. From the same perspective, his subsequent retreat to the primacy of community is disappointing. The proliferation of political subjects and subjectivities is an important component of any *virtù* theory of politics because proliferation, the continual augmentation and amendment of identities, subjectivities, and even sexualities, keeps the contest of identities going. It makes it more difficult for identities to sediment into the comfort and security of constation, it makes it harder for performativities to become naturalized, it actively discourages and contests the ascendance of any identity to hegemony in a political order. The perpetual proliferation of identities heightens our awareness of the strategies of power and discipline to which identity-based politics resort in order to achieve closure. And it enables a *virtù* politics to acknowledge dissonance, to politicize it, and to relax the insistence that otherness in the self and others in the community be assimilated, rejected, or punished in the name of a politics and a way of life that is good, rational, right, or simply (but not more benignly) "ours."

Morally Deep Answers

There is hardly a political question in the United States which does not sooner or later turn into a juridical one.

—Alexis de Tocqueville

There is no more powerful testimony to Sandel's retreat from his initial premise of proliferation, no more powerful illustration of the distance that divides *virtù* from virtue theories of politics, than Sandel's provocative discussion of the state's regulation of sodomy, sexuality and pornography, focusing on *Bowers v. Hardwick*, a privacy case that challenged Georgia's sodomy legislation.[43] The Supreme Court majority rejected the challenge; only the dissenters recognized a right to privacy that protects sodomy, based on the good of voluntarist choice. Sandel argues that voluntarism, liberalism's closest approximation of a conception of the good, is not robust enough to secure a proper respect for the other and that his own "substantive" (no longer "communitarian") approach can do better.

To make his case against voluntarism, Sandel surveys American case law on the right to privacy from *Griswold v. Connecticut* to *Bowers* and argues that the Court's grounding of the right to privacy shifted from a substantive to a voluntarist base. The "right to be free of governmental interference in matters of marriage, for example," has come to be defended in "the name of individual choice," but precedent shows (particularly in the closing paragraphs of *Griswold* but also in the dissent of *Poe v. Ullman*) that, historically, it has also been defended "in the name of the intrinsic value or social importance of the practice it protects." Sandel argues that the dissenters in *Bowers* would have done better to argue for the protection of "homosexual intimacies" on the basis of "the human goods they share with intimacies the Court already protects" instead of arguing in terms of individual right and claiming that "much of the richness of a relationship will come from the freedom an individual has to *choose* the form and nature of those intensely personal bonds."[44]

The problem is that "the voluntarist conception of privacy limits the range of reasons for protecting privacy." Once again, it seems that Sandel's goal is to proliferate political sites, subjects, and strategies. And, once again, the impulse to proliferate is short-lived. Sandel unmasks the false minimalism of liberal practice, showing that some alternative, desirable conceptions of the good are excluded by it, but he does this to secure space for a single substantive alternative that in his view is better able to secure the right to privacy. The substantive alternative justifies the right to privacy not as an individualistic good of free choice but "in the name of the intrinsic value or social importance of the practice" in question.[45]

In the Court's early right-to-privacy decisions, as in *Griswold*, privacy was "accorded constitutional protection in cases that spoke of the sanctity of marriage and procreation." Sandel suggests that "that may not be accidental. . . . only later did the Court abstract privacy rights from these practices and protect them without reference to the human goods they were once thought to make possible. This suggests that the voluntarist justification of privacy rights is dependent—politically as well as philosophically—on some measure of agreement that the practices protected are morally permissible."[46]

But the court's early references to substantive goods are susceptible to a different reading, one that shares Sandel's sensitivity to the dependence that structures the relation between voluntarist and substantive justification without exaggerating the role substantive considerations play in the justification process. After all, *Griswold* appealed mainly to voluntarism; substantive considerations were introduced only in the closing paragraph of the decision. And the dual appeal suggests not that the substantive justification did the real work that needed to be done or that the substantive justification provides the firm ground on which the unsteady voluntarist justification stands; it suggests that the basis of privacy rights was more essentially contested in the early cases than in the later ones.

It might suggest something else as well: perhaps neither voluntarist nor substantive justification is adequate to the task at hand. Perhaps, just as the impossible superimposition of constative on performative utterance secured the Declaration of Independence, so the right of privacy is entrenched in an impossible, unholy union of substantive and voluntarist goods in which the true identity of the wedded couple—substantive or voluntarist?—is finally undecidable.

Sandel, however, like Arendt before him, sees no undecidability here. In *Griswold*, "the justification for the right was not voluntarist but unabashedly teleological; The privacy the Court vindicated was not for the sake of letting people lead their sexual lives as they choose, but rather for the sake of affirming and protecting the social institution of marriage."[47] He dismisses the ambiguity, the structured dualism of the decision. Intent on identifying the authentic *essences* of this case (*Griswold*) and of this practice (of privacy rights) he opposes their *essential* features to those that are merely incidental or accidental. Of the Court's two justifications of privacy, he privileges the substantive justification as essential; the voluntarist justification is inessential, even dispensable. With regard to the right of privacy, he says that it is not accidental that it was first "accorded constitutional protection in cases that spoke of the sanctity" of morally valued practices like "marriage and procreation." It is, instead, essential. Like the friends who participate in the practices of introspection and identification that constitute his politics as friendship, Sandel himself, informally a friend of the Court, sets out to rescue the cherished practice of privacy rights from the confusions of its multiple histories, rituals, and justifications by discovering and enacting (in law and in practice) its true and authentic identity. That true identity turns out to be its entrenchment in a social (not individual or voluntarist), sanctified good; all individualist and voluntarist justifications of privacy are discarded as unsanctified imposters. As with the identification of the communitarian subject, so too with the identification of this substantive practice: features of the practice that do not fit its identity, and even occlude it, are exteriorized. They can now be seen for what they really are: "accidental" complications, confusions, or mistakes.[48]

With the identity of substantive and communitarian practices and subjects thus cocooned, however, their purity is no less protected, nor any less fabulous, than that of their archrival, liberal neutrality. Once again Sandel leaves himself open to the very charge he lodges against Rawls: his communitarian subject is no more open than the removed Rawlsian self to "transformation by experience" and "growth."[49] Subjects and practices that grow and change, whose virtue it is that they go through transformations, are best studied from the vantage point of genealogy, not from an essentialist and essentializing perspective. By treating them in an essentialist way, Sandel makes subjects and practices invulnerable to experiential transformation even while he celebrates and makes a virtue of their supposed vulnerability to the world and to worldliness.

Sandel's essentialism occludes the possibility that *Griswold* and the practice of privacy rights have no true, single, and univocal identity or ground. He never confronts the possibility that this case and this practice are the products of a complex, layered, conflicted, and aporetic genealogy. This never confronted possibility is the same one left out of his account of the true, univocal identity of the communitarian subject. Throughout his work, Sandel leaves out of contention another powerful way of reading cases, practices, and subjectivities, one that treats the curious coincidence of fractious, conflicted, and layered justifications, allegiances, and identities as symptomatic of the perpetual inadequacy of every identity, precedent, and interpretation to secure itself exhaustively and thereby rid itself of its need for supplementation, augmentation, and amendment. From this other perspective, it is unsurprising to find a curious appeal to human goods at the very end of *Griswold:* the sanctity of marriage comes in to hold and to supplement the place of the last instance, the place that god, or sanctity, or essence, *always* occupies.[50]

Sandel looks to marriage and its sanctity to do more than fill a supplementary need. As a prized social institution, marriage (or "heterosexual union") has the power to redeem the other, to give the other the ontological standing necessary to be treated juridically as a bearer of a right to privacy. According to Sandel, the inclusion of the other can and ought to be justified by appeal to the "human goods that homosexual intimacy may share with heterosexual unions" or by demonstrating the distinctive worthiness of this alternative way of life.[51] Note that both justifications depend on highlighting the respects in which the other is like "us." Distinctive worth cannot be assessed from too great a distance or too dissonant a perspective. Failing to make use of these justifications, the dissenters in *Bowers* provided the majority with an opportunity and excuse to ridicule Hardwick's petition, to attribute to him the claim that he had a "fundamental right to engage in homosexual sodomy" and to dismiss that claim as absurd.[52]

Either the other is like "us" or he is "other." Either-or. If he is like us, he gets to share in the goods of our community, which include the right to privacy. If he cannot be *likened* to "us," *made like* "us," then he is rightly the object of ridicule.[53] According to Sandel, the great virtue of his position is that it would "win for homosexuals more than a thin and fragile toleration." It would win for them "a fuller respect" and, "if not admiration, at least some appreciation of the lives homosexuals live."[54] What Sandel does not say is that, since the lives led by homosexuals are as heterogeneous as those led by heterosexuals, this fuller respect could be accorded only to some, to those whose homosexual relationships are intimate in ways that are recognizable to "us" and can be likened to those "we" value as a culture. But the majority of male homosexuals might fail the test of his standard of intimacy, if, as Richard Mohr points out, "traditionally the majority of male homosexual encounters have been impersonal."[55] Sandel's new economy of toleration and respect has a serious, structural inequity at its core: it includes some homosexuals on the basis of their likeness to a standard set by a dominant heterosexual and heterosexist culture. As a result, toleration extends to a much wider variety of heterosexual relations (and even encounters) than to homosexual ones because the varieties of heterosexual difference are less threatening to "us" as heterosexuals. As Rawls might say, their nature is their good fortune (as well as ours).[56]

Just as for Kant, so too for Sandel: the object of respect is not difference but sameness. The enhanced respect and appreciation Sandel envisions is not for the other as other but for the other insofar as he is the same. The effect is to divest the other of his power to destabilize established practices, conventions, and values. The other is worthy only if he can be seen to support the dominant moral, cultural, and political sys tem. The other is included only if he will let us remake him in our own (undistorted) image. If he denies that this image is his essence or acts in ways that inhibit our essentializing needs (as most gay males do, according to Mohr), if he rejects the enlistment of his "assets or life prospects" into this community service, then respect, appreciation, and full juridical protection will all be denied to him. In short, the price of Sandel's broader and deeper toleration is a broader and deeper intolerance. Its insistence on sameness *produces* the repugnance for difference and otherness it seeks to overcome.

Sandel's standard of intimacy has a lot in common with the sodomy laws it opposes. Both regulate sexuality for the purposes of consolidating and privileging particular forms of association. And both maintain the associations they privilege by opposing them to a spectral other who is not at all like "us." The opposition stabilizes the identity, the traditional family or intimate association, that cannot stabilize itself.

The dynamic is clearest in Sandel's discussion of *Stanley v. Georgia*, a pornography case in which the Supreme Court upheld the right to view obscene materials privately, at home.[57] In *Stanley*, the argument for toleration "was wholly independent of the value or importance of the thing being tolerated." Likewise in *People v. Onofre*, in which the Court concluded that if *Stanley* protected privacy for sexual gratification with obscene materials then surely privacy ought to extend to homosexuals whose conduct "once was commonly regarded as 'deviant' conduct." Sandel's critique of liberal neutralism is animated by his objection to this comparison. The "case for toleration that brackets the morality of homosexuality has a powerful appeal," but "the analogy with *Stanley* tolerates homosexuality at the price of demeaning it." The comparison "puts homosexual intimacy on a par with obscenity—a *base thing*," and it takes the interest at stake to be the impoverished "sexual gratification" rather than intimacy, its rich and enriching alternative. The respect and appreciation Sandel valorizes does not extend to pornography and its consumers. They are other. And they are other so that some homosexuals might become the same.[58]

In Sandel's account, pornography's consumers reoccupy the site of deviant conduct so that homosexuality might occupy the site of normal or worthy behavior. Unlike homosexuals, consumers of pornography are opaque; we are completely unable to discern the contours of our own image and values there. "The only intimate relationship at stake in *Stanley* was between a man and his pornography," Sandel says.[59] And ridicule, apparently, is the only voice with which members of Sandel's community speak to the truly other. It seems that the Court's mistake in *Bowers* was to treat homosexuality as other. It made *no* mistake in addressing the other sarcastically and dismissively. It made no mistake in thinking that it was within its provenance to regulate sexuality and define sexual pleasure.

These powers of regulation and definition are the very ones Sandel calls on the Court to exercise. The standards he favors are different from those on which the Court relies, but that difference is not significant. To compare the homosexual relations of *Bowers* to the marital relations endorsed in *Griswold*, Sandel invents a new standard: dropping *Griswold's* reference to the good of procreation (it, apparently is not an essential part of the essence of the decision), he draws solely on the Court's reference to intimacy (abstracting that from its marital context) and dismisses one long-standing ground for the otherness of homosexuality, its character as a form of nonreproductive sexual pleasure. Replacing the good of procreation with the good of intimacy makes homosexuality's nonreproductivity irrelevant. Intimacy is the new standard that all heretofore "deviant conduct" must meet if it is to be included under the sign of the same. Now it is no longer Hardwick but Stanley who is the other.[60] What remains unchanged, however, is the state's role as the authorized definer and arbiter of a distinction between sexual behavior that is merely and (therefore) dangerously erotic and sexual behavior that is socially important or intrinsically worthwhile (if not reproductive, then at least productive and useful). What remains unchanged is the reliance on standards of social importance and intrinsic worth to re-mark a variety of erotic pleasures as illicit. Practices of intimacy support the communitarian ideal to which Sandel aspires. Eroticism, especially as figured by private, stay-at-home consumers of "base" pornography like Stanley, does not.[61]

Sandel implies that his own argument is based on "some measure of [moral] agreement"[62] but his mere assertion of likeness between heterosexual and homosexual intimacy cannot by itself reverse existing patterns of heterosexist discrimination (or substitute for an investigation of them); nor, at a theoretical level, can it contain the motion of likening in one direction (to include Hardwick) and prevent it from proliferating to others (to include Stanley). Surely there are grounds on which Stanley's penchant for pornography could also be likened to the dominant culture's sexual norms and expectations (perhaps if he and his wife partook together?). The unidirectionality Sandel's account simply assumes needs to be defended with an independent argument, but Sandel does not offer one. That independent argument would have to invoke a difference between eroticism and intimacy (between "base" sexual gratification and the goods of marriage), a difference Sandel presupposes in his readings of *Griswold* and *Bowers* but never theorizes. It would have to endorse a Hegelian philosophy of history in order to justify the deployment of particular social institutions, like marriage, as normative standards to which all newcomers must measure up. And, finally, it might address another problematic unidirectionality that pervades, directs, and indeed safeguards Sandel's position throughout: it might try to explain why his essentializing gaze is so thoroughly panoptic, always moving from the (fictive) center of the "we" outward, and never back again.

What line of defense secures Sandel against the reflection of reflection? On his account, to engage with the other in a communitarian or substantive way is to discern patterns of the same in the other (or to fail in the attempt). The subsequent conversion of the other under the sign of the same consolidates this otherwise fleeting image. What we do not see from Sandel's perspective, through his gaze, is the other as an embodiment of a dissonance that is also in ourselves. We do not see patterns of otherness inside the same. The other remains outside, always (daily reinstalled) beyond the pale.

"When politics goes well," Sandel says, "we may know a good in common that we could not know alone."[63] When politics goes that well, though, it is because the other, among us and in us, is being converted, suppressed, recognized, ejected, punished, or reintegrated into the fold. When politics goes that well it is because it is no longer political, it has been converted into a juridical, administrative practice that oversees (and is produced by) an economy of identification whose currency is that of a relentlessly categorizing friendship and enmity.

The *virtù* theorist responds with a call to rouse "enmity toward order," to affirm the difference/otherness that frustrates virtue theorists' will to system and highlights the violence and ridicule to which virtue theories are driven in their frustration. As an antidote, a *virtù* theory might theorize a respect for the other precisely insofar as she is other and *not* the same. Respect for the other might follow from our indebtedness to it for disabusing us of the notion that dominant identities have achieved the reassuring closure and univocality to which they and we aspire. The other awakens differences and resistances within us, inviting us to experience as contingencies the identities and proclivities that constitute us so deeply that we often experience them as natural. Hence Madonna's recent dare: "Every man, at least once in his life, should have another man's tongue in his mouth."[64] The other disrupts. And for this the *virtù* theorist is indebted to the other, the enemy who is also a friend.

The debt turns on a prior commitment to a politics that rejects a will to system and puts in its stead a politics of augmentation and amendment, a democratic and democratizing politics that accords magnanimity and gratitude to the other who spurs its practices of personal and institutional augmentation. It turns on an affirmation of the impossibility of closure and the celebration of the (sometimes precarious and often exhausting) perpetuity of political contest and agonistic engagement with the other within and among us. It turns on a commitment to live life without the assurance that ours is the right, good, holy, or rational way to live. Indeed, because no way of life can constitute itself so exhaustively that all remnants of the other are expelled, it renders much more complicated and tenuous the identification of a way of life as "ours."

It suggests that the real challenge posed by the other is not whether or how to convert, tolerate, protect, or reject those who are not the same, but how to deal with difference, with those who resist categorization as same or other. What if the other is not that which is already established as not "us," as Sandel assumes. What if, instead, it is that which *resists* the binary categorization of same versus other, friend versus enemy? What if it is neither—and both? Perhaps the real outrage of the other is not its unlikeness to "us" but its undecidability, the fact that it calls attention to the *processes* that produce and consolidate difference and otherness into comfortable binary categories of friend or enemy, straight or gay, intimate or promiscuous.

Sandel allows Hardwick to surface so that we might decide *through him* whether homosexuality is same or other. Is he to be tolerated or ridiculed? We need to know. Eccentrics like Rawls's grass counter are interrogated: is it their nature to be this way? We *need* to know. Otherwise we risk the destabilization of the same, a way of life that is maintained through eternally recurrent patterns of identification that are as relentless and unforgiving in Rawls's justice as fairness (both early and later) as they are in Sandel's communitarian setting.

Perhaps there ought to be a fourth relevant description of subjectivity that addresses the othernesses that are not reducible to the stranger but are instead the excess, the ill-fitted, the remainder, that which escapes and resists the standard frame of political subjectivities. This last form of otherness is acknowledged by the *virtù* theorist as she calls for the proliferation of political subjectivities across lines of gender, race, friendship, and sexuality in the hope that it might dislodge the entrenched binaries that engender, and are symptomatic of, ways of life without largesse and politics without magnanimity. In contrast to Sandel's short-lived attempts, a more relentless strategy of proliferation might really contribute to "a fuller respect" for and an enhanced appreciation of the contingency and multivocality that mark every being, every life, every body, even those that fit relatively comfortably into the form of their subjectivity. It might be harder for some to live without the knowledge that their way of life is right, rational, or fair, but it would not be harder for others. It might be difficult to live life this way because it would mean living more politically. To live life more politically is to live with undecidability and proliferation (two sides of the same coin); it is to commit to the project of denaturalizing and deconstructing concretized identities, to rouse enmity toward the orders that vouchsafe them, and to expose the power, violence, cruelty, and arrogance in their resolutions. All this for the sake of a way of life that might never escape these problematics but would at least engage them and might succeed therefore in engendering them a little less insistently, a little less predictably, a little less successfully, maybe a little less violently.

The Rawlsian Supplement

If anything, Rawls's amendments of his position in a series of articles since the publication of *A Theory of Justice* have moved him closer to his communitarian and substantive critics. The rationalism and universalism of the early work are chastened as Rawls relocates the account of justice from an allegedly unsituated original position to the more explicitly situated context of dominant aspects of modern American political culture. His recent method is not unlike Sandel's. He too surveys some of the practices, beliefs, judicial decisions, and conceptions of the good that make up American political culture, examining them with an essentializing gaze, seeking the nuggets of overlap on which a "we" might build a collective life that is founded on something more (something better, deeper, more secure) than a mere Hobbesian modus vivendi.

But the basic elements of Rawls's conception of politics remain unchanged. The scheme is still predisposed to reconciliation rather than politicization, consolidation rather than disruption, the achievement of fittedness rather than a perpetual augmentation. There are, however, three moments in the later work that may appear to respond to some of the concerns *virtù* raises, and I address them by way of three questions. Does Rawls's shift to a political conception of justice make a difference to the *virtù* critic for whom his early work was not political enough? Is his new conception of the self as citizen more compatible with the *virtù* theorist's account of the self? Does his recent recognition that "there is no social world without loss" indicate a new sensitivity to the *virtù* theorist's concerns about the tendency of particular practices to sediment into naturalized identities that remainder others?[65]

When Rawls says that justice as fairness is political he means that it is "not metaphysical." For Rawls, "political" is a negational adjective; a political conception is a partial conception that does not commit its adherents to a comprehensive vision of the good. Rawls's later conception is not political in the sense that it politicizes its citizens and calls on them to augment and amend the terms of their constitution as subjects and citizens.[66] Nor is it political in the sense that it alerts subjects to the significance of power in the consolidation of their institutions, identities, and practices, both public and private.

Indeed, one of the merits of his theory of justice, according to Rawls, is that it presupposes no particular conception of self as subject and is compatible with a variety of forms of subjectivity. In *A Theory of Justice*, Rawls claimed that "embedded in the principles of justice there is an ideal of the person that provides an Archimedean point for judging the basic structure of society."[67] Fourteen years later, in an oblique response to Sandel's critique of that ideal of the person, Rawls moves not to more neutral but to a more plural, proliferating ground:

> If we look at the presentation of justice as fairness and note how it is set up and note the ideas and conceptions it uses, no particular metaphysical doctrine about the nature of persons, distinctive and opposed to other doctrines, appears among its premises, or seems required by its argument. If metaphysical presuppositions are involved, perhaps they are so general that they would not distinguish between the distinctive metaphysical views—Cartesian, Leibnizian, Kantian: realist, idealist, or materialist— with which philosophy has traditionally been concerned.[68]

Justice as fairness is ecumenical; it does presuppose a conception of the person but one that is not "opposed to other doctrines." It is not neutral, exactly, but neither is it controversial. It is general.

But Rawls's amended conception of the person is not so general (how could it be?) as to be compatible also with a *virtù* conception of the self as subject. Rawls constructs a metaphysically general conception of the self through which to envision a quite determinate set of virtues, the set of "cooperative virtues" that a "constitutional regime" requires. He envisions those cooperative virtues as vehicles through which principles of justice "are embodied in human character and [enabled to] regulate political and social life."[69] The well-ordered self becomes the cooperative and self-regulating good citizen, the dissonant self is transformed into the uncooperative subject, and the parts of the self that resist the formation of subjectivity are stabilized into vices of noncooperation. Because this regime institutionalizes cooperation by bracketing all rational and foreseeable *causes* of noncooperation, there is still no room from the regime's perspective (and that is the perspective from which Rawls writes) to envision itself as the producer of those noncooperative selves and subjects; nor does it understand itself to be indebted to them; nor can it imagine any grounds on which to affirm them or the contests they engender as the conditions of a positive possibility; nor, therefore, can it call for their proliferation (in their positivity).

Rawls's proliferation stops here, prior to or apart from any consideration of subjectivity from a *virtù* perspective. The dissonant subjectivities, the multiplicity of selves, bodies, and sexualities that are highlighted from a *virtù* point of view, must all in his view be part of a private realm pluralism lest they complicate the order and the system of cooperation and closure that he seeks for his administrative politics. His later move to an overlapping consensus can be read as part of this pattern insofar as it aims to achieve "compliance by a *concordant fit* between the political conception and general and comprehensive doctrines together with the public recognition of the very great value of the political virtues."[70]

The effect of that concordant fit, Rawls concedes, is that some forms of life will "die out." But, he concludes, this does not compromise the justice or neutrality of his political conception. Citing Isaiah Berlin and Bernard Williams, Rawls says that "there is no social world without loss." No social arrangement can achieve a "neutrality of effect or influence"; that "is an impracticable aim."[71] For Rawls, this is not a political issue; it is a fact of (Darwinian) life. No *virtù* theorist would disagree with the latter claim. But, pace Rawls, the struggle within and among social worlds is internal to political and juridical institutions. The facts of the struggle are political facts; they are the effects and manifestations of power; the quality of the struggle and its outcome will vary depending on the institutions that structure and mediate it; it will depend on those institutions' attitudes toward struggle in political life.

Rawls's strategy here, as in his early work, is to reconcile subjects to the fact of loss rather than to politicize it. If there is no social world without loss, then the fact that justice as fairness cannot support and sustain every form of life does not pose a problem for it. But, as we saw in Chapter 5, justice as fairness is not a neutral bystander in a Darwinian struggle for survival. And its repeated attempts to occupy that role of neutrality are themselves political; they shape the practice of power (and punishment) in the regime.

Left out of Rawls's account is an alternative, more politicizing posture toward loss, one that treats lost forms of life as remainders. This alternative challenges the tendencies of regimes to stabilize certain practices and subjectivities by opposing them to others against whom they are defined and by discouraging the politicizations necessary to keep plural possibilities alive. On this alternative account, punishment and the construction of criminality are highlighted as the effects of a social need rather than as epiphenomenal, prepolitical facts of life. Rawls's construction of remainders as losses once again removes juridical institutions from any active role in or responsibility for the construction of subjectivity. It justifies social or cultural losses at the outset, marking them as the unavoidable costs of any form of human association. There is cause for lament here, Rawls says, but not for struggle. Another potential site of political contest is closed.

Throughout, Rawls seems unaware or untroubled by the fact that his political liberalism maintains itself by daily displacing politics and contestation, by devoting itself primarily to the simple and depoliticized processes of ordering commitments, settling ambivalences, clarifying confusions, and maintaining the concordant fit that is the necessary condition of this regime's positive possibility. Throughout, Rawls is guided only by the bright side of the settlement he seeks to achieve, to identify with us, and to seal with that closure of identification. And no wonder: that settlement promises to satisfy a deep yearning, a yearning for peace and quiet, for the privacy and withdrawal so many liberals have sought throughout the history of liberal thinking.

To that end, Rawls vies with Sandel over who shall be the authorized reader of American political culture. From a *virtù* perspective, it is unsurprising that the positions of these two adversaries should have converged; they were susceptible to a quite damaging likening all along.

Indeed, the terms of their opposition were secured by the need of each to construct his version of the same in opposition to the other. From a perspective that calls precisely that binary into question, in this case, a *virtù* perspective, the opposition between Rawls and Sandel begins to look more like an alliance, one whose success has been the exclusion and marginalization of destabilizing perspectives and characters such as those that I have tried to imagine and give voice to here.

CHAPTER SEVEN

Renegotiating Positions:
Beyond the Virtue-*Virtù* Opposition

The disturbing suggestion, made by Machiavelli [was] that since [*virtù*] was action, it must sooner or later alter the conditions on which it rested and so render itself impossible.

—J. G. A. Pocock

Ethics used to be a coercive, customary manner of ensuring the cohesiveness of a particular group through the repetition of a code—a more or less accepted apologue. Now, however, the issue of ethics crops up whenever a code (mores, social contract) must be shattered in order to give way to the free play of negativity, need, desire, pleasure, jouissance, before being put together again, although temporarily and with full knowledge of what is involved.

—Julia Kristeva

In my effort to subvert some of the established, oppositional positionings in contemporary political thought, I have developed another opposition, between virtue and *virtù*, and positioned myself on one side of it. I have spent the previous six chapters stabilizing that opposition so as to render it a better lever of destabilization. The binary oppositions and adjectival pairs have added up beneath the respective columns of virtue and *virtù* theories of politics: consolidation versus disruption, community versus dissonance, closure versus fissures, stability versus eventfulness, containment versus proliferation, settlement versus unsettlement, reconciliation versus politicization, administration/technique versus politics. The lever of destabilization *virtù* provides is enabled by this stabilizing series of oppositions, a series that is itself vulnerable to subversion, to the disruptions of *virtù*.

The perspective of *virtù* provides a lens through which to isolate and exaggerate certain features of politics and political thought. In particular, it highlights the strategies of consolidation that virtue theorists of politics deploy and the will to order that structures the demands of their theoretical systems. But, once again, the *virtù* perspective is vulnerable to the same charges: it itself is an instrument of consolidation. I have spent the past few hundred pages organizing theorists as diverse and multivocal as Kant, Rawls, and Sandel into the category of "virtue theorists of politics," selecting particular features of their views as central, thrusting others into the background, finessing resistances and excesses so that the virtue aspects of their views stand out more sharply. The same practices are responsible for the production of Nietzsche and Arendt as *virtù* theorists. There is nothing illicit in any of this. Reading is never innocent or passive; it is an engagement, constructive and productive, a practice of knowledge that is never freed of power. Better, then, not to pretend otherwise, better to conclude by acknowledging and engaging the fact that the *virtù* theory of politics developed here maintains itself partly by relying on strategies of consolidation and opposition that it tends to identify with virtue theories and of which it tends to be quite critical.

I raise these issues and concerns because the very categories that set things in motion at the outset of this project now threaten to sediment into problematic patterns of their own. In an effort to offset that tendency, I conclude by reassessing the role of *virtù* as a distinct *alternative* to virtue. What if virtue and *virtù* represent not two distinct and self-sufficient options but two aspects of political life? What if they signal two coexisting and conflicting impulses, the desire to decide crucial undecidabilities for the sake of human goods that thrive most vigorously in stable, predictable settings, and the will to contest established patterns, institutions, and identities for the sake of the remainders engendered by their patternings and for the sake of the democratic possibilities endangered by their petrifications?

The partiality of my governing categories may explain why none of the theories examined here exemplifies the position of virtue or *virtù* without remainder. Nietzsche's and Arendt's accounts both had to be radicalized before they could serve as stable markers of the *virtù* position. The dissonance engendering perspectivism or politicization endorsed by these theorists is aimed at some established settlements, but not at all of them. Each relegates social and economic issues to the herd and to the *oikos*, sites of closure, the fantastic products of powerful forces of normalization amid the sheer massness of modern society. Each looks elsewhere for sites of contest. My characterization of Nietzsche and Arendt as *virtù* theorists depends partly on my treatment of their essentializing claims about bodies and the herd as claims about aspects of subjectivity in modernity and not as claims about modern subjects tout court. The metaphorization resists the closures they assume, proliferating spaces of political and perspectival possibility beyond the public-private distinction, beyond the potential binary of overman and herd.

The partial, arbitrary, and indeterminate character of the categories of virtue and *virtù* can be further illustrated by reversing my first readings of an exemplar of each one. Surely there is a case to be made for reading Arendt, for example, as a virtue theorist of politics and Rawls as a *virtù* theorist?[1] A reading of Arendt that highlighted the nonnegotiability of her public-private distinction and the refusal of her actors to engage private realm identities or resist the private realm's rather broad moments of irresistibility could well conclude that hers is a virtue theory of politics. It might point out that, whereas *virtù* claims to rouse "enmity toward order, toward the lies that are concealed in *every* order, institution, actuality," Arendt herself assigns unsettling practices, like politics, to a rather narrow set of sites and objects, insisting that politics stay there lest it disturb the reassuring identities and roles, the predictabilities, of daily life. Fearful that "total politics" would be "like living without the ground on which we stand,"[2] Arendt does not politicize the private realm; instead, she reconciles us to its determinations, constructs, and closures and to the public-private distinction that keeps them safe. Too much uncertainty would be unbearable: that is the virtue theorist's worry about *virtù* and it is Arendt's concern about action.[3]

To read Arendt as a virtue theorist is to take her word for what and where political action is instead of tracking (as I do) its transgressive movements in her own texts, in her own disciplined accounts of action and its boundaries. The excesses of Arendtian action, if they did call themselves to the reader's attention, would be explained as errors, moments of inattention in an otherwise beautifully rigorous account, slippages that do not compromise the integrity of Arendt's distinctions, accidents that befall her pristine categories from some outside.

To read Rawls as a *virtù* theorist is to emphasize the fact that the institutions of justice provide a very basic structure. Rawls leaves so much to private initiative—religious worship and education, family structures, careers, culture—that disruptions of the scene are virtually guaranteed, even in the absence of calls for politicization. When these disruptions occur, whether in the form of idiosyncrasy or criminality, they are seen not as mysterious, inexplicable threats from some (antecedent) outside but as the usual (albeit sometimes tumultuous) rumblings, perversities, and rewards of an active citizenry living in a vigorous and relatively undisciplined private realm. On this reading, Rawls's return to desert does not fulfil a structural need of his account, it is an unfortunate error that ought not to be taken too seriously.[4]

If what the *virtù* theorist seeks is a proliferation of identities and differences, then there is no reason to think that she will have any trouble finding it here. Rawls's private realm, by far the most time- and attention-consuming space in justice as fairness, is a space of events, even in the Arendtian sense; there, new relations and new realities are bound to spring up. Liberated from their daily battles with injustice, Rawlsian citizens are freer to engage in self-reflection and strongly supported in their experiments in living by sturdy practices of mutual respect whose range of toleration is wider and deeper than those in any contemporary society. Rawls's institutional arrangements may regulate and limit the range of permissible activities, but in so doing they secure—they do not undercut—the conditions for heightened individuality and a spontaneity that may *very* rarely be justifiably diminished for any raison d'etat.[5]

These reversals of my first readings attest to the fact that these theories resist my disciplining of them into the categories of virtue and *virtù*, but they do not undermine the usefulness of the categorizations. Indeed, the reversals highlight, they do not obviate, one stubborn and important difference between Rawls and Arendt: each assigns very different tasks to *politics*. Rawls looks to politics to provide citizens with a settled, even irresistible setting, structured by a law of laws, identification with which is consolidated through "the repetition of a code,"[6] the code of the original position or the overlapping consensus. Rawls would like to stabilize that setting as a *background* that is relatively untouched by action, a stable, predictable background against which the disruptions of individuality (in art, culture, science, industry, and politics in the Rawlsian sense of administration) might even stand out. Arendt, too, assumes and even cherishes a stable, predictable background, relatively untouched by action, structured by a law of laws (the laws of nature), identification with which is also consolidated by the repetition of a code (the codes and behaviors of private realm subjectivity). And she, too, treats that realm as a valuable backdrop against which the distinctiveness of individuality may be more easily and fully appreciated. But Arendt's stable background is provided by the private realm, not by politics.

Does this difference make a difference? I think it does. And the difference is important because the so-called private realm of late modernity fits neither Arendt's description nor Rawls's. Contra Rawls, the private realm is not only a realm of freedom, innovation, spontaneity, and individuality. As we saw in Chapter 5, even his own idealized account of that realm is marked by discipline, normalization, power, and violence. And contra Arendt, the mindless, tiresome, and oppressive repetitions she attributes to the modern private realm are not the determinations of a univocal cycle of nature but are, instead, the imperfect repetitions of codes whose processes of subject (re)production are political.

The important difference between the two is that Arendt's politics has within it the resources to overcome her misconception of the private realm, whereas that of Rawls and the other virtue theorists of politics, because of their displacements of politics with administration or consolidation, does not. Arendt's politics beckons beyond itself to practices of disruption, augmentation, and refounding that surpass the ones she theorizes and circumscribes. That is the most promising part of her politics: its unruly excess, its boundlessness, its transgressive impertinence, its spontaneous, local, emergences. My own augmentation of Arendt's account builds on these excesses, prizing and extending them, marshaling the democratizing force of their politicizations against the sedimentations of the private and the public realm, against the tendency of the state to enforce and maintain those sedimentations in order to facilitate its own project of effective governance, administration, and organization, and against political communities that treat those sedimentations as fragile repositories of meaning and self-realization that must be perpetually protected from (because they are always haunted by?) the dissonance and disruption of the others they engender in their processes of self-consolidation.

By once again underscoring my support for a radicalized Arendtian politics, I do not mean simply to reinstall the binary of *virtù* versus virtue; I mean to get beyond it. As these reversals indicate, each side of the opposition tells only half the story. Arendt and Rawls are *both* right about the private realm, and that is why each of them is wrong about it. As Arendt more or less rightly notes, the private is a realm of compulsory repetitions whose (re)production of selves into subjects unifies the self's original multiplicity, homogenizing the differences that animate action and diminishing the distinctivenesses of individuality. And, as Rawls rightly notes, the private is a realm in which the construction of selves into subjects makes individuality possible, empowering subjects to participate in diverse forms of life, many of which may well be hospitable to numerous innovations and styles. These two characterizations seem to conflict but both are right; the private realm is both these things at the same time.

Likewise, each of these theorists is wrong about politics because, once again, both are right about it. Politics consists of practices of settlement *and* unsettlement, of disruption *and* administration, of extraordinary events or foundings *and* mundane maintenances. It consists of the forces that decide undecidabilities *and* of those that resist those decisions at the same time. To reduce politics to only one side of each of these operations, to depoliticize the opposite side by identifying it with nature (as Arendt does) or with an outside agitation (as Rawls does), is to displace politics, to deny the effects of power in some of life's arenas for the sake of the perceived goods that power stabilizes under the guise of knowledge, respect, rationality, cognition, nature, or the public-private distinction itself.

As we have seen, however, this strategy consistently fails to secure the goods virtue and *virtù* theorists seek. Their displacements of politics tend to disempower the very subjects they seek to empower, leaving them politically, strategically, and even cognitively unprepared to engage or resist or affirm the closures and settlements reinforced by their states or communities. The identities of the criminal, the promiscuous person, or the gay man along with those identities that anchor and dominate them, like law-abiding citizen, responsible adult, or straight male, form a highly settled terrain into which selves are born and constituted as subjects. To live in that terrain is necessarily to negotiate—to repeat, to resist, to engage—the repetitions that constitute differences, impulses, and dispositions into (more or less) stable identities and othernesses. The negotiation is political and the best perspective from which to appreciate that fully is generated not by virtue or *virtù* but by the struggle between them. From a perspective between virtue and *virtù*, the self's relations to itself as (potentially self-realizing) subject and (potentially demonized) other are both politically significant. From this perspective, neither the good fortune of fittedness nor the misfortune of ill-fittedness is de-politicized.

In recasting the relation between virtue and *virtù*, we might follow Max Weber's example. Weber's "Politics as a Vocation" describes two distinct ethics, an ethic of responsibility (which bears some resemblance to the *virtù* theory developed here) and an ethic of ultimate ends (which bears some resemblance to the virtue theory developed here). The two ethics are developed as polar opposites, but toward the end of his essay Weber suggests that perhaps they "are not absolute contrasts but rather supplements."[7] The two ethics come together in a single person for whom politics is (therefore?) a vocation, but they do not produce a subject that is a unified, univocal whole. The miscegenation brings Weber's heroic figure to the point where he must say in proud torment: "Here I stand; I can do no other." The phrase unites freedom and necessity, performativity and constation, existential choice and phenomenal determination. It attests to the beauty and impossibility of self-creation in a world already highly organized and disciplined. It echoes, in reverse order, Zarathustra's proclamation of the same impossible and enabling rift in subjectivity: "I am who I must be; I call myself Zarathustra."

That rift in subjectivity generates the political space that occasions the consolidations, negotiations, politicizations, and augmentations that mark the work of Kant, Nietzsche, Arendt, Rawls, and Sandel. I prefer Nietzsche's formulation to Weber's, however, because Nietzsche begins with an acknowledgment of the constating structures and identities into which human beings are born. As a result, the possibility to which he moves next—that of a performative self-fashioning—is necessarily a self-overcoming. Weber's stand, by contrast, suggests not self-overcoming but a nonnegotiable, principled positioning. The phrase "I can do no other" signals a submission to (an existential) destiny, not a commitment to resist, subvert, or engage it, perpetually, in a practice of creative refashioning.

It is for the sake of the remainders of politics that I value that moment of Nietzschean self-overcoming. Indeed, my own effort to overcome, without invalidating, the virtue-*virtù* opposition is animated by my concern that, once any conception of politics and identity or agency begins to sediment, its usefulness as a lever of critique is diminished and its generative power becomes a force of constraint. Carol Gilligan's ethic of care provides a good example of the problem. Gilligan turns to care, as I turn to *virtù*, seeking a perspective from which differences that are occluded or deprivileged by the dominant perspective (in her case, by Lawrence Kohlberg's ethic of rights) might be acknowledged, perhaps with magnanimity and even with gratitude. Gilligan ends with a call for a dialectic of rights and care; I call for a politics that engages both virtue and *virtù*. But Gilligan does not call for the overcoming of the ethic of care, nor does she conceive of care as an ethic of self-overcoming.[8] Here the parallel lines of our arguments diverge.

Gilligan's binary of care and rights draws on certain elements in the voices to which she attends while downplaying others, but she never confronts the artistry of her constructions. She stabilizes both ethics by mapping them onto existing lines of differentiation, such as feminine versus masculine modes of reasoning, but she never addresses the more multiple and complicating differences of class, race, or religion, nor does she engage the undecidabilities they organize.[9] In short, Gilligan's ethic of care, by decentering Kohlberg's hegemonic ethic of rights, opens up some spaces for difference—but it maintains itself by closing off others. Despite her occasional cautions, care sediments into a feminine mode of thinking and acting, a women's way of knowing, and the sedimentation generates a range of identitarian and normalizing pressures that discipline both men and women into their gendered subjectivities.[10] Gilligan's dialectic of rights and care is not empowered to address or resolve these pressures; it feeds on them. And they increase markedly as care turns from a lever of critique into a constraining norm, a measure of moral maturity that marks true femininity as the ethic of rights marks true masculinity. These are some of the remainders of Gilligan's binary of care versus rights. They cannot be avoided—no ethic is remainderless— but they can be acknowledged, engaged, and perhaps overcome through newer alternative positionings and innovative decentering strategies and proliferations. Some of these are already in play in the voices of Gilligan's subjects, but Gilligan, listening through the filter of care and rights, does not hear them,[11] nor does she call for them.

Eleven-year-old Amy, a subject of Gilligan's first study, calls attention to the impossibility of remainderless choices: "If both the roads went in totally separate ways, if you pick one, you'll never know what would happen if you went the other way. . . . that's the chance you have to take and, like I said, it's just really a guess."[12] Neither the ethic of care nor that of rights captures this insight into the risk, arbitrariness, and chance of (moral) choice and action. Amy's insight is echoed throughout *In a Different Voice* by women faced with hypothetical as well as real dilemmas, but the adults add a new dimension to the problem: feeling a sense of responsibility to the selves and others that will be affected by their actions, they recognize that no matter what they do they will feel guilty. As in the classic tragic situation, their sense of guilt seems to mire them in the impossibility of their situations, making it hard to imagine how they could ever survive or overcome the effects of these experiences.[13] Gilligan sees the possibility of resolution, though. The guilt these women experience has a restorative function when it is assimilated to a broader ethic of care, an ethic that Gilligan calls "the most adequate guide to the *resolution* of conflicts in human relationships."[14] Wrapping it in an intricate layering of care, narrative, connection, contextualism, responsibility, and femininity, Gilligan preserves and stabilizes guilt as an ethical, moral response, transforming it from a symptom of the ethic of rights' incoherences to a sign of moral maturity and competence.

Dilemmas are unsettling because they expose the remainders of systems, calling attention to the moments of incoherence that mark moral and political orders. One response to dilemmas might be to radicalize their unsettling possibilities: what if they are not the exceptions but the rule? what if the instability and undecidability they expose marks all human choices? what if, in spite of all our rules, reasons, and institutions, "it's just really a guess?" This is not Gilligan's response to dilemmas, however. She tries to soothe the ruptures of dilemmas by developing new rules for them.[15] She converts Amy's insight into an ethical lesson about the need for care and nurturance in an unruly world in which our actions, however well-intended or justified, hurt others. In Gilligan's hands, the crisis of the tragically undecidable situation "creates character," producing a "*re*discovery of connection," a return to a (speculative?) beginning that bears within it the saving grace of human relations: "the realization that self and other are interdependent and that life, however valuable in itself, can only be sustained by care in relationships."[16]

Gilligan marshals the resources of guilt, care, and responsibility in response to the incoherences that afflict the model of rationality and moral agency behind the ethic of rights. But in so doing she does not overcome Kohlberg's ethic of rights, she reenables it, ultimately taking it as her dialectical partner. The unstable ethic of rights is restabilized by care; what used to look like incoherences in rationality are now accounted for as sites of care, masculine reasoning is disambiguated and propped up by the nurturant support of its newly stabilized other, the feminine; and what initially appeared to be a displacement of the hegemonic order begins to look more like a refurbishing of it, a reinstallation.

Gilligan's contrast between care and rights does empower some of the remainders of Kohlberg's model, capturing dimensions of moral life that are silenced or deprivileged by its ethic of rights and justice and giving them a voice. But if the goal is to empower the remainders of system, then the binary of care and rights must itself be overcome in turn. Once these levers of critique sediment into norms, they engender remainders of their own, and the only way to remain sensitive to that process is by switching perspectives and positionings yet again. Gilligan stabilizes the opposition of rights and care effectively and to good effect, but she never returns to ask what care looks like from the perspective of rights.[17] Nor does she seek out other perspectives from which to render problematic her new positionings of rights and care. The contest between rights and care is her contest. For the sake of the advances and empowerments it brings, she does not look beyond it.

But the contest between rights and care engenders other contests. Care's claim to an expressive relation to femininity and its ontologizing assumption that feminine reasoning maps onto anatomical women without significant remainder have been resisted by other feminisms that seek to proliferate the contests of gender rather than make their last stand here, in the terrain staked out by care and rights. Thus, Rosi Braidotti writes that "feminism is neither a concept, nor a theory, nor even a systematic set of utterances about women. It is, rather, the means chosen by certain women to situate themselves in reality so as to redesign their 'feminine' condition."[18] The feminism I have in mind does not embrace and repeat the constations of gendered subjectivities, it does not organize itself around them. It announces their indeterminacy, celebrates their perpetual failure to achieve the closures they assume, and seeks their subversion through a series of performative appropriations and negotiations.[19] It gives voice to the dissonances experienced by men and women for whom the binaries of rights versus care, reason versus emotion, or masculine versus feminine are ill-fitting, even oppressive, constraints. It treats those dissonances, not as markers of personal idiosyncrasy or deviance, not as obstacles to be once and for all overcome on the road to identity, but as sites of political contest.

To keep the contest going requires a commitment to a politics of self-overcoming, a politics that contests closure. For Nietzsche, the ancient Greek practice of ostracism provides an institutional expression of that commitment to contest over closure by protecting the agon from domination by any one great individual or hegemon. But the agon is less easily protected in late modern times in part because it is less easily located and in part because it is threatened not by a single individual possessed of great force but by numerous, overlapping forces, some of which are hegemonic in their aspirations, others of which are simply the expressions of the human, all-too-human yearning for a freedom from politics or contest, a freedom Nietzsche identifies with death. Nietzsche's sentiment is captured well by Stuart Hampshire's observation: "Harmony and inner consensus come with death, when human faces no longer express conflicts but are immobile, composed, at rest."[20]

The closures represented by law, responsibility, authority, the state, community, and sex/gender (to mention only a few) are not immobile, however. They are not static, never at rest. They are all performative products, maintained daily, politically, and imperfectly. Sometimes they enable a democratic politics, but their sedimentations also have disempowering effects that are not easily overcome or challenged. To engage them, we must approach them genealogically, switch perspectives, occupy unfamiliar positions, use strange languages, forge uncomfortable alliances, "pairing the most alien things and separating the closest."[21] In this spirit, the politics generated by the engagement of virtue and *virtù* proliferates the sites of action, the perspectives from which we judge it, and the readings we give of the texts that give theoretical renderings of it. The readings of the texts offered here diversify interpretations that have become overdetermined by their location in an established terrain. Alternative readings—particularly in the case of Rawls and Sandel—suggest themselves more readily when these texts are taken out of their apparently antagonistic but also mutually supporting context in the liberal-communitarian debate. The disruptive pairing of each with a *virtù* perspective opens up new spaces for reflection, for dissent, perhaps even for the creation of *new relations and realities*.

This last phrase is Arendt's. It is the fable she fantasizes as the effect of political action's reemergence in modernity. Its quality as a fable is not in itself problematic. All the positions examined here are moved by fable or fantasy. From the perspective of a magnanimous, democratic politics, the test of fables is whether they open up spaces of critical reflection and resistance or seal an already dominant ethic into place. Arendt's and Derrida's fables of the American founding each open up space for a potentially radical democratic politics of augmentation. Rawls's fable of an American founding, by contrast, trades empowerment for justice (in the mistaken belief that justice only empowers, without remainders of disempowerment) and seals the rifts and fissures that might complicate (or politicize) its administrative mission. Similarly, Kant's fable of beginnings entertains the possibility of radical alternatives only to seal dominant conventions more firmly into place.

These closures are always in process, they are never faits accomplis. Rather than resent this condition, a politics of augmentation celebrates it, acknowledging the remainders of the will to closure, extending to them a magnanimity and gratitude that seem to be beyond the reach of most liberals and communitarians. The lesson of the contest of virtue and *virtù* is that politics never gets things right, over, and done with. The conclusion is not nihilistic but radically democratic. To accept and embrace the perpetuity of contest is to reject the dream of displacement, the fantasy that the right laws or constitution might some day free us from the responsibility for (and, indeed, the burden of) politics. It is to give up on the notion that one day a constative truth of sex/gender will emerge and settle the ambiguities and struggles that mark the lives of most men and women. It is to see that human being in the world is always enabled by categories and forms of life against which individuals and communities invariably struggle to find a place from which they might speak, or be seen, or be.

Notes

1. Negotiating Positions: The Politics of Virtue and *Virtù*

1. It is from Bernard Williams that I borrow the language of remainders (and I am extremely indebted to him for it), but my theorization of the concept differs from his. For Williams, remainders are the moral oughts that are *not* acted on in dilemma situations. They exist because of a *value* pluralism that no single systematic or formulaic ethics can encompass. That failure is illustrated only in dilemma or tragic situations (in which there is "no right thing to do"), which are exceptional, not the rule (*Problems of the Self* [Cambridge: Cambridge University Press, 1973], 172–83). On my account, by contrast, remainders include a much broader array of resistances engendered by (a broader variety of) rather ordinary human attempts systematically to organize the world conceptually, categorically, linguistically, politically, culturally, and socially as well as morally.

What difference does this second theorization of remainders make? When we say that the number 100 divided by 11 equals 9, remainder 1, the remainder of the 1 is understood by Williams to have existed prior to the division process and apart from it. The process stumbles on it. To further the analogy, the problem with formulaic ethics would be that they round off to the nearest number without attending to the division's remainder at all. In my view, however, the problem with both Williams's account and that of the theorists of formulaic ethics is that neither sees that the remaindered 1 is produced by the process of division itself, in the absence of which it would not exist as such. The advantage of the latter view is that it directs attention to the *institutional processes* that engender remainders and not just to the complexities of the world in which those institutions operate. Once our attention is directed at institutional processes, it is easier to see that, contra Williams, ordinary situations do not differ in kind from tragic situations. If there *is* one right thing to do in ordinary situations, that is because competing possibilities (and the tragedies they once signaled) have been successfully suppressed by the rules and institutions that govern ordinary situations and constitute them as ordinary.

2. Friedrich Nietzsche, *The Will to Power*, ed. Walter Kaufmann, trans. R. J. Hollingdale and Walter Kaufmann (New York: Random House, 1967), §317.

3. Hannah Arendt, *The Human Condition* (Chicago: University of Chicago Press, 1958), 197, 200, 38.

4. Hannah Arendt, *Lectures on Kant's Political Philosophy*, ed. Ronald Beiner (Chicago: University of Chicago Press, 1982), 8, 19.

5. See Stuart Hampshire, *Innocence and Experience* (Cambridge: Harvard University Press, 1989); Sheldon Wolin, *The Presence of the Past: Essays on the State and the Constitution* (Baltimore: Johns Hopkins University Press, 1989); Nancy Fraser, "Rethinking the Public Sphere: A Contribution to the Critique of Actually Existing Democracy," *Social Text* 25/26 (1991), 56–80; William Connolly, *Identity\Difference: Democratic Negotiations of Political Paradox* (Ithaca: Cornell University Press, 1991); Stanley Cavell, *Conditions Handsome and Unhandsome: The Constitution of Emersonian Perfectionism* (Chicago: University of Chicago Press, 1990); Michael Walzer, *Spheres of Justice* (New York: Basic Books, 1983), and "Philosophy and Democracy," *Political Theory* 9 (1981), 379–99; Judith Butler, *Gender Trouble* (London: Routledge, 1990); Isaiah Berlin, *Four Essays on Liberty* (Oxford: Oxford University Press, 1969), and *The Crooked Timber of Humanity* (New York: Knopf, 1991); Bernard Williams, "A Critique of Utilitarianism," in J. J. C. Smart and Bernard Williams, *Utilitarianism: For and Against*, (Cambridge: Cambridge University Press, 1973), *Problems of the Self* and *Moral Luck* (Cambridge: Cambridge University Press, 1983); and Richard Flathman, *Toward a Liberalism* (Ithaca: Cornell University Press, 1989), and *Willful Liberalism: Voluntarism and Individuality in Political Theory and Practice* (Ithaca: Cornell University Press, 1992).

6. See *Time* magazine cover story: "Why *Roe v. Wade* Is Already Moot" May 4, 1992, 26–32.

7. My analysis of the immediate post-*Roe* period draws on Kristen Luker's *Abortion and the Politics of Motherhood* (Berkeley: University of California Press, 1984).

8. Consider, for example, the recent relocations of the abortion debate in Democratic and Republican party deployments of "family values."

9. While those who are critical of masculinism highlight its weaknesses (for war, rights, and autonomy) in contrast to womanly strengths (for peace, care, and connectedness).

10. Since I first characterized Machiavellian *virtù* in these terms, two similar but much more critical readings of Machiavelli have appeared. See Wendy Brown, *Manhood and Politics* (Totowa, N.J.: Rowman and Littlefield, 1988); and Linda Zerilli, "Machiavelli's Sister's: Women and 'the Conversation' of Political Theory," *Political Theory* 19 (1991), 252–76.

11. Sabina Lovibond, *Realism and Imagination in Ethics* (Minneapolis: University of Minnesota Press, 1983).

2. Kant and the Concept of Respect for Persons

1. John Rawls and Robert Nozick both justify their views in terms of their success in giving appropriate expression to Kant's principle of respect for persons. See Rawls, *A Theory of Justice* (Cambridge: Harvard University Press, 1971), 65; and

Robert Nozick, *Anarchy, State, and Utopia* (New York: Basic Books. 1974), 30–31. Robert Paul Wolff takes a proto-Kantian commitment to the integrity of the self as one of his points of departure. See Wolff, *In Defense of Anarchism* (New York: Harper and Row, 1970), ix, 18–21.

2. Some of Kant's commentators note that Kantian respect for persons is not really for persons but for the moral law in persons, but none discerns the three distinct strands of respect I trace below, nor does anyone remark the didactic and disciplinary dimensions of the practice in Kant. On Kant's conflation of respect for persons and respect for the moral law, see Andreas Teuber's very good essay, "Kant's Respect for Persons," *Political Theory* 11 (1983), 369–92.

3. Kant, "Perpetual Peace," trans. H. B. Nisbet, in *Kant's Political Writings*, ed. Hans Reiss (Cambridge: Cambridge University Press, 1970), 125 (henceforth *KPW*).

4. The role of the state and philosophy in licensing the exercise of *enlightened* reason is outlined primarily in "An Answer to the Question: 'What Is Enlightenment'" and "The Contest of the Faculties," both in *KPW*.

5. Kant, "Speculative Beginning of Human History," in *Perpetual Peace and Other Essays on Politics, History, and Morals*, trans. and ed. Ted Humphrey (Indianapolis: Hackett, 1983).

6. Kant himself is quite clear on this score. The original sin of Eden ought not to be attributed to man's "original parents. . . . instead, he must admit what they did as his own act, and must completely credit to himself the guilt for all evil that arose from the first misuse of reason, for he is probably conscious that he would behave in precisely the same way were he in those circumstances," which he is, daily ("Speculative Beginning," 59).

7. Ibid., 49–50.

8. I focus here only on the first three steps. The fourth step is man's discovery that animals are a means to his ends and his simultaneous awareness, through the idea of contrast, that he and all other rational beings are, unlike animals, ends in themselves. The attribution of man's existence as a historical and political being to an originary disruption of reason is highly reminiscent of Rousseau's account, which Kant admired greatly. It would be easy to make a case for treating Rousseau as a virtue theorist of politics. I focus on Kant because he has a far greater influence than Rousseau on contemporary formulations of virtue theories of politics, both liberal and communitarian.

9. "Speculative Beginning," 50–51.

10. Ibid., 51–53.

11. Ibid., 51–52. As we see in Chapter 6, Michael Sandel's arguments take a similar turn. First, he allows sites of pleasure to proliferate, then he retreats from that proliferation lest eroticism exceed the bounds he prescribes, the bounds not of decency, exactly, but of "intimacy." The similarity between Kant and Sandel on this point is worth noting because each regulates sexuality in the name of practices that conduce to the form of civil association he seeks. For Kant this means that practices of decency, respect, and civility on which republics rely have to be protected against the potentially subversive excesses of eroticism. (Bestiality is the only transgression that results in the expulsion of the offender from Kant's republic: "The criminal guilty of

bestiality is unworthy of remaining in human society." Immanuel Kant, *The Metaphysical Elements of Justice*, trans. John Ladd [Indianapolis: Bobbs-Merrill, 1965], 363.) For Sandel this means that the practices of intimacy that support his communitarian programmatic must be protected from the potentially destabilizing effects of an eroticism that resists confinement to the service of the state or community.

12. "Speculative Beginning," 52.

13. Ibid., 50.

14. The phrasing is from Ludwig Wittgenstein, *Philosophical Investigations*, trans. G. E. M. Anscombe (New York: Macmillan, 1953), §6.

15. In the biblical account, all the birds and animals are brought before Adam to be named by him. And Adam also names Eve. But no one names Adam. *Adam*, in the Hebrew, means, simply, "man."

16. "Speculative Beginning," 52. Actually, Kant ascribes this consciousness of mortality to both husband and wife, whereas the first two steps of reason's disruption are related by him in terms of their effect on man alone. This suggests a presupposition on Kant's part of female passivity with regard to the satisfaction of the natural needs for food and sex, whereas man and woman (husband and wife) are thought to be equally afflicted with the fear of death.

17. "Speculative Beginning," 52.

18. Ibid., 53, 49.

19. Ibid., 51.

20. The same analysis can be applied to reason's first intrusion. With the objects of nourishment withdrawn from him, man finds it necessary to speculate about what objects are appropriate sources of nourishment. Instead of periodic feedings, he now plans meals.

21. "Speculative Beginning," 54–55 and note.

22. Hence my characterization of this process as therapeutic: it gives narrative structure to the chaos of the preconscious or unconscious.

23. Immanuel Kant, *Groundwork of the Metaphysics of Morals*, trans. H. J. Paton (New York: Harper and Row, 1964), 401n.

24. Ibid.

25. Immanuel Kant, *Critique of Practical Reason*, trans. and ed. Lewis White Beck (Indianapolis: Bobbs-Merrill, 1956), 76.

26. Ibid., 73. This recalls Kant's discussion of respect for the sublime in the *Critique of Judgement*, where respect is a kind of awe that leads us to think infinity while at the same time making present to us our own limitations and finitude. It should be noted that Kant doubted that respect for the law was ever successful as an incentive of pure practical reason in the production of maxims willed morally (*Groundwork*, 406–7). His description should be taken as one of an ideal process.

27. *Critique of Practical Reason*, 80.

28. This passage raises provocative questions regarding Kant's claim that respect for the law is the sole incentive to moral action. Here it looks as if it is an incentive of a further incentive, the "moral interest." For the most part, however, Kant leaves moral interest out of the account and relies exclusively on respect for the law to explain how agents come to will maxims morally.

But why does Kant even bother to include a feeling in his account of moral motivation? He wants to distinguish inclination-governed action from action for the sake of duty, but he remains influenced by the Humean belief-desire-action model. On this model, simply having beliefs is an insufficient condition of action. A desire must be introduced to account for the agent's having been brought to act. Kant's obscurity on the subject of respect for the law may be seen as a consequence of this attempt to get away from the Humean model while remaining beholden to it. I am indebted to the late Stanley Benn for this suggestion.

29. *Critique of Practical Reason*, 76, 81. Compare this with Kant's other claim, noted above, that the interest involved in this process, a "moral interest," is analytically distinct from, indeed is produced *by*, respect for the law.

30. *Metaphysical Elements*, 219.

31. *Groundwork*, 428, 402.

32. Immanuel Kant, "On the Common Saying 'This May Be True in Theory, but It Does Not Apply in Practice,'" (henceforth "Theory and Practice"), in *KPW*, 69. Kant's repeated insistence on purity renders even more problematic the place and character of the "moral interest" he introduces to the account.

33. *Groundwork*, 401n. Kant's use of the term "respect" becomes more refined as his thought develops. In the *Groundwork*, he uses the same term, *Achtung*, to denote both respect for persons and respect for the moral law. In the *Doctrine of Virtue*, however, he parenthetically distinguishes respect for the law, *Achtung* (*reverentia*), from respect for persons, *Achtung* (*observatia aliis praestanda*). On this point, see Mary Gregor, *Laws of Freedom* (New York: Barnes and Noble, 1963), 181. In the *Groundwork*, as in the *Critique of Practical Reason*, Kant is primarily concerned to establish the principle of the categorical imperative and to treat respect as an incentive of pure practical reason. Respect for persons as such is therefore not a central concern until Kant turns his attention to ethics and to the maxims that govern relations among persons. The principle of what I call teleological respect makes its first appearance in the *Doctrine of Virtue*, as Kant for the first time distinguishes reverence for the law from respect for persons (though he draws no formal distinction between liberal and teleological respect).

In the quotations from the *Groundwork* Kant's term for respect, *Achtung*, appears as "reverence" as it does in Paton's translation. In my quotations from Kant's other texts, the same term, *Achtung*, appears as "respect." It is important to remember that in spite of the difference between reverence and respect, Kant uses the same term for both. At the same time, however, the difference in the English translation calls attention to a real difference between *Achtung* for the law or the law in persons and *Achtung* for persons in their other dimensions of existence.

34. Ibid., 435–36.

35. *Critique of Practical Reason*, 77.

36. "Speculative Beginning," 52.

37. Immanuel Kant, *Doctrine of Virtue*, trans. Mary Gregor (Philadelphia: University of Pennsylvania Press, 1964), 385–86.

38. The failure of Kantian respect to attend to particular talents and traits of persons is a point on which many theorists of respect focus. See Teuber, "Kant's

Respect for Persons," 378; Bernard Williams, "The Idea of Equality," in *Problems of the Self* (Cambridge: Cambridge University Press, 1973), 235; and Carl Cranor, "Toward a Theory of Respect for Persons," *American Philosophical Quarterly* 12 (1975), 309–19, esp. 310. Problematically, antidotal attempts to direct respect specifically to particular talents and traits often end up treating respect exclusively as an evaluative practice. And, as Stephen Darwall rightly points out with reference to Cranor, that allows the behavior-limiting dimension of respect to recede. See Darwall, "Two Kinds of Respect," *Ethics* 88 (1977), 46. Darwall theorizes two kinds of respect in order to avoid that danger. I believe that my three-part organization of Kantian respect shows that Kant managed to avoid it too, not by rejecting appraisal tout court—Kantian teleological respect appraises the consonance of individual character with the humanity in persons—but by also theorizing respect as a limiting condition on action. Indeed, teleological respect (particularly in its positive, attitudinal dimension) parallels Darwall's appraisal-respect, and the third strand of Kantian respect, liberal respect, parallels Darwall's behavior-limiting recognition-respect.

39. Thomas Hill argues that Kant "sometimes writes as if certain acts amount to 'throwing away' one's humanity [but] he repeatedly implies that a person's humanity remains and so must be respected, even though he defiles, abases, violates, dishonors, rejects it." See Hill, "Humanity as an End in Itself," *Ethics* 91 (1980), 86. Because *most* of Kant's remarks indicate that "a person's humanity remains" no matter what he does, Hill takes that to be his true view (notwithstanding Kant's insistence that those who practice bestiality, for example, be forever banished from civil society. See *Metaphysical Elements*, 363). I prefer to maintain both views at the same time (rather than choose between them) by distinguishing two strands of respect, one unconditional (liberal respect) and the other conditional and subject to withdrawal at any moment (teleological respect). This strategy takes into account more of what Kant actually says about respect for persons while also capturing some of the more didactic and disciplinary dimensions of his remarks.

40. *Doctrine of Virtue*, 435.

41. Immanuel Kant, *Education*, trans. Annette Churton (Ann Arbor: University of Michigan Press, 1960), §§87, 95. Sandel too is tempted by contempt as a response to those whose practices lack moral worth, from his perspective. See my discussion of *Bowers v. Hardwick* in Chapter 6.

Hill argues that Kant is "unusual, at least compared to moral philosophers today, in stressing the importance of attitude and gesture aside from their consequences. Mockery is opposed, whether or not it is effective for the purpose of reform or deterrent, because it reflects a disrespectful attitude toward the humanity of others" ("Humanity as an End in Itself," 97, citing *Doctrine of Virtue*, 467). Once again, Hill bypasses some of Kant's remarks in order to highlight others. He is right about Kant's treatment of mockery. But his conclusion leaves the reader unprepared for Kant's rather different view of contempt, which he treats as a potentially powerful didactic instrument.

42. *Doctrine of Virtue*, 466, 462.

43. *Metaphysical Elements*, 363.

44. *Doctorine of Virtue* 418, 423–24; Gregor, *Laws of Freedom*, 190.

45. *Doctrine of Virtue*, 418; See also *Groundwork*, 430.
46. *Doctrine of Virtue*, 470.
47. *Doctrine of Virtue*, 470–72. In Sandel's practice of friendship, by contrast, confidences and candor are encouraged. One finds that one's friends know one better than one knows oneself. Sandel's community of friends is not threatened or destabilized by the confidence; it is reinforced by it—it occasions community and self-reconstitution. See Chapter 6.
48. It might be objected that this aspect of respect amounts to peer pressure and is therefore in conflict with Kantian morality's requirement that respect for the humanity in oneself be self-imposed. Kant might respond by pointing out that the one friend's withdrawal of respect simply expresses a greater respect for the humanity in the person of his friend than his friend shows for the humanity in his own person, and that the good *example* of the former (not his peer pressure) is what motivates the chastised friend to embark on the path to self-perfection. If his fear of the loss of friendship is what motivates the chastised friend in his self-improvement, it is not perfection that he will attain.
49. As Thomas Hill rightly notes; see "Humanity as an End in Itself," 86.
50. Immanuel Kant, *Lectures on Ethics*, trans. Louis Infield (Indianapolis: Hackett, 1963), 125.
51. *Doctrine of Virtue*, 462.
52. Kant opposes liberal respect to love, characterizing the former as a force of repulsion, the latter as a force of attraction: "The principle of mutual love admonishes men constantly to come nearer to each other; that of the respect which they owe each other, to keep themselves at a distance from one another." Together, the two forces combine to produce friendship, "the union of two persons through equal and mutual love and respect." Friendship is so "delicate," however, and love is potentially so overwhelming that friends need "rules preventing excessive familiarity and limiting mutual love by the requirements of respect" (ibid., 449, 469–70).
This strand of respect as distance is the one to which Kant scholars have been most attentive. But it tends to dominate only Kant's treatment of friendship. Elsewhere, other aspects of respect are central. Friendship is prominent in Kant's moral theory, however. Gregor is right to point out that the "maxim of friendship is," in Kant's view, "the correct moral attitude among men" (*Laws of Freedom*, 200). Perhaps the centrality of friendship in Kant's moral theory is what led many of his readers to generalize from the particular features of the concept of respect as it appears in *that* context.
53. Two people in a relationship of philanthropy, which Kant categorizes under the maxim of love, do not relate to each other as equals for "one is obligated to gratitude" and is in no position to "reciprocally . . . impose obligation." Therefore, the maxim of love is inappropriate as a moral attitude governing human relations. Only in a relation of respect can man "measure himself with every other being . . . and value himself on a footing of equality with them" (*Doctrine of Virtue*, 470–72; 434).
54. "It is our duty to regard them [rights] as sacred and to respect and maintain them as such. There is nothing more sacred in the wide world than the rights of others. They are inviolable" (*Lectures on Ethics*, 193).

220 Notes to Pages 32–37

55. *Groundwork*, 403.

56. *Doctrine of Virtue*, 463.

57. *Groundwork*, 421; *Doctrine of Virtue*, 449.

58. In so willing, we also violate our duty of teleological respect not to be proud. This requires us to "limit our self-esteem by the dignity of humanity in another person" (*Doctrine of Virtue*, 448).

59. Gregor, *Laws of Freedom*, 182.

60. Paton, *The Categorical Imperative* (Philadelphia: University of Pennsylvania Press, 1971), 172.

61. Gregor, *Laws of Freedom*, 203.

62. *Critique of Practical Reason*, 87n.

63. "Perpetual Peace," 104, 98n. In addition to our moral duty to enter civil society, we also have a moral duty to contribute to its maintenance by conducting ourselves in a law-abiding manner ("Theory and Practice," 79–82). See also *Metaphysical Elements*, 372 and Ladd's introduction, Kant also invokes the spectre of lawlessness to legitimate the state's punishment of criminals (*Metaphysical Elements*, 321).

64. "Perpetual Peace," 112, 103, 121n; emphasis added. Kant's aspiration to displace law with moral self-legislation makes politics in his world largely self-defeating. The juridical enforcement of moral ends ceases to be necessary once individuals, moved by reverence-respect for the law, pursue those ends on their own. Indeed, this ultimate elimination of politics (as juridical enforcement) is something Kant, in his more optimistic moments, hopes for: through culture and membership in a "law-governed social order," man's talents are "gradually developed, his taste cultivated, and by a continual process of enlightenment, a beginning is made towards establishing a way of thinking which can with time transform the primitive natural capacity for moral discrimination into definite practical principles; and thus a *pathologically* enforced social union is transformed into a *moral* whole" ("Ideas of a Universal History from a Cosmopolitan Point of View," in *KPW*, 44–45). Kant's optimism does not always get the better of him, however. Often he is inclined to believe that as the species progresses the best we can hope for is not an "ever increasing quantity of *morality* in its attitudes" but an increase in "the *legality* of its attitudes" ("Contest of the Faculties," 187). Either way, the ideal of a postjuridical order leaves its mark: see Chapter 5 for my discussion of the ramifications of Kant's and Rawls's belief that punishment is unnecessary in an ideal regime.

65. Kelly, *Idealism, Politics, and History* (Cambridge: Cambridge University Press, 1969), 116–17.

66. *Doctrine of Virtue*, 387; emphasis added.

67. Ibid., 386.

68. *Critique of Practical Reason*, 171.

69. Among these active promotions would be the satisfaction of what Kant calls "true needs," needs that must be met in order for any person to function as a rational agent. Rawls's primary goods draw on this element in Kant's thinking. On true needs and on the interdependence of Kantian subjects, see Barbara Herman, "Mutual Aid and Respect for Persons," *Ethics* 94 (1984), 577–602, esp. 586–87.

70. In an unpublished paper, Thomas Eagles argues that a plausible reconstruc-

tion of Kant's argument for civil society might rely on a duty "to avoid desperate circumstances." But Eagles stresses that this duty is imperfect and may arguably be fulfilled by entrance into a variety of political arrangements of which Kant's republic is only one. My discussion of the connection in Kant between happiness and perfection is greatly indebted to this paper and to conversations with the author.

71. Kant, "The Metaphysics of Morals," trans. H. B. Nisbet, in *KPW*, 156–57; for a slightly different translation, see *Metaphysical Elements*, 104.

72. "Theory and Practice," 80. It is important to note, however, that there is little in Kant's view to suggest that the aid of others in their pursuit of happiness is related to the duty to respect persons. Kant's discussion of happiness as a means to self-perfection appears in a section of the introduction to *The Doctrine of Virtue* entitled "The Happiness of Others." In this context, the term "respect" makes no appearance. Nor is the duty to further the happiness of others a duty of respect. And the pursuit of happiness as a means to our self-perfection is merely permitted, not required. Why did Kant not argue that the removal of obstacles to the moral development of others is properly a duty of teleological respect for persons? Perhaps because that would resituate autonomy and make it more of a community than an individual end. Or, perhaps because he could not do so without calling into question, or at least attenuating, his insistent separation of the phenomenal and noumenal realms.

73. It is also dependent on international peace. Just as individual men find it easier to pursue their moral ends within a political association than in a state of nature, so morality's progress is facilitated when states are relieved of the pressures posed by dire international circumstances. The duty to pursue perpetual peace and membership in a "lawful *federation* under a commonly accepted *international right*" derives from the same duty—the duty to avoid desperate circumstances—as does the individual duty to join civil society. Only the latter, however, is juridically enforceable ("Theory and Practice," 90–91); see also "Perpetual Peace," 98n.

74. "Idea of a Universal History," 44–46. Unsocial sociability is played out in the dynamic of love and respect that forms the practice of Kantian friendship; it is illustrated by Schopenhauer's porcupines in the passage that heads this chapter. Were it not for his "asocial qualities (far from admirable in themselves)," Kant says man would live forever in "an Arcadian, pastoral existence of perfect concord, self-sufficiency, and mutual love." The implication is that if he did not possess these unseemly features man could live with others in a society governed not by practices of respect but by love, presumably because he would have nothing to hide. In this essay, there is no original Eden that a misuse of reason disrupts. Instead, man is assumed to have always been prevented by his own "far from admirable" unsociability from experiencing a perfect, immediate harmony ("Idea of a Universal History," 44).

75. "Contest of the Faculties," 185, and "Theory and Practice," 87n.

76. "Perpetual Peace," 124.

77. Central to every one of Kant's fables is a faith in the progress of the species. He admits that "history may well give rise to endless doubts about my hopes" and concedes that, "if these doubts could be proved, they might persuade me to desist from an apparently futile task" ("Theory and Practice," 88–89). But it is a postulate

of Kant's argument that no such doubts can ever be *proved*. The confused experiences of the phenomenal world cannot call Ideas of reason into question.

78. Ibid., 89. The thing for which we are meant to hope, however, is precisely this "we" who is doing the hoping; together, we are to yearn for ourselves, for a community that subscribes to shared ends, a "we" that is no longer the fictive subject of a mere fable but a reality that enables the consolation of hope even while it renders it unnecessary. The paradoxical status of the "we" that anchors fables of beginning is a central issue in Arendt's reading of the American founding as well. See Chapter 4.

79. Ibid., 86–87.

3. Nietzsche and the Recovery of Responsibility

1. Friedrich Nietzsche, *The Antichrist*, trans. R. J. Hollingdale (New York: Penguin, 1969), §22 (henceforth *AC*). In this passage, Nietzsche refers specifically to Christianity, which in its desire "to dominate *beasts of prey*" has made the human animal "*sick*" (albeit also more "interesting"): "The sick and weak have had fascination on their side: they are more interesting than the healthy." Friedrich Nietzsche, *The Will to Power*, trans. Walter Kaufmann and R. J. Hollingdale (New York: Random House, 1967), §864 (henceforth *WP*). See also, Friedrich Nietzsche, *The Gay Science*, trans. Walter Kaufmann (New York: Vintage Books, 1974), §4 (henceforth *GS*).

2. Friedrich Nietzsche, *Human All-Too-Human*, trans. R. J. Hollingdale (Cambridge: Cambridge University Press, 1986), §107 (henceforth *HAH*). The identification of birth with freedom is a constant theme of Arendt's work, as well; see Chapter 4.

3. It is only because we have forgotten the origins of our value system "that the highly conditional nature of its right to exist is no longer felt," says Nietzsche, with reference to the English moralists of his day. "Expeditions of an Untimely Man," in *Twilight of the Idols*, trans. R.J. Hollingdale (New York: Penguin, 1969), §5 (henceforth *TI*). Nietzsche himself puns on the first and second senses of "recovery" in *TI*, Foreword.

4. Friedrich Nietzsche, *Beyond Good and Evil*, trans. Marianne Cowan (Chicago: H. Regnery, 1955), §280 (henceforth *BGE*).

5. Friedrich Nietzsche, "On Truth and Lies in an Extra-Moral Sense," in *Philosophy and Truth: Selections from Nietzsche's Notebooks of the Early 1870s*, ed. Daniel Breazeale (Atlantic Highlands, N.J.: Humanities Press, 1979), 81–82.

6. *WP*, §489.

7. "On Truth and Lies," 83–84. A "word becomes a concept insofar as it simultaneously has to fit countless more or less equal cases—which means, purely and simply, cases which are never equal and thus altogether unequal things. Every concept arises from the equation of unequal things."

8. Friedrich Nietzsche, §34, "Self-Surpassing," in *Thus Spake Zarathustra*, trans. Thomas Common (New York: Modern Library, 1960) (henceforth *TSZ*). Hence Nietzsche's claim that the violent history he speculatively constructs in *The Genealogy of Morals* "is in any case present in all ages or may always reappear"; *On The Genealogy*

of Morals, trans. Walter Kaufmann and R. J. Hollingdale (New York: Vintage Books, 1969), 2.9 (henceforth *GM*).

9. See *GS*, §109.

10. *GS*, §109.

11. *WP*, §617. See also "Self-Surpassing," where Nietzsche has Zarathustra say: "Wherever I found a living thing, there found I Will to Power" (*TSZ*, §34).

12. *HAH*, §92. The echo of Machiavelli is striking. Both Machiavelli and Nietzsche posit a strong connection between legitimacy and forgetting and both subvert any semblance of complete legitimacy in modernity by restoring memory to us, by giving an account of the (violent) origins we have forgotten. Like Nietzsche, Machiavelli inquires into forbidden origins—those of political regimes. He too finds that their origins are violent and that the only difference between legitimate and illegitimate regimes is that in legitimate regimes the initial, initiating, acts of violence have been forgotten. See Niccolo Machiavelli, *Prince*, in *The Prince and the Discourses*, trans. Luigi Ricci, ed. Max Lerner (New York: Modern Library, 1959), bk. 2. Neither, however, concludes that, since all institutions have violent and arbitrary origins and are in that sense equally illegitimate, there is no reason to prefer some sets of institutions to others.

13. *WP*, §514.

14. *BGE*, §228.

15. *WP*, §404. This is the message of the *Genealogy*'s third essay, in which the ascetic ideal in the form of the will to truth eventually comes to see the truth about itself.

16. *TSZ*, §56, "Old and New Tables," 25.

17. *TI*, "Expeditions," §5.

18. *GS*, §108.

19. *HAH*, §466.

20. *WP*, §§51, 55; emphasis added.

21. Ibid., §7; *GS*, §357. For Nietzsche there are two kinds of nihilism, one hollow and self-maintaining, the other generative and self-surpassing. The former Nietzsche identifies with Christianity and rejects for insistently clinging to values that are hollow and self-contradictory. The latter he endorses for its insistence (against the self-delusions of the first) that no values are transcendent, objective, or true. To endorse the second sort of nihilism is not necessarily to embrace nihilism as such: Nietzsche endorses it as part of an effort to get past nihilism and on to a new, more viable table of values.

22. *WP*, §§55, 200; *GS*, §4.

23. Nietzsche re-covers the Christian virtue of benevolence with his own ideal, "the ideal of a spirit who plays naively—that is not deliberately but from overflowing power and abundance" (*GS*, §382). Nietzschean "respect for man" is not, like Kant's, "merely for virtuous men" (*WP*, §747); in contrast to the virtue of love understood—as Kant understood it—as "surrender," Nietzschean love is a "bestowal of abundant personality" that does not demand purity and, unlike Kantian love, "forgives the lover even his lust" (*WP*, §296; *GS*, §62).

24. "Not contentment but more power, not peace at all but war; not virtue but

proficiency, (virtue in the Renaissance style, *virtù*, virtue free of moralic acid)" (*AC*, §2).

25. Of his *Genealogy of Morals*, Nietzsche says: "This is offered only as a conjecture for the depths of such subterranean things are difficult to fathom." *GM*, 2.6.

26. *WP*, §773.

27. *GM*, 1.13.

28. Ibid.

29. *WP*, §481.

30. *GM*, 2.2,3.

31. Ibid., 2.4.

32. Ibid., 3.15,13,20; *HAH*, §132.

33. *HAH*, §132.

34. *GM*, 2.22. Can it be anything but ironic that Nietzsche's indictment of the herd for fostering the myth of free will turns on their having *willed* this "myth" into a reality? In this short passage on the madness of the herd's will, the term "will" appears five times. But this should not be taken as a simple self-contradiction. When Nietzsche talks about the *myth* of free will, he does not do so from a position of simple determinism. He means to denaturalize the will, not to deny its existence. Similarly, he does not deny its freedoms, but he does want to point to the will's always conditioned character. Nietzsche is no enemy of the will: the overman he envisions has a powerful will and powerful self-discipline. Nietzsche's point is to condemn the self-defeating madness of the will displayed by the herd caught in the grip of ressentiment, a madness that is mad precisely because it makes further and more powerful willings impossible.

35. Immanuel Kant, "On the Common Saying 'This May Be True in Theory, but It Does Not Apply in Practice'" (henceforth "Theory and Practice," in *KPW*, 72).

36. *GM*, 2.19.

37. *HAH*, §107; *GM*, 2.16.

38. *BGE*, §210; *WP*, §494; *BGE*, §212; and see esp. *GM*, 2.2.

39. *TI*, "The Four Great Errors," §8.

40. *GS*, §41.

41. *WP*, §233; see also *GM*, 3.17.

42. *GM*, 1.10–11. Here, forgetting is an active power, not just a passive inability to remember; hence Nietzsche's admiration for it; see also *GM*, 2.1. Arendt shares Nietzsche's admiration of this power and theorizes a practice of forgiveness that builds on it.

43. *WP*, §235; see also *WP*, §234.

44. Bernard Williams's treatment of remorse and regret as moral feelings provides an interesting counterpoint to Nietzsche's treatment of these topics. It would not be fair to Williams to dismiss (as Nietzsche probably would) his treatments of remorse and regret as merely the effects of ressentiment. Williams turns to remorse and regret because he sees in them not a wallowing in the past but an honest, constructive, potentially transformative disposition to the tragic pasts that all too often hold us captive. Remorse puts us in touch with the remainders of our choices

rather than deny their existence. It is true to our tragedies. See *Problems of the Self* (Cambridge: Cambridge University Press, 1973), 172–83.

Williams's effective re-covery of remorse and regret from forms of self-flagellation to practices of moral healing raises a question for Nietzsche: why does Nietzsche not re-cover remorse along with the other traditional virtues? Why does he see only ressentiment here? Why does he not see transformative and regenerative properties in remorse? I think the answer to that question must have something to do with a point I made in Chapter 1 against Williams (n. 1): tragic situations (situations in which remainderless choice is not possible) are neither as rare nor as exceptional as Williams likes to think. They are typical of the human condition and Nietzsche wants to recast them so that their typicality is clearly manifest, while exploring and affirming a variety of possible responses to them without privileging any single one as ethically superior (which Williams does). There is no obvious reason why a re-covered remorse could not be *one* of those many and varied responses, but Nietzsche seems to assume that remorse is necessarily a reactive disposition, entirely beyond the reach of re-covery for an ethic that replaces reaction with action. As I argue in the following sections of the chapter, Nietzsche looks to action to redeem tragic situations, not to erase or occlude the remainders that preoccupy Williams but to redeem them.

45. The phrase is the famous subtitle of Nietzsche's *Ecce Homo*.

46. Indeed, Nietzsche sees eternal return as a nonresentful way of thinking eternity: it does not seek sources of meaning and salvation outside the present, human world, nor does it deny the contingency and temporality that are the conditions of life. It does not insist that the world be redeemed by something outside itself and it does not put the human species at the center of the universe. Nietzsche seeks an "eternity for everything" (*WP*, §1065).

47. *TSZ*, §57, "The Convalescent," 2.

48. Kant, "Perpetual Peace," in *KPW*, 87.

49. Immanuel Kant, "The Contest of the Faculties," in *KPW*, 180.

50. *TSZ* §42, "Redemption," 1.

51. That Nietzsche means here to praise in particular man's ability to redeem the "It was" is made clear only two pages later in the text when Nietzsche repeats all these phrases, joining them together: "All 'It was' is a fragment, a riddle, a fearful chance, until the creating Will saith thereto: But thus would I have it" (Ibid.; see also ibid., §56, "Old and New Tables," 3).

52. *GS*, §341.

53. *TSZ*, §42, "Redemption," 1.

54. *WP*, §708. Becoming must appear justified at every moment because each present moment is already passing. Once the moment is past, a new redemptive moment must be achieved. Otherwise the stage is set for the reawakening of ressentiment as the passage of time becomes a cruelty that removes the self farther and farther from its greatest moment.

55. *GS*, §341.

56. Walter Kaufmann rejects the comparison of eternal recurrence with Kant's categorical imperative because (a) Kant's formula is logical whereas Nietzsche's is psychological and because (b) Nietzsche is not a moralist but an "immoralist" who

was not concerned with "particular actions" but with "the state of being of the whole man." See Kaufmann, *Nietzsche: Philosopher, Psychologist, Antichrist* (Princeton: Princeton University Press, 1974), 322. Kaufmann is right to point out the first contrast between Kant and Nietzsche, but that difference does not invalidate all comparisons. As for Kaufmann's second objection, it is baffling: Nietzsche is quite explicit in linking the "state of being of the whole man" to particular actions, events, and moments. Indeed, he harbors a deep mistrust for the general. And his rejection of moralism is accompanied by a candid quest for alternative ethical approaches to life.

Beginning from these misleading premises, Kaufmann treats eternal return as a celebratory thought for those who have "achieve[d] self-perfection" (for whom eternal recurrence "coincide[s] with their own Dionysian faith") or for the strong who find in the thought "the last incentive to achieve perfection" (ibid., 322, 325). Kaufmann rightly sees that the thought plays a role in the breeding and preparation Nietzsche endorses (*WP*, §862), but he wrongly assumes that preparation and breeding have an end point at which eternal return ceases to operate as an "incentive" and operates merely as a stamp of approval on a general and already accomplished "state of being."

But Nietzsche's overman is never a fait accompli; he is always in process because ressentiment can never be so thoroughly overcome that it is no longer a temptation and a danger (as Zarathustra would be the first to admit). And these temptations and dangers are necessarily related to or occasioned by "particular actions" (what else could occasion them?). Because Kaufmann thinks, by contrast, that preparation is not perpetual and that self-perfection can be achieved as a fait accompli, he often allows the connection between eternal return and breeding or preparation to recede, he neglects eternal return's character as a test of ressentiment, and he rejects its function as a guide to action, leaving eternal return with only one possible role: to serve as a stamp of self-approval for accomplished overmen. This view paves the way for Kaufmann to argue that the proof that eternal return does not guide particular actions lies in the character of the overmen who think the thought: they "do not deliberate how they should act to avoid unpleasant consequences" (Kaufmann, *Nietzsche*, 323); they "have no thought of the morrow" (ibid., 322). But if that is so, why would they think the thought at all? If they do not require its discipline, why subject themselves to it? The answer is that they are not yet overmen; they do require its discipline; it is part of a perpetual process of preparation that is motored by (what else?) particular actions and events that challenge even the least resentful among us, daily.

That Kaufmann misses this point completely is clear when he offers the following reading of the *Gay Science*'s formulation of eternal return: "Man is to ask himself whether *his present state of being* is such that he would have to answer the demon with impotent anger and gnashing of teeth or whether he could say: 'Never did I hear anything more divine!'" (ibid., 325; emphasis added). But in Nietzsche's text the question is not directed at the subject's present state of being; it asks whether "you have *once experienced* a tremendous moment when you *would have* answered him [i.e., in the midst of which you would have answered, *at the time*] 'You are a god . . .'" (*GS*, §341). It is the particular moment that provides the (momentary) redemption, not the subject's "present state of being" as a whole.

In a more recent reading of Nietzsche, Leslie Paul Thiele highlights the guidance function of eternal return (which he rather unfortunately refers to as a "moral prod"). But he assimilates eternal return too quickly and too simply to Nietzsche's "active nihilism" which, in his view, commands us to "live *in* the here and now, *for* the here and now." See Thiele, *Friedrich Nietzsche and the Politics of the Soul* (Princeton: Princeton University Press, 1990), 204. He fails to see the connection between the thought of eternal return and Nietzsche's treatment of the self as a work of art, a work that serves as a perduring testimony to human creativity, not at all the product of a life lived (nihilistically) merely for the present, though very much a product of a life lived by one who resists the temptation to justify the (often difficult) present in terms of an explanatory (Fallen?) past or a longed-for future.

57. Even the best readers of Nietzsche tend to underrate the import of the moment. Alexander Nehamas emphasizes the role of eternal return as a test for a past we strive to style into a coherence that is appropriate for literary characters. The effort is perpetual because the past—which is always related to and affected by the future—is never settled; it is always subject to the changes the future brings. See Nehamas, *Nietzsche: Life as Literature* (Cambridge: Harvard University Press, 1985), 160–61. In underlining the past orientation of the thought, Nehamas overemphasizes eternal return's evaluative function (which he ties to writing), losing sight of the "tremendous moment"—the action—in the present that makes (momentary) affirmation possible. Alan White, by contrast, responds to Nehamas by overly stressing the transformative function of eternal return, characterizing it as "a challenge for my future," suggestively tying it to dancing rather than writing but thereby underemphasizing the importance of the eternal return in the self's disciplined treatment of its past and present self as a work of art. See White, *Within Nietzsche's Labyrinth* (New York: Routledge, 1990), 110, 113. I agree thoroughly, however, with White's basic claim that "through the thought of eternal return as a challenge, Nietzsche seeks to encourage us to seek a different perspective, a way of viewing our lives that is affirmative without being deceptive or dishonest" (ibid., 69). But I think that Nietzsche seeks more than perspectival shifting. He seeks actions, in the present, that have redemptive power because they are so tremendous or fulfilling that they justify everything that came before them. Deception and dishonesty are dispensed with because their colorings are no longer necessary. In the midst of a tremendous moment, the thought of eternal return can be borne, even celebrated, because ressentiment is momentarily overwhelmed with the affirming joy that attends great accomplishment. None of this is possible, however, without the achievement of a will that can will, an achievement White provocatively identifies with eternal recurrence itself: "Only when I have affirmed my life [in eternal return], have I become one who can will, in the deepest and most comprehensive sense" (ibid., 101).

58. Hannah Arendt, *The Life of the Mind*, 2 vols., ed. Mary McCarthy (New York: Harcourt Brace Jovanovich, 1978), 2:166–69 (henceforth *LM*).

59. Ronald Beiner, "Interpretive Essay," in Hannah Arendt, *Lectures on Kant's Political Philosophy* (Chicago: University of Chicago Press, 1982), 149–50.

60. Ibid., 150.

61. Ibid., 149.

62. *LM*, 2:170.

63. Ibid., 2:172, quoting *GS*, §276, and *TSZ*, "Before Sunrise."

64. *WP*, §585(A).

65. *TI*, "Expeditions," §24; "On Truth and Lies," 96.

66. *TI*, "Morality as Anti-Nature," §1.

67. Ibid. The analogy is justified particularly by Nietzsche's use of metaphorics of dance and music throughout his work to depict the figure he endorses as the subject of a transvaluation of values.

68. *GS*, §290. For the purposes of this chapter, I accept Nietzsche's characterization of the distinction between the castrative self-discipline of the church and the artistic or spiritual self-discipline of his own alternative. Jacques Derrida is right, however, to point out that Nietzsche's implication that "there is no castration operative in [his own] spiritualization" is disputable. See Derrida, *Spurs: Nietzsche's Styles* (Chicago: University of Chicago Press, 1978), 91.

69. *TSZ*, §64, "The Leech."

70. *GM*, 2.22.

71. In their respective discussions of art, there is a great deal on which Nietzsche and Kant seem to agree. This is hardly the place for a detailed account of the subject, but I note Kant's claim (which parallels Nietzsche's) that the artistic imagination "is a powerful agent for creating, as it were, a second nature out of the material supplied to it by actual nature." See Immanuel Kant, *Critique of Judgement*, trans. James Creed Meredith (Oxford: Clarendon Press, 1980), §49. Sally Gibbons directed my attention to this passage, and my brief discussion of the similarities between Kant and Nietzsche on this subject is greatly indebted to her.

72. Ibid., §46.

73. *WP*, §317; *TI*, "Expeditions," §14.

74. Kant, *Critique of Judgement*, §59.

75. *TSZ*, "Zarathustra's Prologue," 5.

76. *TSZ*, §73, "The Higher Man," 13.

77. *TI*, "Expeditions," §11.

78. This is what Zarathustra does (or tries to do) each time he, himself, is confronted with the possibility of eternal recurrence. I take the term "second nature" from *GS*, §290.

79. *BGE*, §212.

80. Nehamas's worry about the inability of Nietzsche's aesthetic judgment of action to condemn immoral acts or excesses of power and exploitation is typical (*Nietzsche: Life*, 166–67). White critically responds to Nehamas (*Within Nietzsche's Labyrinth*, 115–21) and goes on to address these issues in one of the best readings I have seen of Nietzsche on ruling and nobility, both of which, White in effect argues, are re-covered by Nietzsche in *Zarathustra* (129–31). Emphasizing Nietzsche's other texts, Flathman presents another powerful case for reading Nietzsche as the architect of forms of life whose abundance and self-sufficiency are immoral, not in the sense that they violate moral rules but in the sense that they make morality unnecessary, displacing it with an ideal of *personal* self-command and will (*Willful Liberalism: Voluntarism and Individuality in Political Theory and Practice* [Ithaca: Cornell University Press, 1992], 178–84, 201–5).

81. This is similar to the strategy pursued (albeit to somewhat different but complementary ends) by William Connolly in *Identity\Difference: Democratic Negotiations of Political Paradox* (Ithaca: Cornell University Press, 1991). Connolly finds authorization for reading the overman as a part of the self in Foucault, who "shifts the center of gravity of Nietzschean discourse from heroes and classical tragic figures to everyday misfits" (ibid., 187). But Connolly also argues that the collapse of Nietzsche's man and overman "results from the disappearance of the social space in which [the solitary overman] was supposed to reside" (ibid.). My own view is that one does not need to go to twentieth-century conditions or to Foucault to sustain this reading of Nietzsche's overman (though Connolly certainly generates some powerful insights by doing so). Nietzsche himself authorizes the move: if the overman *did* ever achieve the apartness and univocality for which he is often said to strive, he would be over, an end, no longer a beginning; without struggle, he would be without life. Thus, although some of Nietzsche's comments about the overman seem to resist my metaphorization of the figure, they conflict with others that warrant it. The best example in its favor comes from Nietzsche's endorsement (most succinctly developed in "Homer's Contest," which I discuss below) of the perpetuity of contest. An agon dominated by a single genius or overman would cease to be an agon, Nietzsche explains. Similarly, I would argue, the artistic and dancing self for whom Nietzsche writes would cease to create and dance if he were dominated by a single soul. As Nietzsche repeatedly says, this figure has chaos in him, and many souls, and his distinctive style is generated by his internal tumult. Were the overman anything but a *part* of a multiple and chaotic self, were he the total master of a self, he would shut down the internal agon that is the source of Nietzschean creativity.

82. I am indebted to Tom Keenan for this suggestion.

83. Nietzsche's alternative responsibility raises powerful questions for contemporary theory. In particular, it challenges Stephen White's recent distinction between responsibility to the other and responsibility to act in his very well argued book, *Political Theory and Postmodernism* (Cambridge: Cambridge University Press, 1991). White does not address it, but Nietzsche's recovered responsibility resists the terms of his binary. Indeed, from Nietzsche's perspective, White's two responsibilities are in deeper conflict than White imagines. The formation of the multiple self into responsible subjectivity enables responsibility to *act* but usually at the cost of responsibility to *otherness* in the self and in others. One loses one's ear for the other as one is formed (disciplined through increasingly perfect repetitions) into the mode of subjectivity. The alternative responsibility Nietzsche imagines has a better ear for the other than does the responsibility of the moralists and it also (therefore?) generates virtuosic (not, pace White, merely "impertinent") willing and acting, something the responsibility of the moralists actually discourages. This may not be the sort of action White seeks to vouchsafe in his theorization of "responsibility to act," but it does seem to bridge and complicate the categories that structure his argument.

We should not conclude, however, that Nietzsche's not wanting to hold the self responsible *for* acting in White's sense means that Nietzsche has no resources at all with which to respond to ethical concerns like White's. Whereas Nietzsche does not embrace the care and justice White endorses, he does advocate re-covered versions of compassion and magnanimity. True, Nietzsche does not hold his actors responsible for acting compassionately or magnanimously. Instead, he assumes that these excellences will follow from the development of nobility in the soul. As Alan White puts it, "Let us be as charitable to Nietzsche as to Aristotle: let us grant that those who are most noble, admirable and self-affirming will not attempt to exploit others" (*Within Nietzsche's Labyrinth*, 130). Flathman puts the point more positively: the excellences of compassion and magnanimity, among others, *follow from* Nietzsche's ideals of voluntarism, self-discipline, and solitude (*Willful Liberalism*, 199–205).

84. *WP*, §317.

85. Ibid., §95.

86. *HAH*, Preface.

87. *AC*, §11.

88. *WP*, §317. The Nietzsche who authored these two passages on *virtù* is a theorist of radical individuality for whom *virtù*, the personal excellence that is only for oneself, must displace virtue, the herd's self-abnegating excellence that is always for others. Nietzsche's rather lengthy comments on *virtù* provide some of the best support for Flathman's reading of him.

89. Michel Foucault's account of Béasse, a thirteen-year old "delinquent" brought up on charges of vagabondage in nineteenth-century Paris, is a good example of the intricacies of standing apart: "All the illegalities that the court defined as offenses the accused reformulated as the affirmation of a living force." Thus, Foucault argues, Béasse "reinscribed indiscipline [irresponsibility] among the fundamental rights." See Foucault, *Discipline and Punish* (New York: Vintage Books, 1979), 290–91.

90. *WP*, §869; *TI*, "Expeditions," §45. I argue in Chapters 5–7 that the other that virtue theories are most threatened by is not strong, but *undecidable*, which Nietzsche's overman may also be.

91. See the quotation with which this chapter opens.

92. The phrase is used by Sheldon Wolin to characterize Machiavellian *virtù*; see *Politics and Vision* (Boston: Little, Brown, 1960), 217.

93. Nietzsche's re-covery of virtue is unlike his other re-coveries in that it makes use of an alternative term, *virtù*. Elsewhere, Nietzsche simply contrasts, for example, *their* compassion with ours, *their* responsibility with ours. By recovering the term *virtù*, Nietzsche acknowledges a debt to Machiavelli who, in his turn, re-covered the term from Cicero and the Renaissance humanists. Nietzsche turns to Machiavelli for a "cure" from Plato, the consummate architect of virtue politics (*TI*, "Ancients," § 2). Such admiration for Machiavelli was not uncommon at the time. It was shared by many nineteenth-century German intellectuals, led by Fichte. See Max Lerner's introduction to *The Prince and the Discourses*, xli.

94. I focus here not on the civic *virtù* of Machiavelli's *Discourses*—the excellence of a citizen in a republic—but on the rather different princely *virtù* of *The Prince*. Nietzsche re-covers only the latter and it inspires Arendt's vision of politics and action as well.

95. Wolin, *Politics and Vision*, 212–13. The idea that the fortress has this symbolic function is Wolin's insight.

96. Machiavelli, *Discourses*, 2.xxix. Moreover, the ruler's possession of a fortress makes him falsely confident that he can control his subjects through force. Fortresses, Machiavelli advises the prince, are a bad idea for two reasons: first, "they cause you to be more violent and audacious towards your subjects; and next, they do not afford the security which you imagine" (ibid., 2.xxiv). Like Nietzsche, Machiavelli sees that attempts to fix and stabilize an inherently contingent world are not only necessarily deceitful, they are dangerous, provocative of violence and domination. Machiavellian *virtù* consists partly in the wisdom to resist the temptations of this approach.

97. *GS*, §305. Similarly, Machiavelli's prince "must have a mind disposed to adapt itself according to the wind, and as the variations of *fortune* dictate" (*Prince*, 18).

98. For a critical analysis of the problems posed for Machiavelli's politics by his reliance on this masculine-feminine alterity, see Hanna Fenichel Pitkin, *Fortune Is a Woman* (Berkeley: University of California Press, 1984).

99. Actually, he wins for himself a "double glory" if he has both "founded a new realm and adorned it and fortified it with good laws, good arms, good friends, and good examples" (Machiavelli, *Prince*, 24).

100. Mark Hulliung, *Citizen Machiavelli* (Princeton: Princeton University Press, 1983), 30; and John Neville Figgis, *Studies of Political Thought from Gerson to Grotius* (Cambridge: Cambridge University Press, 1956), 85. Echoing Figgis more than Hulliung, Stuart Hampshire faults Nietzsche's aestheticism for its distance from politics, for having "nothing permanently useful to say about political institutions and policies and about their part in limiting tyranny and oppression and averting the destruction of humanity" (*Innocence and Experience* [Cambridge: Harvard University Press, 1989], 156–57). Flathman, by contrast, finds much that is still useful in Nietzsche's remarks about politics, the state, socialism, anarchism, liberalism, and democracy (*Willful Liberalism*, 177–84).

Pace Hulliung, Nietzsche's overman exercises his will to power primarily (even solely) on himself and not on others. If *virtù* is, as Machiavelli says it is, the imposition of form on matter, then those with Hulliung's concerns would do well to note that the matter with which the man of Machiavellian *virtù* works is other people, whereas the matter with which the Nietzschean artist works is the raw matter of self. Finally, pace Figgis, it is not at all clear that Nietzsche's project of making room for individuality under the hegemony of asceticism is devoid of public ends (though its aims are clearly not public in the usual sense of shared and common).

101. *GM*, 2.12.

102. "Homer's Contest," in *The Portable Nietzsche*, trans. and ed. Walter Kaufmann (New York: Viking Press, 1954), 35–37.

103. Ibid., 36.

104. Machiavelli, *Discourses*, 2.Preface; 1.vi.

105. "Homer's Contest," 36–37.

106. Machiavelli, *Discourses*, 1.vi: "If Rome had planned to take away the causes of

riot, it would also have taken away the causes of growth." Expansion is one of the fundamental characteristics of Nietzschean will to power and vitality. In Machiavelli's case, it takes the form of territorial expansion but, as I argue in Chapter 4, there are other varieties of expansion, such as Arendt's account of authority as (constitutional and conceptual) augmentation.

107. Ibid., 1.iv; see also 1.iii, vi.

108. Ibid., 1.vii; emphasis added.

109. Ibid., 1.vi. In short, Machiavelli does not believe that all kinds of internal dissension are productive. He distinguishes "divisions" from "factions." Factions seek the satisfaction of their shared but private interests in the public realm. The rise of factionalism is the mark of corruption in a republic, the mark of the end of devotion to the general good (see, e.g., ibid., 1.viii).

110. *GM*, 2.16.

111. Ibid., 2.9,11.

112. Arendt makes a set of parallel claims with reference to pity, an inherently boundless and therefore destabilizing sentiment on her account, and she too insists on the need for legal and political institutions to act as bulwarks against its manifestation as a political sentiment in the public realm. See Hannah Arendt, *On Revolution* (New York: Penguin Books, 1963).

113. The strategy was to treat "violence and capricious acts on the part of individuals or entire groups as offenses against the law, as rebellion against the supreme power itself." That way, the law "attains the reverse of that which is desired by all revenge": it trains "the eye . . . to an ever more impersonal evaluation of the deed" (*GM*, 2.12).

114. Ibid., 2.10,12. None of the virtue theorists examined here endorses a legal order that is total in the sense of having a law for each and every contingency. But, as I argue below, insofar as the premises and justifications of their legal orders are expressivist, their conceptions of law are, indeed, totalizing—and therefore hostile to struggle. They seek to undermine the very bases of contest by denying, punishing, curing, or otherwise silencing them.

115. Even the man who turns himself into a castle *can*, Nietzsche acknowledges, "achieve *greatness* this way." But there are other avenues to greatness (also durable but perhaps bolder) that Nietzsche prefers.

116. "Enough," but not too much; see *WP*, §480.

117. *GS*, §295. Indeed, for Nietzsche, "duration is a first-rate value on earth" (ibid., §356). Likewise, Machiavelli admires republics because they are not only the most vital (*Prince*, 5) but also the most durable (*Discourses*, 1.lviii) form of political association.

118. *Discourses*, 1.Preface.

119. *GS*, §356. Recall that Nietzsche compares the artist who treats himself as a work of art to an architect in whom "pride, victory over weight and gravity, the will to power, seek to render themselves visible in a building." In Nietzsche's view, "architecture is a kind of rhetoric of power, now persuasive, even cajoling in form, now bluntly imperious."

120. *AC*, §4.

121. Hannah Arendt, *Between Past and Future*, enlarged ed. (New York: Penguin, 1977), 97, 149.
122. See, e. g., *Discourses*, 2.2.

4. Arendt's Accounts of Action and Authority

1. Hannah Arendt, *The Human Condition* (Chicago: University of Chicago Press, 1958), 9 (henceforth *HC*).
2. Peter Fuss highlights the communitarian dimension of Arendt's politics, Seyla Benhabib emphasizes its dialogic moment, and Jürgen Habermas assigns a central role to deliberation and consensus. All overlook the importance of Arendt's debt to elements of the Nietzschean project, in particular, her treatment of action as an intrinsic rather than instrumental good, her identification of action with a virtuosity that is individuating but not subject-centered, her antifoundationalism, and, most important, her commitment to the agonistic dimension of political action. See Peter Fuss, "Hannah Arendt's Conception of Political Community," in *The Recovery of the Public World*, ed. Melvyn Hill (New York: St Martin's Press, 1979); Seyla Benhabib, "Hannah Arendt and the Redemptive Power of Narrative," *Social Research* 57 (1990); and Jürgen Habermas, "Hannah Arendt on the Concept of Power," in *Philosophical-Political Profiles*, trans. Frederick Lawrence (Cambridge: MIT Press, 1983), 171–87.
3. *WP*, §551.
4. *GM*, 1.xiii.
5. Hannah Arendt, *Between Past and Future*, enlarged ed. (New York: Penguin, 1977), 151–52 (henceforth *BPF*).
6. Ibid., 145–53; *LM*, 2:203. For a more detailed account of Arendt's view of the will, see Honig, "Arendt, Identity, and Difference," *Political Theory* 16 (1988), 77–98. As I argue there, the fact that Arendt identifies freedom with worldly appearance even in *The Life of the Mind* argues against the position taken by some of her readers that this last work of hers signals a reevaluation of her dismissive attitude toward the inner self.
7. *BPF*, 151.
8. *HC*, 246, 205. Compare Nietzsche: "In Pericles' famous funeral oration . . . he tells the Athenians: 'Our boldness has gained us access to every land and sea, and erected monuments to itself for both good and evil'!" Nietzsche notes with approval "this 'boldness' of noble races, so headstrong, absurd, incalculable, sudden, improbable . . . their utter indifference to safety and comfort" (*GM*, 1.xi). This short passage contains within it many of the essentials of Arendt's view of action: disdain for the concern for (physical) safety and comfort, the glorification of performances that are spontaneous and surprising, and the claim that the glory of action is not a function of its goodness.
Arendt's use of the term "sui generis" to describe action is not careless. It follows from her controversial claim that "the faculty of action is *ontologically* rooted" in "the fact of natality" (*HC*, 247; see also *LM* 2:217). The ramifications of her gesture to an ontological ground are discussed below.

9. *LM*, 1:192–93. Arendt's assertion that political judgment is directed at particulars echoes both Kantian and Nietzschean aesthetics; see Chapter 3.

10. *HC*, 179.

11. *LM*, 1:29–31; *HC*, 206; see Hannah Arendt, *On Revolution* (New York: Penguin Books, 1963), 49–54 (henceforth *OR*), for a graphic description of the violence of bodily need and poverty and their abortive effects on what Arendt claims might have been a grand *political* revolution in France.

12. *HC*, 40. The former emphasis is more characteristic of *On Revolution*, the latter of *The Human Condition*. For a more sustained discussion of Arendt's treatment of the body as a signifier of necessity, see Honig, "Toward an Agonistic Feminism: Hannah Arendt and the Politics of Identity," in *Feminists Theorize the Political*, ed. Judith Butler and Joan Scott (New York: Routledge, 1992), 215–35.

13. *BPF*, 156.

14. *HC*, 179. George Kateb coins the term "self-surprising" in his penetrating study of Arendt's political thought, *Hannah Arendt: Politics, Conscience, Evil* (Totowa, N.J.: Rowman and Allanheld, 1983).

15. *HC*, 179. Arendt's phrasing here implies that action reveals an antecedently existing "who," but the phrasing is misleading and atypical; see my discussion of performativity below.

16. Ibid., 176.

17. *LM*, 2:217; see also "On Violence," in Arendt, *Crises of the Republic* (New York: Harcourt Brace Jovanovich, 1977), 179. Arendt's description of the actor as, in effect, "born again" is typical of the Christian tone of her rhetoric whenever discussing our "capacity for beginning." She describes "the fact of natality" as "the miracle that saves the world" (*HC*, 247). And she says that "the purpose of the creation of man was to make possible a beginning" (*LM*, 2:217). Arendt's rhetoric is likely influenced by her belief that freedom and "religious conversion" are historically connected: "There is no preoccupation with freedom in the whole history of great philosophy from the Pre-Socratics up to Plotinus, the last ancient philosopher. And when freedom made its first appearance in our philosophical tradition, it was the appearance of Paul first and then of Augustine which gave rise to it" (*BPF*, 145–46; see also *LM*, 2:6). Notably, Arendt also argues that it was the Christian conception of "human secular time" as "rectilinear" that made "such phenomena as novelty, uniqueness of events, and the like conceivable at all" (*OR*, 27).

18. *HC*, 73. Arendt describes "the laborers who 'with their bodies minister to the (bodily) needs of life' [here quoting Aristotle's *Politics* 1254b25] and the women who with their bodies guarantee the physical survival of the species" (*HC*, 72).

19. Ibid., 24.

20. Hanna Fenichel Pitkin, "Justice: On Relating Public and Private," *Political Theory* 9 (1981), 342. Arendt often fails to distinguish clearly her (admittedly admiring) descriptions of the practice of agonal politics in the polis from her account of her own vision of politics, and her critics often mistake the first for the second: for example, Pitkin notes that Arendt's account of action is "individualistic." But the citation on which Pitkin relies (*HC*, 41) is one in which Arendt describes the agon of the polis; where Arendt describes her *own* view of action, even in the early, some say too agonal, *Human Condition*, she says that it is always "in concert" (*HC*, 200).

21. Arendt does seem *at times* to be reluctant to denaturalize labor and work in this way. But this reluctance is offset by numerous passages in which she does treat labor, work, and action as the mentalities Pitkin describes (Pitkin cites *HC*, 46, 83n, 199, 255, and 322 in "Justice," 351 n. 77). And, when reluctant, it is because Arendt wants to secure some important differences among labor, work, and action that are not necessarily threatened, in my view, by a characterization of them as mentalities. Briefly, Arendt is at pains to hold on to the sense in which laboring and working describe not only a mentality but also a particular set of substantive concerns. Thus, she does not oppose the admission of householders into the public realm, but neither does she oppose merely the admission of the householding mentality; she opposes the admission of "householding activities" as an identifiable branch of human activity and concern, not just a mode of thinking. The question then is, can what would otherwise be deemed "householding activities" take on a truly different aspect (become substantively changed) if approached with a different mentality, say, from the mentality of work or action instead of that of labor? Most of the time, Arendt implies that the answer is no, that private realm concerns are stubbornly resistant to transformation; at other times, however, she seems less insistent on this.

22. *LM*, 1:187, 70; *WP*, §490. Nietzsche would, however, reject Arendt's reification of this multiplicity into three distinct mental faculties.

23. *LM*, 2:69.

24. *HC*, 175, 220, 234.

25. *HC*, 244, 184–93. This means that the agon cannot serve as a stage for the vain posturing attributed by critics to Arendt's agonal actors. See Pitkin, "Justice"; Patricia Springborg, "Hannah Arendt and the Classical Republican Tradition," in *Thinking, Judging, Freedom*, ed. G. T. Kaplan and C. S. Kessler (Sydney: Allen and Unwin, 1989); and Wendy Brown, *Manhood and Politics* (Totowa, N.J.: Rowman and Littlefield, 1988).

26. *HC*, 244.

27. Ibid., 244–46. Arendt's characterization of these precepts as "moral" appears curious given her otherwise consistent insistence that action be safeguarded from the intrusion of moral standards and practices. She may use the term to indicate that forgiving and promising operate in the public realm in a way that is *analogous to* morality's operations in the private realm. In *The Human Condition* she says, "In so far as morality is more than the sum total of *mores*, of customs and standards of behavior solidified through tradition and valid on the ground of agreements, it has, at least politically, no more to support itself than the good will to counter the enormous risks of action by readiness to forgive and to be forgiven, to make promises and to keep them" (245).

28. Arendt's third example is that of declaratives, as in declarations of independence that found new regimes in the act of speech and writing; see below.

29. I draw the terms "performative" and "speech act" from J. L. Austin, whose account I discuss below; see *How to Do Things with Words* (Cambridge: Harvard University Press, 1962).

30. *HC*, 237, 244.

31. Ibid., 244.

32. Ibid., 236–37. This view is unchanged in *The Life of the Mind:* "In the realm of action . . . no deed can be safely undone" (2:30).

33. *HC*, 240.

34. Ibid., 241; *WP*, §235.

35. *HC*, 240.

36. *GM*, 2.10–11.

37. *OR*, 206.

38. On Austin's account, for example, discursive practices postulate a vast array of political and cultural institutions that set many of the conditions for discursive felicity, for example, distinguishing and sanctioning the distinction between those who are in authority and those who are not; that is, they identify the authorized speaker of the performative "I call this meeting to order" as the chairman of the board, and they forbid, punish, fail to comprehend or sanction the interrogation of anyone who impersonates the chair and usurps his performative privilege.

39. *GM*, 2.1.

40. For Arendt, autonomy is the impositional construction and promising the nonimpositional and largely self-realizing alternative.

41. *HC*, 245; Arendt's reference is to the first two aphorisms of the second essay of the *Genealogy*. She also says that "Nietzsche saw with unequaled clarity the connection between human sovereignty and the faculty of making promises" but claims that Nietzsche could not appreciate the power inherent in promising because of his "modern prejudice to see the source of all power in the will power of the isolated individual" (ibid.).

42. The same point can be made with reference to Arendt's "stories," the stories that spectators of virtuosic action tell to immortalize great actors and commemorate events. It is curious that Arendt, so insistent that plurality is the sine qua non of the public realm, seems to assume that the spectators will produce and agree on a single story of each action and that the meaning and force of those stories will be clear and unproblematic. It is likely that Arendt's conception of the role of stories in the public realm is unduly influenced by her understanding of the Greek model, in which an authoritative poet (e.g., Homer) gives the authoritative account of political action.

43. It should be noted that all these arguments and those that follow below apply equally well to forgiving, Arendt's other performative "precept" of action.

44. A version of this objection was first suggested to me by William Connolly.

45. "Signature, Event, Context," in *Limited Inc.*, trans. Samuel Weber and Jeffrey Mehlman (Evanston, Ill.: Northwestern University Press, 1988), 13. The last quoted phrase is from the slightly different translation in Jacques Derrida, *Margins of Philosophy*, trans. Alan Bass (Chicago: University of Chicago Press, 1982), 322.

46. "Signature, Event, Context," 14.

47. Derrida is drawing on Austin, *How to Do Things with Words*, 12–16.

48. "Signature, Event, Context," 15.

49. Ibid., 17.

50. Eventually, both become illocutionary *doings*.

51. "Signature, Event, Context," 15.

52. Ibid.

53. Admittedly, once he has analyzed them, Austin sends his performatives out (as it were) into the world and appreciates the idiosyncratic uses to which they are

put, as well as the odd effects they often have. Derrida's criticisms do not deny this; they simply suggest that Austin's *initial* confinement of his analytic gaze has effects that resonate throughout the theory, effects that are at odds (or ill at ease) with Austin's well-known appreciation of the idiosyncratic and the offbeat.

54. *HC*, 176–79, emphasis added.

55. Elsewhere, Arendt tries to attenuate the opposition, seeking "to make the extraordinary an ordinary occurrence in everyday life" (ibid., 197). Derrida's treatment of the signature as both fabulous and ordinary is relevant in this context; see below.

56. Of course, *privileging* the extraordinary, no less than banishing it, contributes to the protection of the ordinary. I discuss Arendt's public-private distinction as a way of protecting the private realm from action's disruptions below.

57. *BPF*, 95.

58. *OR*, 130.

59. "Signature, Event, Context," 5.

60. Ibid., 9.

61. *HC*, 184

62. Other readers of Arendt attribute the uncontrollability of Arendtian action to the plurality of the audience that receives the performance (e.g., Kateb, *Hannah Arendt*, 14–16). On my reading, by contrast, dissemination is not an external accident that befalls Arendtian action; it is *inside* the phenomenon, an inherent, structural feature of language and action, regarded as speech or writing in the public realm.

63. "Signature, Event, Context," 9, 13–19.

64. A much abbreviated version of this section and the next two, appeared as "Declarations of Independence: Arendt and Derrida on the Problem of Founding a Republic," *American Political Science Review* 85 (1991), 97–113.

65. *OR*, 117–18. This view, that Arendt's account of authority is antimodernist, is the standard interpretation. See Richard E. Flathman, *Authority and the Authoritative: The Practice of Political Authority* (Chicago: University of Chicago Press, 1978), and Richard B. Friedman, "On the Concept of Authority in Political Philosophy," in *Concepts in Social and Political Philosophy*, ed. Richard E. Flathman (New York: Macmillan, 1973).

66. The rise of the secular meant that there was a longing even on the part of "very religious people" to establish politically a "secular state" to secure their "posterity" (*OR*, 229–30). Arendt celebrates this, as did Machiavelli. Both see in the rise of the secular a regained opportunity for political actors to exercise *virtù* in virtuoso performances that win them glory, the human world's only immortality.

67. Ibid., 183–84. Arendt is quoting Rousseau, *The Government of Poland*, trans. and ed. Willmore Kendall (Indianapolis: Hackett, 1985), 3, and *On the Social Contract*, trans. and ed. Donald A. Cress (Indianapolis: Hackett, 1988), bk. 2, chap. 7.

68. *OR*, 44; see also 33, 118, 123.

69. Ibid., 149–50.

70. Ibid., 196.

71. Ibid., 198.

72. Ibid., 199, 185–86.

73. Ibid., 190–96.

74. Ibid., 192. Arendt consistently claims that truth is coercive and therefore illicit in the realm of politics (e.g., *BPF*, 107–8; *LM*, 1:61). It seems that she agrees with Nietzsche's claim that "before reason one may submit and acquiesce" (*WP*, §95).

75. I note in passing that Arendt's description of performatives as a form of utterance that creates something de novo, her identification of this form of utterance with politics, and her characterization of politics as world building all suggest that her account draws on the model of the originary performative: the Divine utterance "Let there be . . . ," on the biblical account, is the first of a series of performatives whereby God created the world.

76. *OR*, 130; emphasis mine. Arendt's implied distinction between an "argument in support of an action" and an action that appears in words indicates that she assumes that only performative utterances are speech *acts*. Austin began with this assumption but later found he could not maintain it.

77. Ibid., 192.

78. Ibid., 193, 195.

79. Ibid., 195–96, 181, 175.

80. Ibid., 175.

81. Hannah Arendt, *On Violence* (New York: Harcourt Brace Jovanovich, 1970), 47.

82. *OR*, 199, 193–94.

83. *BPF*, 95.

84. Flathman, *Authority and the Authoritative*, 71, 263 n. 6.

85. *BPF*, 92, 141.

86. *OR*, 166; emphasis added.

87. Arendt repeatedly says in *On Revolution* and elsewhere that the only politics available in modernity are revolutions (e.g., *OR*, 171, 238). But she is also impressed by civil disobedience which she sees as a moment of politics in modernity.

88. See ibid., 116–17, 260.

89. This new conception of authority is formally similar to the traditional Roman conception. For, although Arendt claims that in Rome authority was sustained by the particular traditional and religious beliefs of that society, she also claims that it was "the very coincidence of authority, tradition, and religion, all three simultaneously springing from the act of foundation, [that] was the backbone of Roman history from beginning to end" (ibid., 201). Thus, both the traditional and modern conceptions of authority, on her account, are born of the act of foundation. And this is no coincidence; according to Arendt, the American idea that authority could inhere in the act of foundation was inspired by the example of Rome (ibid., 199).

90. Ibid., 174.

91. *BPF*, 141.

92. *OR*, 167. Arendt makes no note of it, but the phrase "in the Presence of God and one another" instantiates the same incongruous unification of a constative and performative utterance as did Jefferson's "We hold these truths to be self-evident." This suggests that the confidence the parties had in each other was not "granted and confirmed by no one and as yet unsupported by any means of violence"; it was guaranteed by God and his presence.

Indeed, Arendt never mentions it, but the Mayflower Compact was drawn up in Britain under the sanctioning and supporting gaze of British juridical institutions *before* the colonists left for the uncertain and unknown New World. Moreover, it was signed on board ship, *before* the colonists disembarked in America. It would seem that the colonists' "confidence . . . in their own power" was perhaps a little less hardy than Arendt estimates it.

93. Ibid., 213.

94. Jacques Derrida, "Declarations of Independence," *New Political Science* 15 (1986), 10.

95. Ibid., 12; emphasis added. This claim that signatures require "countersignatures" again renders problematic Arendt's faith in the power of the "we" to ensure its own action. For in Arendt's process there are only cosigners, and cosigners on Derrida's account are not sufficient to get us out of Sièyes's vicious circle. The parties to the Mayflower Compact acknowledged this when they combined "themselves together into a 'civil Body Politick'" which was not, as Arendt claims, "held together *solely* by the strength of mutual promises"; these promises were made, as Arendt well knows, "in the Presence of God and one another." The parties invoke the presence of God because they need the validation of his witness, of his countersignature.

96. Ibid., 12.

97. Kant too was aware of the problem. In "The Contest of the Faculties" he notes briefly that the ideal political constitutions thought up by philosophers such as Plato, More, Harrington, and Allais have never "been tried out in practice." This, Kant explains, is because "it is the same with political creations as with the creation of the world: no-one was present at it, nor could anyone have been present, or else he would have been his own creator." See Kant, "The Contest of the Faculties," in *KPW*, 188n.

98. Derrida, "Declarations of Independence," 9.

99. Ibid., 10.

100. *OR*, 193–94.

101. Hannah Arendt, "Understanding and Politics," *Partisan Review* 20 (1953), 378.

102. Arendt reserves the meritorious name "speech" for performative utterances in the public realm.

103. Machiavelli makes a similar point when he argues that violence attends every founding, including those of legitimate regimes.

104. Derrida, "Declarations of Independence," 10.

105. *OR*, 196.

106. *LM*, 2:217.

107. *OR*, 195, 39.

108. See Jacques Derrida, "Devant la loi," in *Kafka and the Contemporary Critical Performance*, ed. Alan Udoff (Bloomington: Indiana University Press, 1987).

109. *OR*, 202; emphasis added. See also *BPF*, 123. Arendt is not the only one to note the etymological and conceptual connections between authority and augmentation (see Friedman, "On the Concept of Authority," R. S. Peters, "Authority," and Carl J. Friedrich, "On Authority," in *Concepts in Social and Political Philosophy*), but she alone reasons from them to an account of authority as deeply tied to a *practice* of augmentation.

110. *OR*, 233

111. Ibid., 250, 253.

112. Ibid., 171, 151–52. Only a republican politics, according to Arendt, recognizes that the source of its legitimacy and power is in the popular performative act of constitution, "not in majority rule or consent (both of which imply submission and acquiescence), not in an external absolute" (ibid., 166). Since Arendt thinks that this commitment to power is unique to republicanism, and that this power is the source of authority in modernity, it seems that on her account only republican regimes can be legitimate. Thus, her re-covered conception of authority for modernity may be as essentialist as was her conception of traditional authority (although not for the reasons that Flathman gives.) But it is also more viable, requiring, on the one hand, a common subscription to a set of authoritative practices more at home in the modern world than the religion and tradition of ancient Rome and, on the other hand, a commitment to a project still valued in the modern era, that of world building.

113. Ibid., 225.

114. This leads one recent critic of Machiavelli, Mark Hulliung, in *Citizen Machiavelli* (Princeton: Princeton University Press, 1983), to argue that Machiavelli's republicanism does not deserve the admiration of his modern readers because Machiavelli's commitment to republicanism follows not from any love of liberty or political participation but from his belief that republics are best suited for successful expansion and conquest. As Hulliung sees it, Machiavelli's expansionist agenda is greedy and self-serving, the agenda of a man hungry for power, in the usual, pejorative sense. And there is a case to be made for this view. But the case is not terribly persuasive. It ignores the fact that Machiavelli, for good republican reasons, preferred the ancient Tuscan mode of expansion to that of Athens, Sparta, and Rome. Pitkin aptly summarizes Machiavelli's account, given in the *Discourses*, 2.iv: "The Romans made alliances in which they always reserved to themselves 'the seat of authority and the reputation of command'. As a result, their allies soon 'found that without realizing it they had subjected themselves with their own labors and their own blood'. Athens and Sparta simply conquered their neighbors outright, turning them into subjects rather than allies. The ancient Tuscan cities formed an egalitarian alliance, carrying over into their foreign relations the mutuality and reciprocity that characterized their republican domestic politics." See Pitkin, *Fortune Is a Woman* (Berkeley: University of California Press, 1984). 237–38.

115. Arendt does recognize, however, that Roman expansion took the form of both territorial acquisition and augmentation (see *OR*, 201).

116. Pitkin, *Fortune Is a Woman*, 88, citing *Discourses*, 1.xliv.

117. *OR*, 255

118. Ibid., 198–204.

119. Jacques Derrida, "Deconstruction in America: An Interview with Jacques Derrida," *Critical Exchange* 17 (1985), 24–25.

120. Pitkin, *Fortune Is a Woman*, 275–79. The return to beginnings will be violent only in regimes that are corrupt, Pitkin argues. Others will respond to nonviolent forms of reinvigoration.

121. The absence in the American republic of something like a ward system that would allow citizens to participate in the political activity of augmentation does not

mean that the republic lacks authority. It does mean that "the true seat of authority in the American Republic" is the Supreme Court, which is, "in Woodrow Wilson's phrase, 'a kind of Constitutional Assembly in continuous session'." Consequently, Arendt argues, the American concept of authority is very different from that of Rome: "In Rome the function of authority was political, and it consisted in giving advice, while in the American republic the function of authority is legal, and it consists in interpretation" (*OR*, 200). This substitution of legal for political authority, together with the failure of the American republic to vouchsafe spaces of freedom for popular participation in politics, marks, according to Arendt, the loss of the American republic's revolutionary spirit.

122. Leo Strauss, *Thoughts on Machiavelli* (Chicago: University of Chicago Press, 1978), 44.

123. Friedrich Nietzsche, *The Use and Abuse of History*, trans. Adrian Collins (Indianapolis: Bobbs-Merrill, 1949), 24.

124. *HC*, 220, 234, 200.

125. Ibid., 246.

126. Machiavelli thought that the greatest founders in history were foundlings; this was to their advantage, for it allowed them to mythologize their origins and enhance their mystique. Pitkin adds that Machiavelli's "founder must be a foundling, conceptually, because he must be the unmoved mover, his autonomy construed as having no human antecedents" (*Fortune Is a Woman*, 79, 57).

127. Pitkin, "Justice," 336; see also Kateb, *Hannah Arendt*, 17–18.

128. Arendt insists that "this whole sphere" of politics be "limited," that it "not encompass the whole of man's and the world's existence" (*BPF*, 264).

129. *LM*, 2:37–38, 101–2; emphasis added. I have argued elsewhere that on Arendt's account the will is both self-generating and capable of bringing its own activity to an end; see "Arendt, Identity, and Difference," 81. However, the final quotation here has persuaded me that Arendt did not attribute the latter feature to the will but to action.

130. Seyla Benhabib also metaphorizes Arendt's public realm, but Benhabib metaphorizes only the discursive moment in Arendtian action and leaves its agonistic other behind. For Benhabib, agonistic public space is a *place*, but discursive public space, Arendt's more "modernist" notion, "is a *space* not necessarily in any topographical or institutional sense. . . . [It] emerges whenever and wherever men act together in concert" ("Hannah Arendt," 193–94). Because Benhabib limits the metaphorization, because she does not identify spaces of politics *in* the (so-called) private self, she continues to treat Arendt's notion of political space as, literally, a *public* (intersubjective) space. And because she cleanses Arendtian action of its agonistic character, she renders Arendt's concept of political action into more of a conversation and less of an event; there is less for action to disrupt and it becomes, once again, difficult to imagine what the topics of "political" conversations might be. In my view (what Peter Fuss calls) the agonal and the accommodational elements of Arendt's thinking require each other: those who favor Arendt's accommodational politics cannot have it cleansed of the agonal other they would like to dispel. And this is, perhaps, one of the best things that can be said about Arendt's conception of politics.

131. As I argued earlier in the chapter, there are Arendtian grounds to deessential-

ize labor and work, to treat them as activities that engender certain mentalities that, if left undisrupted, are prone to sedimentation.

132. Nancy Fraser, *Unruly Practices: Power, Discourse, and Gender in Contemporary Social Theory* (Minneapolis: University of Minnesota Press, 1989), 76.

133. *BPF*, 3–4.

134. I borrow this phrasing from an objection posed to me by Michael Rogin.

135. Judith Butler, "Performative Acts and Gender Constitution: An Essay in Phenomenology and Feminist Theory," in *Performing Feminisms*, ed. Sue-Ellen Case (Baltimore: Johns Hopkins University Press, 1990), 271–80.

136. Pitkin, "Justice," 336.

137. *OR*, 47; see also Butler, "Performative Acts," 274.

5. Rawls and the Remainders of Politics

1. The goal of Rawls's project is "to settle a fundamental disagreement over the just forms of social institutions within a democratic society under modern conditions." See Rawls, "Kantian Constructivism in Moral Philosophy," *Journal of Philosophy* 77 (1980), 518.

2. Sheldon Wolin coins the term "megastate" to good rhetorical effect in "Democracy and Operation Democracy," in *The Presence of the Past: Essays on the State and the Constitution* (Baltimore: Johns Hopkins University Press, 1989), 192–207.

3. John Rawls, *A Theory of Justice* (Cambridge Mass.: Harvard University Press, 1971), 222 (henceforth *TJ*).

4. See Nancy Fraser, "Rethinking the Public Sphere: A Contribution to the Critique of Actually Existing Democracy," *Social Text* 25/26 (1991), 56–80, esp. 65–70. Arendt would not endorse Fraser's multiple publics but, as the argument of Chapter 4 indicates, she would prefer the decentering strategy to its alternatives.

5. My point is not that the decentering strategy is necessarily and always better. Obviously, that depends on the form it takes in any particular setting. But neither is the recentering strategy so obviously a boon to democratic politics that it need not defend itself against this powerful alternative. For recent arguments in favor of an extrastatist politics, see William Connolly's "Democracy and Territoriality," in *The Rhetorical Republic*, ed. Frederick C. Dolan and Thomas Dumm (Amherst: University of Massachusetts Press, 1993); and James Der Derian and Michael J. Shapiro, eds., *International/Intertextual Relations: Boundaries of Knowledge and Practice in World Politics* (Lexington, Mass.: Heath, 1989).

6. Justice as fairness "comes as close as a society can to being a voluntary scheme." It "meets the principles which free and equal persons would assent to under circumstances that are fair" (*TJ*, 13).

7. Rawls's provisions for political participation and civil disobedience are not exceptions to this reconciliation strategy, they are part of it. Both address the state. Both are appropriated by the Rawlsian regime to help consolidate allegiance to the two principles of justice. And both are likely to wane, not flourish, in justice as fairness, where the potentially alienating effect of Rawlsian reconciliation (passive

consumerism in a bureaucratic state) is in tension with Rawls's hope that membership in a political association might be experienced as an intrinsic good.

8. *TJ*, 541.

9. Criticisms of Rawls's early attempts to secure the priority of the right over the good have been ably made by his communitarian critics, most notably Michael Sandel. For a superb analysis of the epistemological and political issues at stake in this part of the liberal-communitarian debate, see David Paris and Patrick Neal, "Liberalism and the Communitarian Critique: A Guide for the Perplexed," *Canadian Journal of Political Science* 23 (1990), 419–39. I focus less on the battle between the right and the good for priority than on the fact that both sides in this debate displace politics in order to secure the outcome they seek. In my view, this displacement poses a more serious problem for Rawls than for his communitarian critics because Rawls's depoliticizations undermine the very ends he seeks to secure. By contrast, Sandel's depoliticizations *do* serve the ends he seeks. The problem is that his depoliticizing strategies are ultimately unsuccessful.

10. Communitarian theorists and some of those influenced by Nietzsche have been more insightful than most liberals in seeing the tendency of communities to treat their own ideals (as well as others') as norms by which others ought to live (or by which their own norms are threatened). "Politicizations" are any responses that engage or contest this tendency.

11. The "distribution of natural assets is a fact of nature." "Neither just nor unjust," it is as contingent as "one's initial starting place in society" (*TJ*, 104–7). The echo of Nietzsche is powerful ("No one gives a man his qualities"). For Nietzsche, as for Rawls, desert is a practice that ought not to survive the death of god.

Rawls's unmasking of desert raises an important question: is desert's arbitrariness (its vulnerability to infinite regress) typical of other social and political practices? Assuming that desert's vulnerability is unique, Rawls simply replaces the practice with something more sturdy. Justice as fairness responds to its own institutionally generated "legitimate expectations" instead of rewarding antecedent moral worth.

But Rawls notices a similar instability in the practice of promising. He responds differently in this case, perhaps because as a contract theorist of a sort he can ill afford to discard the practice of promising. Following J. L. Austin, Rawls characterizes promising "as an action defined by a public system of rules" which is "a set of constitutive conventions" (ibid., 344), but he concludes that "a bona fide promise is one which arises in accordance with the rule of promising *when the practice it represents is just.*" Rawls goes beyond Austin's contextual assurances to guarantee promising with another principle. Because promising "is simply a constitutive convention," it needs to be secured by the principle of fidelity which "is a moral principle, a consequence of the principle of fairness" (ibid., 346, emphasis added). The principle of fairness takes the place of Kant's law of laws and serves as a guarantee, a reliable anchor that stabilizes and secures this contingent, merely conventional practice. Contra Arendt, who praises the binding power of promises, Rawls's position implies that, as Michael Sandel puts it, "it is not *promises* that bind," it is the principle of fidelity; See Sandel, *Liberalism and the Limits of Justice* (Cambridge: Cambridge University Press, 1982), 111 (henceforth *LLJ*).

By contrast with Arendt, for whom contracting and promising are appropriate political practices *because* of the aporia that marks each and every performative utterance, Rawls insists that the aporia must be closed if promising and contracting are to render a meaningful service to politics. Contra Derrida, Rawls believes that it is possible and necessary to fill the place of the last instance, legitimately and nonfoundationally, without violence or arbitrariness. Rawls fills the place of the last instance by resorting to the place of the first instance, the original position.

12. The phrase is from Robert Nozick, *Anarchy, State, and Utopia* (New York: Basic Books, 1974), 225.

13. *TJ*, 102. The willingness of those who are better off to share the fate of those who are less so enhances the voluntary character of the scheme. It effectively provides "a fair basis on which those" who are better off "could expect others to collaborate with them when some workable arrangement is a necessary condition of the good of all" (ibid., 103).

14. Nietzsche, a better psychologist than Rawls, knows better: he warns that we continue to inhabit the houses of God long after his death.

15. *TJ*, 446; emphasis added.

16. The claim that Rawls's regime seeks the closure of political space, that Rawls displaces the political with the juridical or the administrative, is not unique to the perspective of *virtù*. Similar charges have been made from a variety of perspectives by several of Rawls's critics. See Michael Walzer, "Philosophy and Democracy," *Political Theory* 9 (1981), 379–99; Benjamin Barber, *The Conquest of Politics: Liberal Theory in a Democratic Age* (Princeton: Princeton University Press, 1988); Chantal Mouffe, "Rawls: Political Philosophy without Politics," in *Universalism and Communitarianism: Contemporary Debates in Ethics*, ed. David Rasmussen (Cambridge, Mass.: MIT Press 1990); Michael Sandel, *LLJ*; Seyla Benhabib, "The Generalized and the Concrete Other," in *Feminism as Critique*, ed. Seyla Benhabib and Drucilla Cornell (Minneapolis: University of Minnesota Press, 1988); and Sheldon Wolin, "Contract and Birthright," in *Presence of the Past*. In general, these theorists worry that Rawls fails effectively to secure a place in justice as fairness for constitutive political goods like shared reflection, deliberation, accountability, resistance, or collective action. Whereas Sandel and Benhabib focus on the epistemological and political closures enabled by Rawls's modeling of political subjectivity on the classic (male) liberal individual, Walzer, Barber, and Mouffe argue that Rawls's failure to safeguard the political is rooted specifically in his privileging of philosophy over politics. Wolin criticizes Rawls not for privileging philosophy over politics but for reducing politics to political economy (*Presence of the Past*, 142).

For most of these theorists, the charge that Rawls displaces politics is part of an attempt to secure a different displacement of politics, one that consolidates politics into legislature (Walzer) or participation in institutionally established sites (Barber) or the establishment (not the subversion or proliferation) of stable political and civic identities (Sandel, Benhabib) or localism (Wolin). Of this group of Rawls critics, Mouffe is the only one to call for a radical proliferation of political space and action. Perhaps because each is invested in an alternative displacement, none traces the processes or mechanisms whereby Rawls represses dissonance in justice as fairness, nor does anyone note the regime's production of remainders in Part III of *A Theory of Justice*.

17. Wolin and Walzer worry that the original position (in its contractual capacity) erases the past that politics must confront or express. Benhabib and Susan Okin worry that it homogenizes or erases gender difference, thereby disabling real political engagement or inclusion; see Susan Moller Okin, *Justice, Gender, and the Family* (New York: Basic Books, 1990). None sees the self's isolation in the original position as a sign that the position serves a mantra-like function.

18. Rawls's two principles of justice state: "First: each person is to have an equal right to the most extensive basic liberty compatible with a similar liberty for others. Second: social and economic inequalities are to be arranged so that they are both (a) reasonably expected to be to everyone's advantage [the difference principle], and (b) attached to positions open to all." The two principles are lexically ordered so that the first principle's equal liberty may not be traded off for greater social and economic advantage (*TJ*, 60–61).

19. Ibid., 86. "The aim is to use the notion of pure procedural justice as a basis of theory" (ibid., 136). This, along with the priority of liberty, evidences Rawls's commitment to the priority of the right over the good.

20. Ibid., 19.

21. Simplicity is one of the attractions of the move to treat complex problems of economic distribution by choosing principles of justice in a choice situation that is purely procedural, and it is the reason for Rawls's decision to limit the application of justice to the basic structure. He confines his discussion of liberty to "constitutional and legal restrictions" where "liberty is a certain structure of institutions" (ibid., 202). For more on this strategy, see David R. Mapel, *Social Justice Reconsidered: The Problem of Appropriate Precision in a Theory of Justice* (Urbana: University of Illinois Press, 1989).

22. The parties are to "evaluate principles solely on the basis of general considerations" (*TJ*, 137). The veil expresses the moral conviction that "if a knowledge of particulars is allowed, then the outcome is biased by arbitrary contingencies" (ibid., 141).

23. *TJ*, 141, 15.

24. Ibid., 12, 139, 263.

25. Ibid., 141–42.

26. *LLJ*, 127.

27. *TJ*, 121.

28. I am well aware that Rawls does not think that he can achieve that ideal. He certainly knows that the two principles of justice do *not* follow perfectly from the original position. But his idealization of strict deduction affects the regime that lives under its unrealized spell. The ideal has important effects, particularly with regard to the citizens' attitudes toward the presence of politics and dissonance in their regime.

29. Sandel makes the point as well: since the parties to the original position are similarly situated (identically situated would be more accurate, Sandel suggests), "the 'deliberations' of the parties proceed in silence" (*LLJ*, 129). See also Benhabib, "The Generalized and Concrete Other," 89–90, and Walzer, "Philosophy and De-

mocracy," 389. Note that Rawls's ideal of strict deduction is subverted, not secured, by his reliance on the incompatible languages of choice and acknowledgment.

30. *LLJ*, 129–30.

31. Nor, therefore, can it be understood to "come second" in any chronological sense. It is merely second on my list. Note that the undecidability of the original position means that Rawls cannot attain the freedom from politics of (mis)interpretation he sought at the moment of founding.

32. But Rawls's deessentialization of desert surpasses his commitment to set principles that "accommodate our firmest convictions" and "provide guidance where guidance is needed" (*TJ*, 20).

33. Ibid., 53, 19–20.

34. Ibid., 135.

35. Henceforth, a certain indeterminacy is no longer a flaw. The two principles constrain the process of founding in the second stage but the process is no longer strictly deductive. "It is not always clear which of several constitutions, or economic and social arrangements, would be chosen. But when this is so, justice is to that extent likewise indeterminate" (ibid., 201). It may be the case that, when this is so, justice is to that extent, likewise, politicized. In the frame of indeterminacy there is room for contest and for power to play a role in settling arrangements that the rationality of the original position leaves unsettled. Once the constitutional arrangements are settled politically, however, this space of contest is closed. There is some debate among Rawls's critics as to whether the frame of indeterminacy is too narrow or too broad; see Richard E. Flathman, *The Philosophy and Politics of Freedom* (Chicago: University of Chicago Press, 1987), and, for the contrary view, Thomas W. Pogge, *Realizing Rawls* (Ithaca: Cornell University Press, 1989).

36. *TJ*, 196–98.

37. Since at each stage citizens are allowed access to more, not less, information, it might seem that the movement from one stage to the next is not a closure but an opening up of political space. It is true that the space of political contest expands as the breadth of indeterminacy and information expands in each successive stage of the founding, but it is also the case that as the citizens move from one stage to the next the previous stage's contests are closed, settled, rendered inaccessible from their new vantage point.

38. In a critique of Rawls that is kindred to mine, focused not on Rawls's effective closure of political spaces but on his closure of the spaces of moral argument and contest, Stanley Cavell argues that the finality condition is a product of Rawls's mistaken and unfortunate analogy between games and promising. The rules of games may be final and nonnegotiable, but in "the moral life the equivalent finality is carried not by a rule but only by a *judgment* of moral finality, one that may be competently opposed, whose content may then enter into a moral argument, one whose resolution is not to be settled by appeal to a rule defining an institution." See Cavell, *Conditions Handsome and Unhandsome: The Constitution of Emersonian Perfectionism* (Chicago: University of Chicago Press, 1990), 113.

39. The impossibility of perfect repetition is explored to different ends by Wittgenstein and Derrida. See Wittgenstein's discussion of rule following in *Philo-*

sophical Investigations, trans. G. E. M. Anscombe (New York: Macmillan, 1953) and Derrida's treatment of iterability in "Signature, Event, Context," in *Limited Inc.*, trans. Samuel Weber and Jeffrey Mehlman (Evanston, Ill.: Northwestern University Press, 1988).

40. *TJ*, 139; emphasis added. The echo of Nietzsche's themes of perspectivism and eternal return is striking. The most obvious difference between Rawls and Nietzsche on this point is that Nietzsche proliferates perspectives, refusing to grant to any single one sovereignty over the others, whereas Rawls privileges the original position as the sovereign perspective of justice.

41. Ibid.; emphasis added.

42. *TJ*, 141. When I say that Rawls advocates *the* original position, not *an* original position, I do not mean to imply that he prohibits any tinkering with the version of the original position presented in *A Theory of Justice*. On the contrary, he invites his readers to adjust his account in reflective equilibrium and elsewhere. But whether or not we make adjustments, once we decide on the structure and constraints of the original position, what we have decided on is the structure of a sovereign perspective.

43. *GM*, 2.10.

44. Rawls's regime does have a "public system of penalties," however, even at the ideal level. Its purpose is not to punish violations of law (violations of law do not become an issue until Rawls moves from ideal to partial compliance theory) but to solve the assurance problem (*TJ*, 240).

45. "It is an important [albeit secondary] feature of a conception of justice that it should generate its own support. That is, its principles should be such that when they are embodied in the basic structure of society men tend to acquire the corresponding sense of justice" (ibid., 138).

46. Ibid., 177. "The scheme of social cooperation is more or less regularly complied with and its basic rules willingly acted upon" (ibid., 6; see also 138, 572, 576-77).

47. "Finally we checked to see in the third part if justice as fairness is a feasible conception. This forced us to raise the question of stability and whether the right and the good as defined are congruent. These considerations do not determine the initial acknowledgement of principles in the first part of the argument, but confirm it" (ibid., 580).

48. Ibid., 584; see also 515.

49. The strategy serves another purpose too: it gives a new urgency to the Rawlsian insistence on the truth of expressivism. "Our" free and equal rationality is a source of protection, defense, and reassurance for the "we" that is faced with the other. Rawls never asks whether "our" insistence helps to *produce* the other against whom the "we" then defines itself.

50. *TJ*, 314-15; emphasis added.

51. John Rawls, "Two Concepts of Rules," *Philosophical Review* 64 (1955), 3-32, quotation from 3. These arguments distinguishing individual punishments from the practice are not made explicit in *A Theory of Justice* though they are implied by what Rawls does say in the paragraph quoted above. Rawls discusses these issues more explicitly in "Two Concepts of Rules," which I draw on here. His early view of the

practice of punishment as an incentive scheme that is future oriented seems to ground his later reliance on penal institutions to solve the assurance problem in *A Theory of Justice*. But his rejection of a strictly incentive view of punishment is supplemented in the later work by reasons that relate to his theory of justice. His early, strictly retributivist (past-oriented) view of individual punishments seems to be unchanged in the later work but, as I argue below, it has a different resonance in the context of justice as fairness.

52. These two reasons derive directly from Rawls's vision of justice as fairness. I earlier noted a third, more general reason for the rejection of the simple incentive view of punishment at the outset: that view cannot rule out the punishment of the innocent in particular cases.

53. *TJ*, 572–75.

54. Ibid., 567–71. Rawls's three reasons for compliance are all grounds of congruence. All are supposed to be uncontroversial since they follow from the thin theory of the good.

55. Ibid., 575.

56. Ibid., 576; emphasis added. Kant makes a similar point, but with a sharper resonance: in Kant's republic, citizens can improve their situations "if they are able and entitled to do so by their talent, industry and good fortune." In this respect, all citizens are equal and therefore they ought to be happy: "He can be considered happy in any condition so long as he is aware that, if he does not reach the same level as others, the fault lies either with himself (i.e. lack of ability or serious endeavor) or with circumstances for which he cannot blame others, and not with the irresistible will of any outside party. For as far as right is concerned, his fellow subjects have no advantage over him." Against the background of established right, individual malcontentedness is just that: it has no standing, it does not merit political articulation, it has no claim on the system. See Kant, "On the Common Saying 'This May Be True in Theory, but It Does Not Apply in Practice,'" *KPW*, 76–77.

57. Rawls's justification of limiting the freedom of the intolerant also appeals to the hypothetical, original agreement: Their freedom may be limited "for the sake of equal liberty under a just constitution the principles of which the intolerant themselves would acknowledge in the original position" (*TJ*, 220). This means that some intolerant conceptions of the good are not just wrong (or intolerable), they are "irrational" (ibid., 149–50). Since even a racist cannot deny this he, in a sense, wills his own suppression or at least he *would* will it—or give up his racist programmatic— were he to take up the standpoint of the original position. Thus, "by limiting his actions" we actually express our "respect for him as a person" provided we do this only "when this proves necessary" and "only as the principles we would both acknowledge [in the original position] permit" (ibid., 519).

The same point is made by Kant in response to Beccarria. See Kant, *Groundwork of the Metaphysics of Morals*, trans. H. J. Paton (New York: Harper and Row, 1964), 158. In both the Rawlsian and Kantian accounts, the suppression of the intolerant and the criminal is *completely* justified by considerations of right and rationality to which all human beings have access and from which no one has the wherewithal to dissent.

58. David Mapel has suggested a more generous reading. According to Mapel,

the confinement of justice to the basic structure means that the system is very loosely arranged and that communities may educate their children into a vast array of belief systems, even into beliefs that are intolerant and unjust, as long as they do not act on them. Some will act on them, however, and when they do it is clear that social unions or the family are the source of criminality, not individual character, and not the system itself qua basic structure. In my view, the more generous reading may apply to Rawls's justification for limiting the freedoms of the intolerant but it does not apply to the practice of punishing criminals. Rawls explicitly attributes criminality to bad character. Mapel is right, though, to argue that Rawls aspires to looseness in the arrangements of justice; if my emphasis differs from his it is because I want to highlight the tight moments that enable the loosenesses Mapel admires in his *Social Justice Reconsidered.*

59. Rawls devotes no more than five or six pages to punishment in *A Theory of Justice* (240, 270, 314–15, 575–77).

60. Sandel makes a similar point. Indeed, his criticisms of Rawls's account of punishment are similar to those developed here, though his interest differs from mine: Sandel responds to Rawls's reintroduction of antecedent moral worth by arguing that it is an inconsistency that would have to be ironed out in reflective equilibrium. But he never asks why antecedent moral worth makes its reappearance *here.* Happy to mark its return, he does not try to identify the pressures that drive Rawls's account to this inconsistency, nor is he any more concerned than is Rawls about the way this theorization of punishment constructs criminality and affects those who are punished as well as those who are not (*LLJ*, 89–90).

Thomas Pogge also notes the apparent inconsistency in Rawls's account, but he irons it out, see Pogge, *Realizing Rawls*, esp. 76–85. Defending Rawls against the charge that in his regime "there is no Desert at all" (the capital 'D' denotes "moral deservingness"), Pogge points out that Rawls "counteracts this impression by insisting that entitlements arising under the criminal law do involve Desert" (ibid., 83). The return of Desert in retributive justice is a virtue, for Pogge, its inconsistency with Rawls's earlier rejection of the practice notwithstanding. Fortunately for Pogge's Rawls, the inconsistency is a product of Rawls's having burdened himself "with a stronger commitment than necessary" (ibid., 76). Rawls can justify his distributive scheme as "an unmoralized system of incentives" without involving himself in a radical deessentialization of Desert (ibid., 83). Indeed, Pogge argues, it is rational to "'unmoralize' economic benefits" while maintaining a moralized penal system. Intent on improving the Rawlsian depoliticization of crime and punishment, Pogge too fails to ask what it is about criminality and punishment that drives Rawls back to Desert after his initial eagerness to dispense with it.

61. Stanley C. Brubaker argues that liberals cannot punish (by which he means that they cannot justify punishment) because they reject the ground of antecedent moral worth that, from Brubaker's perspective, makes sense of punishment, see Brubaker, "Can Liberals Punish?" *American Political Science Review* 82 (1988), 821–36. Brubaker is mistaken on two important points. First, as we have just seen, Rawls reintroduces antecedent moral worth to ground punishment and is therefore able, presumably, to punish to Brubaker's satisfaction. And second, there may be good ethical

reasons to prefer a practice of punishment that is a little less justified than the practice Rawls and Brubaker envision. The achievement of closure in justifying punishment tends to depoliticize the practice and to demonize the wrongdoer: the other is treated merely as a means. Perversely enough, it is Rawls's attempt to escape this last problem (as posed by utilitarian justifications of punishment) that leads him to justify punishment with reference to the (antecedently) bad character of the wrongdoer.

62. Of course, no regime can control the expectations to which it gives rise. Rawls's distinction between legitimate and illegitimate expectations is meant to stabilize this criterion of stability. Now the regime is only responsible for *some* of the expectations to which it gives rise. But, even so, how do we distinguish legitimate from illegitimate expectations? What difference is there between propensities that are regime-encouraged and those that are extrainstitutional? Is a legitimate expectation one that was *intended* by the framers or the lawmakers? Or is it typical of the general *effects* a particular piece of legislation has on the population? Should we rely on statistical studies to determine the frame of a reasonable response?

63. "The satisfaction of their rancor would make them better off" (*TJ*, 534).

64. Ibid., 144, 530. Envy is produced by a "lack of self-confidence in our own worth combined with a sense of impotence. Our way of life is without zest and we feel powerless to alter it" (ibid., 535). The self-respect that justice as fairness secures provides both the needed antidotes. Self-respect implies, first, "a person's sense of his own value, his secure conviction that his conception of the good, his plan of life, is worth carrying out [read: self-confidence in one's own worth]. Second, self-respect implies a confidence in one's ability, so far as it is within one's power to fulfill one's intentions [read: one feels empowered to alter one's life]" (ibid., 440).

65. Ibid., 245.

66. The same argument applies to envy: the fact that many people in justice as fairness feel envious does not mean that there is anything amiss in the arrangements. It probably means that the envy in question is of the inexcusable variety.

67. *TJ*, 576; emphasis added.

68. There is no reason to reconsider the basis of the scheme "so long as the conception of justice is not so unstable that some other conception would be preferable" (*TJ*, 576–77). Since punishment is a stabilizing institution, the citizens' reliance on it is not, on Rawls's account, in itself a reason to think that some other conception would be preferable.

69. Ibid., 240.

70. Appendix to *The Critique of Pure Reason* in *KPW*, 191; original emphasis deleted, new emphasis added.

71. Rawls's distinction between the bad character and the person who is hard hit by bad luck is reminiscent of the nineteenth-century English distinction between the deserving and the undeserving poor. The undeserving poor were those who did not deserve to be helped (by public or private charities) because they *deserved* to be where they were. Their poverty was attributable to character flaws (like alcoholism) or weaknesses they could do something about if they wanted to. The poverty of the deserving poor, by contrast, was due solely to bad luck. They were poor through no (character) fault of their own, and so they had a claim to help and charity. As in

Rawls, the pairing of the contrasting categories stabilizes each one, making both charity and condemnation possible, thereby satisfying both of the urges experienced by the relatively well off when they are confronted by the poor. In contemporary American politics, the character-luck distinction continues to operate, crystallized in the figures of the urban teen mother contrasted with the unemployed auto worker.

72. From similar concerns regarding Rawls's focus on the "idea of expressing our nature," Cavell reasons to a somewhat different conclusion: "But doesn't this assume a limitation in the kinds of scoundrel or saint there may be, in particular that there are none touched with the satanic, with an intolerance precisely for membership, for reciprocity in the intelligible, or any other, realm?" My argument suggests that although Rawls does indeed begin from an expressivist assumption, the effect of the assumption is (pace Cavell) precisely to turn mere scoundrels or rogues into beings that *are* touched with the satanic or, as in Rawls's vocabulary, with the mark of bad character and are therewith treated accordingly, which is to say, they are exorcised. Perhaps the argument developed here can provide Cavell with the clarification he seeks "of the grounds on which the scoundrel may and must be discounted" (Cavell, *Conditions Handsome and Unhandsome*, xxxiv, xxxvii).

73. Justification not in Rawls's sense of "everything fitting together into one coherent view" (*TJ*, 579) but in the less strict sense of giving reasons.

74. See Williams, "A Critique of Utilitarianism," in J. J. C. Smart and Williams, *Utilitarianism: For and Against* (London: Cambridge University Press, 1973), 75–150.

75. Rawls implies that punishment simply maintains intersubjective order, that the problem is to establish the conditions of cooperation among already well-ordered selves. The intrasubjective dimension of punishment is most apparent when Rawls turns his attention from bad characters to bad faith. The punishment that is directed at bad faith (not characters) is part of a daily, intrasubjective, self-ordering process. In providing for the penal mechanism, the parties seek to ensure themselves against being the sort of character who is unwilling or unable to share in the goods of justice as fairness. The problem of bad faith, or the assurance problem, is posed by the citizens' suspicion that others might be free riding, and it is a problem even at the ideal level (*TJ*, 240; see also 497, 577.) A well-ordered society is especially vulnerable on this count: it relies heavily on rational self-interest as an incentive for allegiance, but rational self-interest is also a great incentive for free riding. For a reading of *Hobbes* that emphasizes the role of self-interest in creating, not solving, the free-rider problem, see William Connolly, *Political Theory and Modernity* (Oxford: Blackwell, 1989).

76. Once again, Cavell's reading of Rawls dovetails with mine. He too worries that one of the effects of Rawls's particular model of conversational justice is "the deprivation of a voice," the subtle silencing of the voice of the other (*Conditions Handsome and Unhandsome*, xxxvii). Cavell explores these effects through Ibsen's Nora and raises powerful doubts about the Rawlsian project (ibid., 101–26). But, by turning to Ibsen, Cavell also leaves room for Rawls's readers to dismiss the critique as one that runs parallel to Rawls's concerns without intersection. Hence my decision to trace the deprivation of voice as it manifests itself in Rawls's own text, repeatedly.

77. As these questions indicate, my broadly Nietzschean critique of Rawls should by no means be confused with the early wave of Rawls criticism that also drew on Nietzsche. Allan Bloom, for example, saw in the aristocratic elements in Nietzsche's thought the resources for a critique of Rawls that is very different from my own. See Bloom, "Justice: John Rawls vs. the Tradition of Political Philosophy," *American Political Science Review* 69 (1975), 642–62.

78. In other words, Rawls is no longer granted his assumption that criminality is epiphenomenal. It is assumed, instead, that societal needs and Rawls's expressivist wager itself play a role in the production of criminality. Thanks to Michael Shapiro for pushing me on this point.

79. But also by the absurdity of its effects, in this instance.

Note that Rawls could argue that, in the event of his expressivist wager's failure, the result is also likely to be not more punishment but more politics—since when punishment ceases to function well as a stabilizing mechanism citizens are well advised to seek alternative arrangements, to refound their regime. But since Rawls does not permit the frequency of punishments in itself to be taken as a signal of the regime's inadequacy, and since punishment is so well justified in and by the regime and its citizens, the regime could conceivably maintain itself as a stable entity even if it punished frequently. Thus, the problem is that punishments would have to be quite frequent and ineffective before refounding became a viable alternative, especially since the regime's institutions so discourage refounding.

80. As Richard Flathman repeatedly reminds me.

81. Women are among the most obviously silenced others in this regime, but I do not focus directly on them because I prefer (for better or worse) to trace problems in Rawls's account through those others that *are* present in his text. As Okin points out, however, the absence of women from *A Theory of Justice* is a serious issue, not simply because Rawls neglects to ask whether there are any gender-specific needs to which justice ought to answer (like the need to regulate distributions *within* households, not just among them), but because Rawlsian justice assumes a gendered family structure as one of the necessary conditions of moral development. See Okin, *Justice, Gender, and the Family*, 89–110.

82. So much so that subjects will take part in increasingly complex activities. This is the speculation of Rawls's Aristotelian principle (*TJ*, 430).

83. Ibid., 420–23. Does responsibility do for the intrasubjective self what the principles of justice do for intersubjective relations? Could there be a difference principle to adjust claims among early and later selves? How would the justification requirement work? More important still, does Rawlsian responsibility *produce* the enduring subject that the original position—whose parties are to deliberate as heads of families—presupposes? Does the possibility of contractual deliberation in Part I depend on the antecedent success of Part III, and is Rawls's theory therefore caught in the aporia of founding I discuss in Chapter 4? Must it presuppose its outcome in order to stabilize itself at the founding moment?

Finally, is there reason to think of Rawlsian responsibility as both a product and a necessary condition of punishment? Punishment only works if the self faced with it is able to reason and to make calculations in the long range. But Nietzsche argues that punishment itself is what ingrains the habit of long-range calculation in human beings. Likewise, Rawls's constructivism implies that the self is not unified and continuous by nature. Rawls argues that it is in the self's interests to treat itself as an enduring subject, but it cannot really calculate as an interested being until it has become an interested being, until it is ordered into a subjectivity that can bear the burden of interests, and of interestedness. By insisting that responsibility (self-unification in time) is a matter of right, Rawls seeks to bypass this circularity. The "essential unity of the self" is assumed; it is "already provided by the conception of right" (ibid., 563). In short, Rawls seems to rely on the principle of responsibility to do for the self what the principle of fidelity does for promising: as principles of right, both are empowered to save the self as interest bearer and as promiser from the aporias of circularity and infinite regress, respectively.

84. But this test of responsibility—which requires that the self make choices in the present that it will be able to affirm later—assumes that the present self can predict with confidence the later self's desires and criteria of judgment. As Sandel points out, it assumes a continuity of identity that is possible only under the improbable assumption that the self is not a subject, that it is not at all constituted by its ends or changed in any way by its experience in the world, that it is not at all determined or even affected by the effects of earlier choices (*LLJ*, 163). But Rawls knows that the assumption is improbable. He admits that desires change over a life: "We can certainly decide now to do something that we know will affect the desires we shall have in the future" (*TJ*, 415). Indeed, he hopes that the assumption is false, after all, he wagers that those who live in justice as fairness will change quite remarkably over a life. Does this mean that Rawls's optimistic wager poses a conceptual problem for his account of responsibility? Does Rawlsian responsibility require that the self treat itself as the very unity Rawls hopes and wagers it is not?

85. *TJ*, 418.

86. Ibid., 94, 143. Does this effective lowering of expectations also contribute to the closure of the gap between expectations and experience?

87. Ibid., 422.

88. And its irrationality serves the same end: the regime is not obligated to engage these emotions; they are not symptoms of injustice.

89. A rational plan is one expressly "designed to permit the harmonious satisfaction" of our "interests." We formulate a rational plan "by rejecting other plans that are either less likely to succeed or do not provide for such an inclusive attainment of aims" (*TJ*, 93).

90. Just as rationally well-ordered selves are that much more, not less, discomfited to experience outlaw impulses inside the self.

91. The Reagan administration's justification of its increases in relative inequalities—benefits would trickle down to the least advantaged, it argued—was consistent with the difference principle's requirements, and members of the least-advantaged classes may well have accepted the justification. It is hard to resist the state's expertise. But, by the time it became clear that Reaganomics was not going to deliver on its promises, the least advantaged were substantially less empowered to protest. There is reason to think that their disempowerment was in part a product of the

practice of justification, which is no substitute for (though it may have a part to play in) practices of politicization.

92. In short, the price of Rawlsian justice may be, contra Sandel, not the simple loss of community but the more worrisome move to a managed population. Sandel might argue that the latter move is made more easily when communities have been broken down. With only dislocated individuals left, the state finds it easier to organize them as it sees fit. But Sandel does not actually make this argument. He leaves Rawls's state centricism aside. Is that because he, too, counts on the state to support the politics that he seeks?

93. *GS*, §262.

94. *TJ*, 127. In the last instance, Rawls does say that these "shortcomings" are "simply part of men's natural situation" and not attributable to defects or moral failures, and so the subject knows that "there is no cause for self-reproach. There was no way of knowing which was the best or even a better plan" (ibid., 422). But the moral packaging is not so easily undone.

95. Ibid., 432–33. The case is not so fanciful. The *Santa Barbara News Press* (October 17, 1989, p. A2) reported that David Wimp of Riverton, Wyoming, spends as many as six hours a day counting on his calculator: "One plus one, plus one, plus one, plus one, plus one." Having reached three million he began to count backward. "Once he hits zero, he'll start counting to five million." It took Wimp five years to count to his first million, but he is much quicker now. Thanks to Peter Digeser for bringing this story to my attention and for helping me think about its ramifications for Rawls's account.

96. *TJ*, 432, emphasis added. Sidney Maskit suggests that, given Rawls's appeal to nature and the grass counter's apparent fascination with nature, this scenario might be read as a conflict between two nature lovers.

97. I develop this distinction between liberal and teleological respect in Chapter 2 to organize Kant's account of respect for persons.

98. *TJ*, 432, 337–38.

99. *WP*, §349. The Nietzsche that authors this passage is the one brought to the fore by Flathman in his *Willful Liberalism*. Flathman's Nietzsche celebrates mutual opacity as a condition of individuality. From this Nietzschean perspective, Flathman brings out the tension in Rawls between the deep *privacy* (to the point of inaccessibility) that marks individual conceptions of the good and the belief that in justice as fairness the "formation and pursuit of conceptions of good . . . can and should be informed, disciplined, and controlled by mutually agreed and strictly enforced conceptions of right or justice (the 'reasonable')" (ibid., 168). My own reading of Rawls, here situated in the parallel tension between the expectations/psychologies generated by the original position's deliberations and the actual workings and experience of justice as fairness, highlights the information, discipline, and control that structure relations among citizens at the level of the good.

100. Adam Swift has suggested (in conversation) that Rawls could respond by charging that his citizens' request that the grass counter justify himself is itself an instance of the sort of politicization a *virtù* theory claims to celebrate. Do they not ask the grass counter to reflect on his subject position and on the effects his activity has on

those around him? Are these reflections not political by the *virtù* theorist's standards? These questions are effective in that they highlight important differences between interventions whose purpose is to consolidate forms of life and those that effectively disrupt them. The political intervention of Rawlsian citizens in this case is for the sake of the former; the actions a *virtù* theory might call for would be for the sake of the latter. In any case, were Rawls indeed willing to treat this encounter between citizens and the other as a *political* encounter, that in itself would constitute a significant departure from his position.

101. I do not mean to imply by this that either arrogance or a sense of instability is behind Rawls' treatment of this example. On the contrary, I take his intent to be to show that justice as fairness has dimensions of community support and interaction that other versions of a liberal society might (to their detriment) lack. I criticize the example at length because I think it gets away from Rawls and speaks—beyond his intentions—to the problem of relating to the other in a society founded and dependent on closure, reconciliation, and the displacement of politics.

102. *GS*, §305.

103. Cavell, *Conditions Handsome and Unhandsome*, xxxvii.

104. *TJ*, 126, 53.

105. See Isaiah Berlin, "Two Concepts of Liberty," in *Four Essays on Liberty* (Oxford: Oxford University Press, 1969), esp. 118, where Berlin also distinguishes technique and politics in a way that overlaps my distinction between virtue and *virtù*.

106. Richard E. Flathman, "Moderating Rights," in *Toward a Liberalism* (Ithaca: Cornell University Press, 1989), 166–67. Hence Flathman's embrace of a "chastened citizenship" and his rejection of withdrawalism (the other option that tempts him): in a statist context, withdrawalism endangers individuality instead of safeguarding it (see the superb "Citizenship and Authority: A Chastened View of Citizenship," in ibid., 65–108). I am very sympathetic to Flathman's accounts of rights, authority, and, particularly, citizenship. My only reservation is that his rejection of a more activist, less chastened citizenship ("high citizenship") is due to his acceptance of two problematic assumptions that do indeed animate most theories of high citizenship (like Arendt's, on some readings of her work, and Benjamin Barber's) but need not do so. The assumptions are (a) that the practice of citizenship always engages—or, worse, is managed by—the state; and (b) that it always aims to bind or consolidate individuals into a political community. My deployment of the *virtù* perspective is part of an effort to make room for practices of citizenship that are not state centered or state centering—in their proliferation of political sites, they are, in fact, state decentering—and for understandings of politics as an activity that resists consolidations instead of finessing them. If there is "high citizenship" here, it does not operate at the same heights as the practices Flathman rejects.

107. Flathman goes so far as to imply that subscription to authority (which he figures too decisionistically; hence my use of "reconciliation" rather than "subscription" to authority) is always cause for regret because subscription is never justified without remainder: "To subscribe to authority is to commit oneself to take actions that one would not take if considered exclusively on the merits of the actions themselves. [This dimension of subscription is what Rawlsian expressivism tries to

erase, in my view.] Under suitable circumstances, there may on balance be convincing reasons for such a commitment; I at least do not see how a reflective person could make that commitment without regret" ("Citizenship and Authority," 104). To make that commitment without regret is to be so reconciled to the state apparatus that one is beyond sensitivity to its remainders. I take Arendt's account of authority as augmentation to provide a possible avenue through which to engage those regrets. Flathman, however, resists any attempt to theorize authority in a way that might diminish its felt impositions (and that is, indeed, one of the dangers and temptations of Arendt's deauthorizing theorization of authority).

108. Its ability to do so effectively is called into question by Amy Gutmann, who points out that envy and resentment persist in conditions of relative deprivation; see Gutmann, *Liberal Equality* (Cambridge: Cambridge University Press, 1980).

109. Wolin, *Presence of the Past*, 148.

6. Sandel and the Proliferation of Political Subjects

1. And also because many misread Sandel as himself an advocate of radical situatedness. See, for example, John Gray, "What Is Dead and What Is Living in Liberalism?" *Post-Liberalism: Studies in Political Thought* (Routledge, forthcoming).

2. *LLJ*, 183.

3. Ibid., 57–58.

4. Ibid., 56–58. According to Sandel, Kant repairs this sort of dispossession with the pure will of practical reason: "Practical reason finds its advantage over theoretical reason precisely in this voluntarist faculty, in its capacity to generate practical precepts directly, without recourse to cognition" (ibid., 176). Rawls's mistake, presumably, is to follow Kant's lead here as elsewhere.

5. Richard E. Flathman, *The Philosophy and Politics of Freedom* (Chicago: University of Chicago Press, 1987), 86.

6. For a reading of Sandel that emphasizes this corrective quality and confines communitarianism perpetually to an antidotal function, see Michael Walzer, "The Communitarian Critique of Liberalism," *Political Theory* 18 (1990), 6–23.

7. *LLJ*, 85.

8. Ibid., 84; see also Joel Feinberg, *Doing and Deserving* (Princeton: Princeton University Press, 1970).

9. *LLJ*, 180.

10. Ibid., 84.

11. Ibid., 96.

12. Nozick, *Anarchy, State, and Utopia* (New York: Basic Books, 1974), 228, quoted in ibid., 78.

13. *LLJ*, 78–79.

14. Ibid., 79–80. Sandel goes on to argue that not only the difference principle but also Rawls's idea of social union commits him "to an intersubjective conception he otherwise rejects" (ibid., 80–81).

15. Ibid., 141. Rawls's recourse to fraternity may be an attempt do some of the

work Sandel thinks Rawls has left entirely undone. Rawls says that his difference principle "does seem to correspond to a natural meaning of *fraternity:* namely, to the idea of not wanting to have greater advantages unless this is to the benefit of others who are less well off" (*TJ*, 106).

16. *LLJ*, 144.

17. Ibid., 143. Like Rawls, Sandel makes no mention of how or whether this sharedness applies to problems as well as to achievements, to punishments as well as to rewards. Presumably it applies only to the latter because both Rawls and Sandel assume that the resistances and vices possessed by this constituted self are not part of its community constitution but come from some "outside" source.

18. The proviso also prevents the loss of community that occurs as community becomes a broader, more encompassing category—as in "the community of human-kind."

19. As Ludwig Wittgenstein puts it: "When one draws a boundary it may be for various kinds of reason. If I surround an area with a fence or a line or otherwise, the purpose may be to prevent someone from getting in or out; but it may also be part of a game and the players supposed, say, to jump over the boundary; or it may shew where the property of one man ends and that of another begins; and so on. So if I draw a boundary line that is not yet to say what I am drawing it for." See Wittgenstein, *Philosophical Investigations*, trans. G. E. M. Anscombe (New York: Macmillan, 1953), §499.

20. Patricia Williams, *The Alchemy of Race and Rights: Diary of a Law Professor* (Cambridge: Harvard University Press, 1991), 111–15.

21. To honor one's enemies is the lordly way in the first essay of the *Genealogy;* see *GM*, 1.10.

22. *LLJ*, 143.

23. Ibid., 149.

24. Ibid., 143.

25. As in Rawls, justification resolves political problems like resentment—without remainder.

26. I leave aside the important issue of whether Sandel's communitarianism conflates or confuses an epistemological need to assume situatedness with a normative call for community as a political good. See Walzer, "Communitarian Critique of Liberalism," for the most succinct and direct treatment of these issues with regard to communitarianism in general.

27. *LLJ*, 146, 152–53. Hence Sandel's criticism of Rawls and of Ronald Dworkin for speaking abstractly of "the common interest" and of general "social ends." There is, he says, "no such thing as '*the* society as a whole', or '*the* more general society', taken in the abstract, no single 'ultimate' community whose pre-eminence just goes without argument or further description" (ibid., 146).

28. Sandel does not raise the issue but the question, On whose behalf am I the guardian of these talents? necessarily implies another question: Are these attributes indeed *talents?* The answer will depend on the community to whom they belong. Audacious art may signal talent in one community, prurience in another. In the former the talent would be nurtured, perhaps even supported by the community; in

the latter it would be discouraged, possibly punished, and its products almost certainly censored. The former might proclaim proudly its role in the development of this talent, the latter might mourn the fact that it and one of its members have been assaulted (from some outside) by such unfortunate and deviant impulses. Sandel is right that the question of belonging is important, but it is more important than even he thinks it is.

29. *LLJ*, 152–53.

30. Ibid., 181.

31. Sandel does not explicitly discuss the relation between identity and agency. His failure to do so is problematic largely because of the way he treats identity, as a kind of univocal membership in a community of belonging. To say that one has not achieved agency in the absence of *that* kind of identity is (rightly) very controversial. I attribute a somewhat different position to Sandel, according to which agency and the affirmation it makes possible are necessary conditions of the communitarian identity Sandel seeks. It would be even better, however, to abandon the hierarchical ordering of agency and identity altogether and say that agency and identity are always inextricably intertwined because the self is always already a subject and is therefore always already positioned in a set of identity problematics its involvement in which presupposes *and* produces some sort of agency.

32. Is David Duke's politics of resentment merely a mistake? Is there some perspective or setting from which he would drop his objections against welfare programs and affirmative action?

33. *LLJ*, 152–53.

34. The strategy echoes Kant's reliance on respect as distance to produce new and subtle proximities as well as his reliance on reason as a power of consolidation divested of its powers of dissolution.

35. *LLJ*, 152; emphasis added.

36. *LLJ*, 179–81, 172.

37. This is not to say that Sandel's "Who am I?" is not, in Rawls's view, also a paradigmatic moral question. The point is that Rawls's focus is not on moral questions per se but on how to conceive of a political association whose terms are morally secure.

38. *LLJ*, 159.

39. Once identity is turned into something that can be got right, however, it also becomes something that can be got wrong. And yet Sandel never discusses the political or juridical consequences of making the wrong decision. He never mentions punishment. He does not enter the fact of the community's (broader) institutional power into the calculus, nor does he examine the effect of that power on the subject's deliberations and choices. Sandel finesses these problems by returning as always to the standpoint of the intersubjective conception.

40. William Connolly gives these questions about identity and its relations to difference and otherness the attention due them in his *Identity\Difference*, see esp. chap. 6. My reading of Sandel's communitarianism is indebted to Connolly's discussion of civic liberalism in chap. 4 of *Identity\Difference: Democratic Negotiations of Political Paradox* (Ithaca: Cornell University Press, 1991).

41. In this criticism, Sandel overlooks two important features of Rawls's argument, both points he and Rawls share, at least formally. First, Rawls does presuppose a basic unity from which plurality is then generated. As I argue in Chapter 5, Rawls domesticates Kant's postulate of unsocial sociability into a postulate of plural and often circumstantially conflicting conceptions of the good. This domestication of Kant's deep ambivalence about sociability allows Rawls to posit a phenomenal commonality Kant himself does not venture, a shared understanding of membership in a just political association as an unambiguous good. Second, the principle of unity present in Rawls's account, while it may not be attached specifically to human nature, is very much attached to Rawls's practice of deliberative rationality (which has as its object the unification of the self as deliberative subject) and more generally to his conception of reason. Similarly, the unity of the self Sandel wants subjects to come to know is accessible through deliberation (which Sandel identifies with introspection with friends, not with individual choosing).

42. Arendt's belief that identity-based regimes can successfully close the spaces of politics shows that she, like Sandel, attributes an enormous power of closure to identity. In this regard, she departs from Nietzsche, who treats identity as an instrument of the will to closure that is very powerful but never quite successful. I discuss Arendt's hostility to identity-based politics in more detail in Honig, "Toward an Agonistic Feminism: Hannah Arendt and the Politics of Identity," in *Feminists Theorize the Political*, ed. Judith Butler and Joan W. Scott (New York: Routledge, 1992).

43. *Bowers v. Hardwick*, 478 U.S. 186 (1986), 191; Michael J. Sandel, "Moral Argument and Liberal Toleration: Abortion and Homosexuality," *California Law Review* 77 (1989), 521–38.

44. "Moral Argument" 524, 534; *Poe v. Ullman*, 367 U.S. 497, 547, (1961); *Griswold v. Connecticut*, 381 U.S. 479 (1965).

45. "Moral Argument," 531, 524.

46. Ibid., 537.

47. Ibid., 527. The social institution of marriage is a less pure example of a nonvoluntarist good than Sandel's deployment of it implies. As Joseph Raz points out, the good of marriage in contemporary Western cultures has become quite bound up with the good of freely choosing one's own partner. See Raz, *The Morality of Freedom* (Oxford: Clarendon Press, 1986), 203.

48. Once again Sandel prefers to opt for a principle of unity that is "essential to our nature" and for an account wherein *conflict* is an "[un]happy accident," one that befalls communities from some outside, from some extracommunity source.

49. *LLJ*, 78–79, 94, 161, 172.

50. This view of *Griswold*'s final appeal as a supplementation might also support Walzer's case (in "Communitarian Critique of Liberalism"), but Walzer would probably domesticate the undecidability on which my reading insists in order to treat the communitarian moment of the decision as a corrective for its otherwise (and therefore) authentically liberal character.

51. "Moral Argument," 537.

52. *Bowers v. Hardwick*, 191, quoted in "Moral Argument," 537. The Court not

only rejected the claim as absurd, it argued that the claim was "at best, facetious." For a brief but powerful reading of this part of the *Bowers* decision, and of its "unusual power to offend," see Eve Kosofsky Sedgwick, *Epistemology of the Closet* (Berkeley: University of California Press, 1990), 6–7.

53. I say "rightly" because I take Sandel to agree with the Court that the notion of a right to sodomy is absurd. For Sandel, the "obvious reply" to the Court's ridicule is not to defend the notion of a right to sodomy but to reject the claim that the case is about a right to sodomy at all: "*Bowers* is no more about a right to homosexual sodomy than *Griswold* was about a right to heterosexual intercourse" ("Moral Argument," 537). To claim *either* of these as rights, Sandel implies, would indeed be ridiculous. But Sandel's position presupposes a false analogy between (or a false attribution of likeness to) heterosexual and homosexual intercourse. In a heterosexist culture, a right to heterosexual intercourse might appear to be absurd. But in that same culture, against a background of long-standing, violent, patterned, institutional and juridical discrimination against homosexuals, a right to sodomy is not absurd, no more absurd surely than the laws that outlaw the act. A right to sodomy can be made to appear absurd, though, if we assume that sexuality is a voluntaristically chosen, freely practiced, leisure activity instead of something more akin to a form of life or if we think of the state as the unquestionably legitimate regulator of sexuality. Sandel's agreement with the Court's ridicule of a right to sodomy follows from both assumptions, the first of which commits him to a voluntarism he otherwise rejects, the second, to a statism that he never really examines critically.

54. "Moral Argument," 537.

55. Mohr, *Gays/Justice: A Study of Ethics, Society, and Law* (New York: Columbia University Press, 1988), 67.

56. I use the word "nature" only to paraphrase Rawls. I do not mean by my use of the word to support a naturalist or essentialist view of sexuality.

57. *Stanley v. Georgia*, 394 U.S. 557 (1969).

58. "Moral Argument," 536; emphasis added.

59. Ibid., 536.

60. Sandel's implied inclusion of Hardwick and his exclusion of Stanley is problematic because the sodomy act that started *Bowers v. Hardwick* was not at all an intimate act in Sandel's sense. It was a pick up, an encounter that, *on Sandel's scale*, is much more like Stanley's relationship to his pornography than like the marital relationship of *Griswold*. Kenneth Karst (who also supports the extension of protection to homosexuals on the basis of a standard of intimacy, and whose reading of *Griswold* and *Bowers* importantly informs Sandel's) tries to get out of this problem by arguing that the justification for protecting sodomy on the ground of intimacy extends to casual sodomy since it may lead to more serious things, and eventually to intimacy. In other words, casual sodomy can be *likened* to homosexual intimacy which can be likened to heterosexual marriage. Likening has unlimited possibilities for Karst, if not for Sandel. See Karst, "The Freedom of Intimate Association," *Yale Law Journal* 89 (1980), 641, cited in Mohr, *Gays/Justice*, 67. For a cogent critique of Karst, see Mohr, *Gays/Justice*, chap. 3.

61. Eroticism is hardly exhausted by this figure, however. For an analysis of the

generative power of the erotic, see Audre Lorde's *Uses of the Erotic: The Erotic as Power* (New York: Out and Out, 1979). On the self-defeating character of prohibition when it comes to sexuality, fantasy, and the erotic, see Judith Butler's discussion of the Helms amendment in "The Force of Fantasy: Feminism, Mapplethorpe, and Discursive Excess," *Differences* 2 (1990), esp. 111.

62. "Moral Argument," 537.

63. *LLJ*, 211.

64. *The Advocate*, Interview, Spring 1991.

65. John Rawls, "The Priority of Right and Ideas of the Good," *Philosophy and Public Affairs* 17 (1988), 251–76.

66. The closest the later Rawls comes to this position is when he claims that political liberalism is compatible with a classical republicanism that insists that democratic institutions (no matter how well designed) require the support of a vigorous civic life to prevent them from falling prey to those with undemocratic intent. But this position maintains Rawls's identification of politics with the state and its institutions, as well as his distinction between public and private, citizens and subjects. And how are we to interpret the claim that political liberalism is *compatible* with civic republicanism? The institutions Rawls describes in *A Theory of Justice* tend to treat citizenship as a relatively passive consumerism; Part III, Rawls's fuller account of the regime, presupposes that. Does this new compatibility with civic republicanism mean that Rawls is actually in favor of redesigning the institutions of justice as fairness to reflect the need for a greater activism as well as redesigning his account in Part III, which assumes that a life lived privately in the private realm is not only compatible with, but is actually one of the goals of his just institutions? More likely, it means that those so inclined will find opportunities for greater political participation should they seek them out.

67. *TJ*, 584.

68. John Rawls, "Justice as Fairness: Political not Metaphysical," *Philosophy and Public Affairs* 14 (1985), 230 n. 22.

69. Ibid., 237.

70. John Rawls, "The Idea of an Overlapping Consensus," *Oxford Journal of Legal Studies* 7 (1987), 25; emphasis added.

71. Rawls, "Priority of Right," 264–65.

7. Renegotiating Positions: Beyond the Virtue-*Virtù* Opposition

1. As I suggested toward the end of Chapter 5, my contrasting classification of Rawls and Arendt as virtue and *virtù* theorists, respectively, is not itself unproblematic, particularly in view of the fact that Rawls's and Arendt's positions on the administration of justice have surprising but extensive moments of overlap. Here I take the argument a step farther by asking whether my classifications of them as virtue and *virtù* theorists are reversable.

2. *BPF*, 264.

3. Hence Arendt's "basic gratitude for everything that is as it is; for what has

been *given* and was not, could not be, *made;* for things that are *"physei* and not *nomoi,"* for things that are "beyond dispute or argument." See "'Eichmann in Jerusalem': An Exchange of Letters between Gershom Scholem and Hannah Arendt," *Encounter,* January 1964, 53. I discuss this exchange in detail in "Toward an Agonistic Feminism: Hannah Arendt and the Politics of Identity," in *Feminists Theorize the Political,* ed. Judith Butler and Joan W. Scott (New York: Routledge, 1992).

This gratitude may well be the source of Arendt's concern, mentioned elsewhere, that the agon in Greece was in danger of being out of control. Bhikhu Parekh notes the concern in *Hannah Arendt and the Search for a New Political Philosophy* (Atlantic Highlands, N.J.: Humanities Press, 1981), 192–93, chap. 8 n. 1. See also Arendt's "Philosophy and Politics," posthumously published in *Social Research* 57 (1990), esp. 73, 82.

4. This is the perspective on Rawls (suggested to me by David Mapel) I considered and rejected in Chapter 5 because of its failure to make sense of the importance (both explicit and implicit) of Rawls's return to antecedence and desert in his treatment of criminality. I resurrect the perspective here to acknowledge that it is a plausible reading of Rawls and that, as such, it calls attention to the insistences and remainders of my own reading of Rawls. But to sustain this reading of Rawls as a *virtù* theorist, one must treat his turn to antecedence and desert as errors that can be eliminated from the theory without loss or violence to its vision. I am not sure this last effort can succeed, because to do so would be to give up on Rawls's commitment to justice as fairness as a form of moral association.

5. In "The Basic Liberties and Their Priority," *The Tanner Lectures on Human Values,* ed. Sterling McMurrin (Salt Lake City: University of Utah Press, 1982), Rawls makes the compelling claim that no abridgement of free speech in the history of the United States has ever been justified.

6. The phrase is Julia Kristeva's, drawn from the longer passage that heads this chapter; see, Kristeva, *Desire in Language* (New York: Columbia Press, 1980), 23.

7. Max Weber, "Politics as a Vocation," in *From Max Weber: Essays in Sociology,* ed. Hans H. Gerth and C. Wright Mills (New York: Oxford University Press, 1946), 127.

8. Carol Gilligan, *In a Different Voice: Psychological Theory and Women's Development* (Cambridge, Mass.: Harvard University Press, 1982), 174. There is certainly a sense in which Gilligan's ethic of care is all about self-overcoming—it is an other-regarding ethic—but that sense of self-overcoming is quite different from Nietzsche's call for a shifting of perspectives and habits as part of a practice of perpetual self-transformation.

9. Gilligan's focus on gender as the site of difference is complicated by the authors of *Women's Ways of Knowing,* who attend to the significance of class and institutional power, along with gender, in knowledge practices. See Mary Field Belenky, Blythe McVicker Clinchy, Nancy Rule Goldberger, and Jill Mattuck Tarule, *Women's Ways of Knowing: The Development of Self, Voice, and Mind* (New York: Basic Books, 1986). Gilligan herself notes the need to introduce "variables of culture, time, occasion, and gender" to her abortion dilemma study. And Lawrence Kohlberg argues that gender difference shows up as *the* differentiating difference only "without

controlling for education and job differences" while still maintaining that the abstract rationality of his own ethic of rights represents a more advanced level of moral reasoning. See Kohlberg's "Synopses and Detailed Replies to Critics," with Charles Levine and Alexandra Hewer, in *Essays on Moral Development* (San Francisco: Harper and Row, 1981), 347.

10. Gilligan insists that "the different voice [she] describe[s] is characterized not by gender but theme." Unfortunately, this insistence does not undo the effect of her "empirical observation" of that different voice's "association with women," an observation that leads to claims like this: "Women, however, define their identity through relationships of intimacy and care" (*In a Different Voice*, 2, 164).

11. Does caring make it harder rather than easier to listen to the other? This formulation of the problem was suggested to me by Stanley Cavell. The possibility that caring and listening conflict raises difficulties not only for difference feminism but also for Stephen White's effort to draw on an ethic of care to nourish the disposition to the other he favors. Indeed, the conflict between caring and listening may well be illustrated by White's own construal of the other as a stable subject to whom "we" relate intersubjectively. The other as liminal moment, site of undecidability, intrasubjective dissonance, is absent from White's discussion and this facilitates White's provocative and admirable account of two kinds of responsibility (to the other and to act). But in locating the other intersubjectively, White resolves or sidesteps some of the most difficult questions that otherness poses for moral and political systems. Care for the other (even the light care White endorses) presupposes *and produces* an intersubjectivity that otherness (particularly in its intrasubjective forms) often resists and disrupts, not because it is "ineffable" or "unspeakable"—as Michael Brint suggests in *Tragedy and Denial* (Boulder, Colo.: Westview Press, 1991), 8—but because it is undecidable. To locate the other intersubjectively is to decide its undecidability and resolve, without really investigating or engaging, the most profound challenges that otherness poses to moral and political systems: the other marks the remainders of system, the sites in which knowledge shades off into power, power into violence, voice into silence. That is why otherness appears as a specter to those whose identity and form of life are bound up with existing systems of (inter)subjectivity. What assumptions and operations have to be in place for the other to be (only or even primarily) a potential object of care? Doesn't care turn the other into the receptive object of our need to act out of a sense of responsibility to it, a mirror of our desire? Doesn't care thereby close spaces of dissonance and resistance even while addressing some otherwise silenced voices? Is it *because* care closes spaces of dissonance that White is so drawn to the practice?

12. Gilligan, *In a Different Voice*, 32. In the first study (25–32), Gilligan contrasts Amy's and Jake's responses to moral dilemmas and finds that Jake's approach is mathematical and logical whereas Amy's is narrative. Underlying this contrast, however, is a more fundamental distinction that is less easily assimilated to Gilligan's ethic of care, a distinction between a moral reasoning that dissolves remainders in the closure of resolution (as illustrated by Jake's reflections) and one that sensitizes us to the remainders that prevent resolutions from achieving the satisfaction of closure (as illustrated by Amy).

13. Ibid., 101. Gilligan's theorization of the special relationship among women, guilt, and dilemmas raises a provocative question: do women find themselves in dilemma situations more often than men do and, if they do, is that because they live in a world where men make the law that regulates and reproduces the hierarchically ordered and gendered subjectivities and practices that constitute them? Gilligan does not pose these questions in this way because she is less interested in interrogating the gendered subject positionings and institutional pressures that produce the guilt these women experience than she is in tracking and stabilizing it.

14. Gilligan, *In a Different Voice*, 105; emphasis added.

15. Bernard Williams pursues a third, possibly hybrid, strategy in which tragic situations "are not merely exceptions, they are exceptional" (*Moral Luck* [Cambridge: Cambridge University Press, 1981], 60). They are the ineliminable products of value conflicts that no rule can adjudicate because values are plural and incommensurable. In that sense, tragic situations are to be expected, they are not exceptions. But they are exceptional, nonetheless, because the circumstances that generate value conflicts are infrequent; for the most part, moral rules govern daily conduct successfully and uneventfully.

The exceptional-exceptions distinction notwithstanding, Williams, like Gilligan, elides the possibility that these exceptional situations have a lot more in common with ordinary ones than might first appear to be the case. Once the possibility is posed, another question (posed by neither Gilligan nor Williams) can surface: why are some subjects more likely than others to find themselves in dilemmas? Perhaps it is not simply bad moral luck. What rules, forces, and institutional pressures combine to reproduce that outcome?

16. Gilligan, *In a Different Voice*, 126–27; emphasis added.

17. Answer: from the perspective of rights, care's profound sensitivity to the violences of resolution is likely to translate into indecision and even paralysis in the face of the need to act. The point is relevant to Stephen White's project (though he does not raise it), which draws on Gilligan's ethic of care to support an ethic of responsibility to act.

18. Rosi Braidotti, *Patterns of Dissonance: A Study of Women in Contemporary Philosophy* (New York: Routledge, 1991), 147.

19. Judith Butler, *Gender Trouble* (New York: Routledge, 1989), is a good example of this recent development in feminism.

20. Hampshire, *Innocence and Experience* (Cambridge: Harvard University Press, 1989), 189.

21. Friedrich Nietzsche, "On Truth and Lies in an Extra-Moral Sense," in *Philosophy and Truth: Selections from Nietzsche's Notebooks of the Early 1870s*, ed. Daniel Breazeale (Atlantic Highlands, N.J.: Humanities Press, 1979), 90.

Index

Library of Congress Cataloging-in-Publication Data

Honig, Bonnie.
    Political theory and the displacement of politics / Bonnie Honig.
        p.   cm. — (Contestations)
    Includes bibliographical references and index.
    ISBN 0-8014-2795-9 (alk. paper). ISBN 0-8014-8072-8 (pbk.)
    1. Political science.   2. Political science—Philosophy.   3. Liberalism.   4. Democracy.
I. Title.   II. Series.
JA71.H62   1992
320'.01—dc20   92-56772